D0908639

Amway Forever

Amway Forever

THE **AMAZING STORY** OF A **GLOBAL** BUSINESS PHENOMENON

Kathryn A. Jones

WILEY

John Wiley & Sons, Inc.

Published by John Wiley & Sons, Inc., Hoboken, New Jersey.
Published simultaneously in Canada.

For general information on our other products and services or for technical support, please
contact our Customer Care Department within the United States at (800) 762-2974,
outside the United States at (317) 572-3993 or fax (317) 572-4002.

Wiley also publishes its books in a variety of electronic formats. Some content that appears
in print may not be available in electronic books. For more information about Wiley
products, visit our web site at www.wiley.com.

Library of Congress Cataloging-in-Publication Data:

Jones, Kathryn A., 1956-
    Amway forever : the amazing story of a global business phenomenon / Kathryn A.
Jones.
        p.   cm.
    Includes bibliographical references and index.
    ISBN 978-0-470-48821-8 (hardback); ISBN 978-1-118-107751 (ebk);
    ISBN 978-1-118-107768 (ebk); ISBN 978-1-118-107775 (ebk)
    1. Amway Corporation.   2. Direct selling—United States.   I. Title.
HF5439.H82J66 2011
381'.130973—dc22

                                                                    2011014330

Printed in the United States of America
10   9   8   7   6   5   4   3   2   1

For my parents,
Samuel and Wanda Jones

Contents

CONTENTS

Acknowledgments

This book would not exist without the vision of Debra Englander, executive editor at John Wiley & Sons, Inc., who proposed the idea of telling the story of Amway's rise to a global powerhouse. Her commitment and confidence in the book spurred me forward.

I also want to thank my agent, Grace Freedson, who has worked tirelessly on my behalf and has been a writer's dream.

Jennifer MacDonald, Wiley's development editor, has been efficient, cordial, and very detail oriented, which every writer hopes for in an editor.

Thanks also to Stephen Duthie in Amway's communications department. To all the former and current Amway distributors who spoke with me on and off the record, thank you for your time and insights.

Introduction

Selling a Dream

mway Corporation marked its 50th anniversary in May 2009 with a glitzy celebration at the MGM Grand on the Las Vegas Strip. Spotlights swept across the crowd of well-dressed people who had come from all over the world for the event. A movie theater–sized screen splashed the Amway logo against a cobalt blue background. Cameras flashed and music pulsated. The upbeat mood and excitement inside the auditorium felt similar to the energetic vibe at a national political convention or a religious rally.

One charismatic speaker after another extolled the virtues of hard work and the freedom that comes from owning one's own business. It was both a patriotic message and one infused with an almost sacred belief that the opportunity for wealth and success is a universal right. And Vegas turned out to be the ideal setting for the company that has inspired millions of people to bet on the hope that someday they, too, can hit the entrepreneurial jackpot and become as rich and successful as the Amway business owners who have received Rolex watches and bejeweled pins for building immense networks of salespeople around the globe.

The evangelists of enterprise preached to the faithful that day because most of the thousands of people gathered were "Diamond" Amway distributors, meaning its top producers. Among the speakers were the company's co–chief executive officers, Steve Van Andel and Doug DeVos. They had followed their fathers, Amway founders Jay Van Andel and Rich DeVos, in an unusual dual-family succession into top management, and they uncannily reflected their fathers' characteristics. Like his father, Jay, Steve is lanky and fair-haired and speaks in a low-key but self-assured manner. Doug DeVos, like his father, Rich, sports a boyish smile, diminishing hairline, and forceful, gregarious speaking style. Their words pumped up the crowd and fed the sense of euphoria that typically hovers over Amway gatherings. "Owning your own business is a chance to change your life . . . and if you can change your life, you can change the world," Steve said, arms stretching outward. "Amway in its essence came from one thought and one desire—to give people an opportunity and to improve their lives through a business of their own. When you introduce the concept of freedom and free enterprise, people change. They put aside their differences and become a part of a group, one unified group of people, behind a cause, behind a dream, and pursuing that dream."[1]

Doug also delivered a rousing message about personal freedom, emphasizing key words like a minister speaking to his flock: "We have an idea to keep us alive—all of us—of *freedom* . . . and *free enterprise* . . . and the power of having a business of *your own*," he said, pacing back and forth across the stage and gesturing for emphasis like a politician. "Because the Amway idea is alive and well, and what happens to us from this day forward . . . well, it's up to us, isn't it? *Right?* And as we look forward, Steve and I know all of you . . . *together* . . . believe we are just getting started."[2] Then Rich DeVos, the billionaire who's revered by Amway distributors as the company's iconic patriarch, took the stage to look back on a half-century of business. In his 80s and balding, with age spots on his scalp, Rich got a second chance at life after a heart transplant in 1997. "*Now* is our time," he said. "And when you're in this business, you learn to work with where you are now. So now we're going to move on and you're all going to go home and think back, I hope, of the good time you had, but most of all of the people out there who don't know yet about what they're missing. And you're going to be the *missing link* in bringing it to them and their life will change because of you, as many others have already." DeVos, who's known as a naturally gifted and persuasive speaker, not to mention a crackerjack salesman, paused to let the words sink in. He smiled and said he liked to think of himself simply as the "Amway guy." "When I meet people, they say, 'What do you do?' and I say, 'I'm the Amway guy. I've been in it a long time,'" Rich explained. "'I believe in it. And I like it.'"[3]

Then Rich shocked the audience by saying that Amway's cofounder and his old friend, Jay Van Andel, would like to "wrap it up." What could Rich mean? Jay died from Parkinson's disease in 2004. He and Rich, who became friends in high school, had shared a rare lifelong business partnership. They made an odd but effective couple—Jay, the nerdy, straight-A's numbers cruncher, and Rich, the glib, fun-loving extrovert. The partners, though, over the years repeatedly said they were stronger together than they would have been on their own. The combination of Jay's analytical mind and Rich's persuasive speaking and selling skills proved ideal for a business like Amway.

There was a flicker onstage and suddenly Jay appeared, reincarnated through technology in a life-sized hologram. A company called Digital Illusions LLC stitched together seven clips from archival footage to create a two-minute speech in high definition.[4] It was a "wow" moment for many of those in the audience as the deceased Van Andel's image materialized, much like Obi-Wan Kenobi's spirit appeared in the *Star Wars* sequel to dispense advice to young Luke Skywalker. "The volume of that applause not only is gratifying to me, but it lets me hear how much we've grown since Rich and I held our first Amway convention in 1961," Van Andel's lifelike visage said. "At that time I think the entire audience could have easily fitted on this stage." These days, it takes an auditorium or even a stadium to hold an Amway gathering. "When Rich and I started Amway in our basements of our homes, we had a dream," Jay's image went on to say. "We dreamed that everyone should have the opportunity to be in business for themselves. Today, I look at this tremendous group, this great crowd, and see all of you as fulfillment of that dream." The audience gave Jay Van Andel's eerily realistic hologram a standing ovation. Then it flickered off. Rich and Doug DeVos and Steve Van Andel stood together onstage, arms raised like rock stars, to thunderous applause. A laser light show pulsed, and a shower of special effects sparks rained down upon them.[5]

In Vegas, Amway Diamond distributors and executives also were treated to private performances by Elton John and the Blue Man Group. They roamed the slick "Experience Amway" exposition hall, complete with product experts and samples. They talked about how "the business" had transformed lives. Their personal stories sounded like testimonials at a revival. But the spirit that filled them was the spirit of free enterprise—and, of course, the prospect of making even more money—as they schmoozed in the city where millions of people every year gamble on dreams.

The anniversary gala underscored that five decades after the company's founding, few corporate names inspire such passionate reactions as "Amway." The direct-selling pioneer grew from humble beginnings peddling soap and vitamins into the world's largest and arguably most influential multilevel marketing, or MLM, company with a line of more than 450 products, from cosmetics and skin care lines to water purifiers to cookware. Although Amway started out selling soap, detergent, and other household products, beauty and health care products now account for most of its business. Along the way to the top, Amway sparked its share of copycats and the company spawned other MLMs, but it still reigns as the supreme example of a direct-sales machine adept at packaging and selling not only products, but also dreams, to individuals who believe they are on a divine mission to chart their own destinies. The words of founder Jay Van Andel still resonate in the videos he left to inspire others: "We've learned that Amway principles translate into many languages and transcend many cultures," he said. "Being rewarded in proportion to how much you do is a universal language for people around the world. Our goal must be to make the lonely and the frustrated and the scared have that sense of hope and security that we can bring them. That's why you're here. That's what we're all about. We have to believe in ourselves. You can't predict the future, but you can follow your dreams."[6]

Following their dreams had led Amway's founders to enormous riches as well as controversy. From its inception, Amway was caught in the crosshairs of government regulation and legal challenges. Some of the company's own former distributors have accused Amway of running an illegal pyramid scheme. Yet, despite the allegations, the giant direct seller has continued to survive, operate, prosper, and spread its philosophy of free enterprise—and universal dreams of prosperity—around the globe.

When I first got involved in this book, my publisher expected that the company would cooperate and provide access to company executives. My knowledge of Amway before writing this book was minimal. I've never bought anything from Amway or knew much about the company except that it sold soap. Despite more than a year of back-and-forth communications between Amway and the publisher, however, efforts failed to convince the company to allow unfettered access to its managers, employees, and archives.

Objectivity and distance are important because, until now, most books about Amway have been authored by its founders, corporate or personal friends, and current or former independent business owners, or IBOs. They tend to fall into two categories. Some were written by mega-distributors such as Dexter Yager, who says he loves Amway and the IBOs in his group and wants to share with others how to get started with their own Amway businesses. On the other end of the spectrum, some Amway IBOs or people involved with other MLM businesses had a negative experience, lost their money, and want to warn others away from MLM schemes. Both perspectives convey a valuable side of the Amway narrative, but they don't tell the complete story. Emotion clouds objectivity, and people get very emotional about money, especially when they make—or lose—a great deal of it.

My research took me across the United States, to Europe, and to Asia to visit some of the markets where Amway has established a presence and shown a remarkable ability to adapt to other cultures and consumer attitudes. Over the past year I've interviewed dozens of current and former Amway distributors, attorneys, consultants, authors, government officials, and others, and pored over hundreds of pages of legal documents. I've listened to motivational tapes and watched video footage of Amway seminars and rallies all over the world. I wanted to tell the Amway story as much as possible through people, but I did run into limitations. Because I did not have the company's blessing, many Amway distributors, who are loyal and protective to the max, refused to talk to me. Some did so only if their names were not used. "IBOs are not allowed to do mass market advertising, and appearing in a book might be considered by some as just that," an IBO in Europe told me. As a result of the media-shy company's refusal to grant access to its leaders and employees, I have had to rely on secondary sources more than I would like to with the caveat that I took into account each person's subjectivity, experiences, and motives.

That said, what follows is neither an exposé nor an authorized corporate biography, but an unbiased, journalistic look at the rise, stumble, and rise again of a dynamic and controversial company that has changed the world of direct selling forever. Whether it's changed that world for better or worse is up to the reader to decide.

Chapter 1

Capitalism and Controversy

Amway's gateway to the world begins in an unlikely place—a small Midwestern township called Ada, Michigan, 12 miles east of Grand Rapids. Founded as a French-Canadian trading post and home to a historic covered bridge over the Thornapple River, Ada is best known these days for the sprawling world headquarters of Alticor Inc., parent company of Amway. The complex of office buildings and manufacturing plants stretches for more than a mile. Its busy visitors center has become a local tourist attraction with its giant see-through metal globe in front and 50 flagpoles flying the flags of affiliates' home countries. In the spring, the garden around the globe is planted in tulips, a nod to Jay and Rich's Dutch heritage. The business partners are immortalized in life-size bronze statues that stand in the headquarters lobby.

Selling Directly to Buyers

The company that Jay and Rich created casts a goliath's shadow over the direct-selling industry, but Amway wasn't the first company to sell directly to buyers. Others, such as Fuller Brush, Stanley Home Products, Avon Products, and Tupperware, preceded it. But Amway took the multilevel marketing (MLM) concept and ran with it around the world. It not only laid the foundation for other MLMs, but also helped spark some of the business trends taken for granted today—working from home, shopping from home, globalization, and shifting the activities of selling and distribution away from brick-and-mortar structures and traditional systems. The Direct Selling Association (DSA), the industry's major trade organization, says that a record 16.1 million Americans worked as direct sales representatives as of 2009. That was up by 1 million people from 2008's sales force. People are "looking to earn extra money on their own terms and at their own pace," says Neil Offen, the DSA's president and chief executive officer.[1]

Business icon Donald Trump, British airline tycoon Richard Branson, and billionaire Warren Buffett have limited involvement in MLMs and direct selling as well. The Trump Network in 2009 began selling nutritional supplements, healthy snack foods, and skin care products. The marketing materials make the network sound a lot like, well, Amway:

> It's an opportunity. An opportunity for you. And an opportunity to help rebuild a country founded on that very premise. It's a chance to turn a land overwhelmed by stress and ill health to one of strong bodies, bright minds, and free spirits. A chance for you to promote wellness and entrepreneurialism. Even more, a better way of life. This is far more than a financial opportunity. This is a chance to live and promote something you can believe in.[2]

Branson's Virgin Group in 2009 sold its Virgin Vie at Home skin care and makeup division to its management team. And in 2003 Buffet's company, Berkshire Hathaway, purchased The Pampered Chef, a direct seller of kitchen gadgets and cookware.

Amway, though, stands out from the pack of direct sellers for its distinctive culture and ideology. What sets Amway apart isn't that it sells products in a nontraditional—and often controversial—way. It's that it sells its sellers, who are called independent business owners (IBOs), on the dream that the company's founders and executives spoke of in Las Vegas. And not just any dream, but the "American dream"— the idea that if you are motivated and work hard enough, you deserve success and it will come your way. Call it bootstrap capitalism with a blend of "soap and hope," a marriage of manufacturing and motivation. "Rich DeVos and Jay Van Andel didn't set out to sell products," says Pat Williams, senior vice president of the Orlando Magic national basketball team, which Rich owns. "They sell *confidence*. They fire up people to believe in themselves, and those people sell the product."[3] The founders espoused the quintessentially American ideal of hard work, perseverance, taking risks, and overcoming obstacles at a time in the late 1950s when the fear of Communism and socialism was spreading. Indeed, the very name *Amway* is a compressed version of "American way." It's direct selling wrapped up in a flag, along with spiritualism and family. Former distributor Stephen Butterfield, who is now deceased, put it this way:

> Here is obviously a new power in American life: a corporation with immense popular appeal, a grass-roots following among all classes and trades, an explosion of political and religious energy such as has not been released since the growth of industrial unions in the 1930s. What makes this power all the more remarkable is that corporations have never been very dear to the hearts and minds of the American people.[4]

One of the reasons for Amway's power is that it embraced social networks long before anyone heard of the Internet, Facebook, or Twitter. "We probably were one of the original social networks, before there was technology associated with it," Steve Van Andel says.[5] Its primary social network was and still is the one-on-one connection, at first person to person and later tied to the Internet.

Exporting a Sales Model

The Amway way isn't just the American way anymore, however. It's spreading into a global phenomenon under its rallying cry of economic "freedom." As Kaoru Nakajima, one of Amway's major distributors in Japan, puts it: "I was a salaried man working in a company for eight years. Now I am my own boss. Now I am free."[6] Peter Muller-Meerkatz, who with his wife, Eva, amassed one of Amway's largest distributor networks in Europe, adds: "We believe in capitalism. We are convinced that democracy and free enterprise are the world's only economic hope. Why wouldn't we want to share it?"[7]

Amway certainly did share it, exporting its direct sales model— "the Plan," as Amway IBOs call it—to much of the world. The company operates in 80 countries and territories and the breakdown of its domestic and international business has flipped. At the end of the 1980s and the beginning of the 1990s, 70 percent of Amway's business was in the United States. By 2009, however, 90 percent of its sales came from outside the United States.[8] Two-thirds of its business is in Asia.[9] Its single largest market is China, which accounts for more than a third of its more than $9 billion in annual sales.[10] The company's success there is due in part to tapping a vast market of more than a billion people who are breaking away from old feudal systems and are part of a culture that encourages family members to support a relative's business venture. Amway says it's committed to help budding entre- preneurs in the world's most populous country. "We want to be successful in China and we are here in China to stay for the long term," says Eva Cheng, executive vice president responsible for Amway markets in Greater China and Southeast Asia. "We are not just here for a few years to make some quick bucks and then go away."[11] Indeed, the company has been adept at gaining access to markets—including China's—where governments at first resisted its entry. Chinese law limits direct selling, so Amway had to break with its traditional way of doing business and set up government-mandated storefronts. They proved so successful that Amway may open additional retail outlets in other countries. (It still has no plans to sells its products in the United States through stores, however.) Another Eastern country, India, represents a huge market as well. "Our business is based on people and how many people there are," Steve Van Andel explained. "Well, there's a lot of people in India and there's a lot of people in China. . . . We're available to most of the world's population, so now we've got to take a look at the markets we're in and to try to figure out how to get better market share."[12] There are still parts of the world without Amway, but that could change. "We're not everywhere yet, you know—the Middle East, Northern Africa, sub-Saharan Africa," Doug says. "It's just a matter of time, I think. Those things are going to happen."[13]

Alticor, Amway's parent company, overcame weak economic trends in recent years to report record 2010 sales of $9.2 billion thanks to strong growth in China, India, Korea, North America, and Latin America.[14] An estimated 12,000 people a day sign up to become Amway IBOs around the world. The company employs more than 14,000 worldwide—4,500 of them in the United States—and 300 scientists, who hold about 700 patents. More than 3 million IBOs are active in 80 countries and territories. Moreover, Amway operates factories in Michigan, California, China, and Vietnam. Access Business Group, a wholly owned Alticor subsidiary, oversees packaging design, makes bottles and labels, and contracts to manufacture products under a third-party—and confidential—arrangement for some very large consumer brands. Beyond manufacturing, Alticor owns several downtown Grand Rapids hotels through the Amway Hotel Corporation: the luxury Amway Grand Plaza Hotel, the JW Marriott Hotel, and Courtyard by Marriott. The company's *Enterprise II* yacht is a floating conference center for those in the Diamond Club, and a resort on Peter Island in the Virgin Islands awards sales leaders with luxury, vacation-style meetings.

Once known mainly as a direct seller of soap and detergent, health and beauty now account for most of Amway's sales. Amway's Nutrilite product ranks as the world's best-selling brand of dietary supplement,[15] and Artistry, Amway's facial skin care and cosmetics brand, ranks as one of the top five worldwide beauty brands with $1 billion in global sales.[16] Major markets are China, Japan, the United States, South Korea, Russia, Thailand, Taiwan, India, Malaysia, and Ukraine. Private and very closely held by the DeVos and Van Andel families, Amway doesn't disclose profit figures. But, in terms of sales, if Amway were a public company, it would rank in the Fortune 500—No. 253, to be exact, in 2010— elevating it on par between Starbucks (No. 241 with $9.77 billion in revenues) and eBay (No. 267, with $8.7 billion in revenues).[17] Among private companies, in 2010 Amway was ranked second on Forbes's annual list.[18] Along the way, Amway's founding families have grown very wealthy. As of early 2010, Rich DeVos had an estimated net worth of $4.5 billion, ranking him at No. 176 on *Forbes*'s list of the world's billionaires.[19] Money has brought Amway and its leaders political clout, influence, and access to those in power. Amway's founders have been major contributors to the Republican Party and conservative causes. Rich's son, Dick, who was co-CEO with Steve Van Andel from 1993 to 2005, resigned from the company to pursue his own business and political interests, and in 2006 made an unsuccessful run for Michigan governor in the state's most expensive gubernatorial campaign in its history. The founding families cultivated close relationships with former presidents Ronald Reagan, Gerald Ford, and the Bushes, especially George H. W. Bush. Former Amway distributors—including former House Whip Tom DeLay, who in January 2010 was sentenced to three years in prison for money laundering—have been elected to Congress. In addition to political contributions, the DeVos and Van Andel families and Amway also have used their wealth for philanthropic projects, from building a children's hospital in their hometown to paying for cleft palate surgery in Thailand to helping educate children in rural provinces of China.

A Fuller Picture

That's all quite a transformation from the once little soap company born in a Grand Rapids suburb, leading Richard L. Lesher, former president of the U.S. Chamber of Commerce, to call Amway "one of America's most spectacular business success stories."[20] Conceived of in the shell of an abandoned gas station with $500 in cash, Amway's plan sounded simple enough: recruit people to sell products such as soap and cosmetics and sell others on the Amway system. Then they, in turn, would be recruited to sell the products, and so on and so on. To become an Amway IBO, one had to be sponsored into Amway by another IBO, who then received a cut of the new level of the business. And if others could be recruited, then the next distributor got a cut of *their* business. And so the MLM pyramid-shaped feeding chain of commissions built into multiple levels as distributors "upline" could make money on the layers of salespeople below them, or "downline." Other names frequently used to describe the business model are "network marketing" and "direct marketing." Whatever the terminology, Amway has been remarkably successful with its approach of building a network of salespeople through building and taking advantage of relationships. In his book *Believe!*, Rich DeVos noted that person-to-person selling has gotten a "bad rap" but is a time-honored profession:

> We happen to think that personal service beats making the customer stand in line. . . . I respect the man who is in a business where the customers need not beat their way through traffic, park way out in a crowded parking lot and run through the rain or snow to get their goods.[21]

While Rich paints a folksy picture of direct selling, others view the company and its business model in a much darker light. Litigators, competitors, and disgruntled former distributors who morphed into Amway whistle-blowers have accused the company of operating a pyramid scheme that sells people on unrealistic dreams that, in reality, are built on a system where those at the top earn the pharaoh's wealth while those at the bottom struggle to get ahead and often fail.

Numerous Internet sites are devoted to exposing Amway as a "scam." Critical bloggers repeatedly refer to the company as "Scamway" (a Google search on "scamway and Amway" turned up 13,000 results). There's even an "Amway Wiki" (www.amwaywiki.com) site, a collaborative repository of information, both positive and negative, about Amway; its parent company, Alticor; and Quixtar, the name Amway adopted for its North America operations in 2000 before deciding to go back to the Amway name. Early in 2010, when Robert Pagliarini, author of *Your Other 8 Hours*, posted a positive blog, "Why You Should Join Amway," on CBS MoneyWatch.com, the discussion thread that followed set a record for the blog with 582 comments by people either praising or condemning the MLM. CBS Interactive stepped in, though, when the comments turned into a classic Internet flame war. Stephen Howard-Sarin, vice president of business and finance brands for CBS Interactive, posted the last response, No. 583, in the discussion thread: "Thank you, now stop."[22]

Despite the razzle-dazzle recruiting rallies and glamorous get-togethers that spotlight Amway's top success stories, few people make dramatic profits working as Amway distributors. Amway's brochure, "A Business Opportunity for Entrepreneurs," boasts that since 1959 it has paid out more than $33 billion in bonuses and incentives world-wide and that in 2010 more than 309,000 North American IBOs received a bonus check. But check the fine print. In the footnotes to the accompanying table of annual compensation, the company discloses that "approximately 0.18% of IBOs in North America achieved at least Gold Status" ($12,303 a year) and "approximately 0.26% of IBOs in North America achieved at least Founders Platinum status" ($40,125 a year). Moreover, the average monthly gross income for "active" IBOs was $115 (approximately 66 percent of all IBOs of record were found to be "active").[23]

Jay Van Andel often remarked that anyone who thought he or she would get rich quick with Amway was mistaken. "If you are looking for a magic bullet—a surefire gimmick that will make you a millionaire overnight—you're looking in the wrong place," the cofounder wrote in his memoir, *An Enterprising Life*.[24] Rich said pretty much the same thing. "I have never tried to make it sound easy," he wrote in his memoir *Hope from My Heart*. "It isn't easy. It wasn't easy for us. When people came to us with the expectation of quick prosperity, I told them to look elsewhere."[25] But try telling that to the throngs of recruits who pack auditoriums and stadiums and watch a parade of wealthy Diamonds and Crown Ambassadors onstage. They are people like Butterfield, a former English professor-turned-Amway-distributor, whose 1985 book, *Amway: The Cult of Free Enterprise*, was the first of a string of exposés. "I liked the idea of making money, lots of it, without having to show up for work . . ." Butterfield said. "I wanted to be plucking the fruit from the money tree, not sitting on the outside of the circle chewing pits while others feasted."[26]

Multiple Transformations

To its supporters and believers, Amway remains a symbol of free enterprise—an "empire of freedom," as one best-selling book put it[27]—and the resilient spirit of entrepreneurship under attack by big government. As one top distributor, Ron Puryear, says about walking away from his previous job and following his dream: "I chose freedom."[28] At the heart of Amway's success is helping people to feel good about themselves, he adds:

> We are a stand-on-your-feet-and-cheer-each-other's-victories people. And our cheering isn't phony or contrived. We know how hard each of us works. We know what it takes to stay motivated, to go out night after night when it's easier to stay home and watch television. We know what those first hard years cost in time, energy, and commitment.[29]

Leonard Kim, who is a marathon runner and with his wife, Kim, formed a leading global sales organization in South Korea, says that some people mistakenly think the Amway business will "give you a fortune right away. However, in reality, the business is a like a long marathon."[30] The key to productivity and making money, Jay and Rich believed, was to motivate people like Puryear and Kim, who didn't want to work for someone else in a big company, and to show them the way to self-sufficiency. Amway set up a highly decentralized organization and eschewed top-level bureaucracy to encourage people down the chain of command to work harder because they were working for themselves. "The A. L. Williams Company (a whole life insurer) and other members of the direct selling industry, such as Amway Corporation, Tupperware, and Mary Kay Cosmetics, have stopped trying to fine-tune bureaucracy in the search for productivity," University of California at Davis management and sociology professor Nicole Woolsey Biggart says in the first full-scale study of the industry, *Charismatic Capitalism: Direct Selling Organizations in America.* "Instead, they have adopted a form of organization that dates from this nation's colonial past and have shaped it to fit the circumstances and aspirations of contemporary Americans."[31] Avon Products Inc., founded in 1886, remains the world's leading direct seller, with $10.4 billion in revenues and more than 6 million distributors.[32] (Amway made an unsuccessful bid to acquire Avon in 1989 for $2 billion.) Unlike Amway, it relies on single-level and multilevel compensation plans.[33] Ranked third behind Avon and Alticor is Germany's Vorwerk & Co. KG, which includes JAFRA Cosmetics. It's followed by Mary Kay Inc., Herbalife Ltd.,

Primerica Financial Services Inc., Tupperware Brands Corp., Natura Cosmeticos SA of Brazil, and Oriflame Kosmetiek B.V. of Sweden. Other top 100 direct-sellers are in Japan, Peru, and Mexico.[34] The most common sales categories overlap with Amway's: beauty products, nutritional aids, cookware, and replenishable household products.[35]

While worker ants in Corporate America may have lost faith in working for someone else, belief in Amway's system at one time was shaken, too. Growth stalled in the 1980s in America as some "black hat" distributors cast the company in a bad light with their cultlike recruitment tactics and exaggerated promises of wealth. Those practices left many Amway distributors in the hole while top-of-the-food-chain distributors grew very rich. Amway's critics say the real money has been made by those who built their own pyramid-shaped sales organizations based on pushing non-Amway tools or "peripherals," including motivational books, CDs, suits, jewels, and tickets to motivational rallies. According to critics, by letting some mega-distributors and so-called "Amway motivational organizations" grow unchecked for years, Amway allowed renegades to tarnish the company's image. As part of its transformation, top Amway executives said they are "reasserting" their roles to oversee distributor behavior and establish "boundaries" for conduct. "The biggest issue is when people don't feel they're being told the truth," Steve Van Andel says. "Somebody's misleading them, or at least not telling them everything there is. And that's the cause of a lot of issues."[36]

People who tend to get lumped by the media into the category of Amway "critics" haven't stopped raising questions, even though Amway has taken some of them to court. Ironically, for a company that shies away from media coverage except when it's to its advantage, Amway has been embroiled in controversy and lawsuits for decades. It's been sued by its own distributors, competitors, foreign governments, and the U.S. government. That's true of many large international businesses, of course, but few companies have been accused and investigated of operating a pyramid scheme—an accusation it has fought in the courts and so far defeated time and time again. In the best-known and most significant challenge, the U.S. Federal Trade Commission (FTC) in 1975 charged that the company was, indeed, running an illegal pyramid scheme. But because the core of Amway's business is based on the sale of products, not just direct payments to join, and because of other procedures Amway had in place, the FTC in 1979 ruled the operation to be a legal enterprise.[37] The order not only gave Amway the green light to continue business, it also had the effect of legitimizing the MLM model and creating a whole new business genre based on the "Amway rules" laid down by the FTC (this is discussed in detail in Chapter 6, "Toppling the Pyramid"). Other businesses adopted those rules, and MLMs proliferated in the United States and around the globe.

Despite the federal government's pronouncement that Amway's sales model was legal, lawsuits against the company continue under state statutes related to pyramid schemes. Rival Procter & Gamble also accused Amway of running an illegal pyramid operation, contending that it primarily sells products to its distributors rather than making retail sales to consumers. Some of Amway's former IBOs have made similar charges in lawsuits. Amway's business model also has come under scrutiny in Canada, the United Kingdom, India, and other countries for a variety of alleged practices, from price-fixing to avoiding paying customs duties to playing hardball with vocal critics. And in 2007, former distributors for Quixtar—the name Amway was using for its North American operations at the time—filed a class-action lawsuit also alleging the company and some of its top-level distributors operated a pyramid scheme. In November 2010 a settlement was announced under which Amway agreed to pay $34 million in cash and $22 million in products to the distributors. The settlement also included amending the complaint to remove the term *pyramid scheme* from the case.[38]

Influences on Public Perception

Still, public perception can be slow to fade. When I told people I was working on a book about Amway, their typical responses were, "Isn't that a pyramid scheme?" and "Don't they sell soap?" Amway management grew more press-shy over the years, not feeling it got a fair shake in the media and dodging persistent accusations that it ran an illegal pyramid scheme despite the FTC ruling. "There was a very adversarial feeling between ourselves and the media early on, during the first publicity crises," Jay wrote in his memoir. "Rich and I were incensed at first, then frustrated by the power newspapers and television had over the American public. The newspapers and television had the ability to define us for the public—to present a false image of what we were all about at Amway."[39] Jay went on to say that mainstream media had a "bias" against Amway because it and other network marketing firms rarely advertised in those outlets.

In 2007 the company began a two-year global transformation and rebranding—or "retro-branding," as Steve and Doug call it—to return to the Amway name.[40] Its parent company, Alticor, created a single, global brand—Amway Global—and invested more than $200 million to boost compensation to IBOs and an advertising campaign to bolster its reputation. The company now is called just "Amway," but it's a new Amway, company executives insist. "We are reintroducing a $1 billion start-up company," says Steve Lieberman, vice president and managing director of Amway's U.S. and Canadian businesses. "The company is switching from being distributor focused, where distributors are the only ones carrying our messaging to the public. We're becoming distributor and consumer focused. So we're taking our message directly to consumers."[41] It's doing so by airing "The Power of Positive" national television commercials to "reintroduce" shoppers and potential distributors to the company.

Amway also has been working its way into popular culture in a variety of ways. For example, Amway Global sponsored the Tina Turner Live 2008 North American Tour as part of a stepped-up marketing strategy to raise awareness of Amway business opportunities and products in North America. It also sponsored the YMCA National Wellness Campaign, two professional soccer teams (the San Jose Earthquakes and the LA Sol), the U.S. Rock and Roll Marathon, and Skate Canada. The home of the NBA's Orlando Magic has a new name, Amway Arena. Amway also has tried to jack up its credibility and once-low profile with celebrity endorsements. In spring 2010 Amway Global launched the first of a line of healthy snack products with musician and TV and radio personality John Tesh. Tesh's wife, actress Connie Sellecca, athlete and model Gabby Reese, and world soccer star Marta also signed similar endorsement contracts. Amway regularly has been a sponsor at the Olympics and was among the companies sponsoring the U.S. Pavilion at the 2010 World Expo in Shanghai, which drew 73 million visitors, a record for an international expo.[42] The company lined up Olympic champions such as Chinese hurdler Liu Xiang to be a spokesperson for its line of health supplements, Nutrilite. Amway also has partnered with one of the most enduring symbols of American wholesomeness, the Miss America organization, to sponsor scholarships. Teresa Scanlan, Miss America 2011, is acting as an ambassador for Amway's Artistry cosmetics line. There's even an Amway Global Visa credit card now with the blue and red logo. "We're beginning to register again with the general public," Lieberman says.[43] Consumers, though, still can't go online and buy directly from Amway. They still must buy through an IBO's online site.

It could take more than a national TV campaign and PR blitz, though, to turn around enduring perceptions about Amway's business and convince ever more people to sell its products and its form of marketing to the world. Ironically, the company's alleged distrust of the media and its secretive insider culture may have given its critics ammunition to attack it. Whether Steve Van Andel and Doug DeVos can create a new, more open Amway and continue to grow in the United States and abroad remains a large challenge for its future and survival as a network marketer that depends on selling its products—and itself—to the world.

■ ■ ■

Jay Van Andel and Rich DeVos were determined to hold onto their sense of hope for the future and security by working for themselves. They were aspiring entrepreneurs from an early age who chased their own dreams and cemented a mutually beneficial partnership and friendship that lasted a lifetime. Later, others would study and try to emulate the company with varying degrees of success. Yet Amway stands alone as a direct-selling and social phenomenon that, more than 50 years later, still draws people with its alluring message of financial independence and personal growth. Dreams, though, like soap bubbles, are fragile. Alongside the much-hyped Amway success stories, there are also others: the disappointments from when bubbles burst. That, too, is part of the American way.

Chapter 2

An Adventurous Partnership

Jay Van Andel once remarked that his life of enterprise began not with a buck but with a bankruptcy.[1] The business failure triggered a series of events that put Jay in the proverbial right place at the right time—the point where aspiring entrepreneurs often discover a window of opportunity to start something big, something that will make a difference, something that will be remembered.

Jay Van Andel

For Jay, the path to that point began long before he was born and an ocean away in the Netherlands. In 1909 Christian Van Andel, Jay's paternal grandfather, was living with his wife, Elizabeth, and two sons,

James and Christian Jr., in the Dutch city of Haarlem situated along the banks of the River Spaarne west of Amsterdam. For centuries, the town, which dates to the Middle Ages, has been the center of Holland's tulip-growing region. Christian worked hard at his bicycle shops and blacksmith business, but the family still struggled financially. He decided to follow the lead of other Europeans who had fallen on hard times. At age 50, he left in search of new opportunities, and in 1910 moved with his wife and sons to America. Christian's sister had already left Holland and urged them to join her in Chicago.

The city on the shores of Lake Michigan was like another world for the close-knit family, thrust from a small Dutch community with a slow-turning, picturesque windmill into a whirling mass of people, engines, and industry. Decades earlier, the Industrial Revolution had transformed Chicago into a manufacturing and trade center and the hub of the nation's rail system. By the time the Van Andels arrived, Chicago ranked as the fourth-largest city in the world behind London, New York, and Paris. It was booming largely due to immigrants. More than three-quarters of its population either were foreigners or had one parent born in another country.[2] Elevated trains crisscrossed the city, transporting carloads of passengers between homes and factories. Streetcars clanked almost bumper to bumper along the downtown streets. Author and muckraking journalist Upton Sinclair in 1906, four years before the Van Andels' arrival, had published his novel *The Jungle*, which exposed unsanitary and dangerous working conditions in Chicago's meatpacking industry. In the novel, an immigrant family from Lithuania moves to the city to pursue the "American Dream." Instead, they find an urban jungle of corruption and exploitation. Here's how Sinclair described Chicago through the fictional family's eyes:

> They were on a street that seemed to run on forever, mile after mile—thirty-four of them, if they had known it—and each side of it one uninterrupted row of wretched little two-story frame buildings. Down every street they could see, it was the same—never a hill and never a hollow, but always the same endless vista of ugly and dirty little wooden buildings. Here and there would be a bridge crossing a filthy creek, with hard-baked mud shores and dingy sheds and docks along it; here and there

would be a railroad crossing, with a tangle of switches, and locomotives puffing, and rattling freight cars filing by; here and there would be a great factory, a dingy building with innumerable windows in it, and immense volumes of smoke pouring from the chimneys, darkening the air above and making filthy the earth beneath.[3]

Working conditions in Chicago's factories often were appalling in their disregard for workers' health and safety. George Pullman, the developer of the luxury Pullman rail cars, had died in 1897, three years after Pullman workers went on strike, and unions were gaining strength to fight workplace injustice. Christian Jr. found a job painting Pullman cars, but working conditions hadn't improved much. The fumes and dirty, back-breaking work gave him health problems. He knew little English and the language barrier also proved too difficult to overcome, so he turned to farming. When his younger brother, James, was old enough to strike out on his own, he left Chicago and moved to more familiar territory—Holland, Michigan, a town settled by Dutch immigrants and that is known for its annual tulip festival. James, too, was interested in machines and especially vehicles, but he decided to sell them rather than make them. In 1921 he opened an auto dealership in Holland and sold Chevrolet automobiles, International Harvester trucks, and Gray Motor Corporation's new four-door touring roadster, which cost $490, and four-door sedan, which cost $895.[4]

James married a woman of Dutch descent, Petronella "Nellie" Van der Woude. They shared a similar family background. Her father had gone bankrupt in the Netherlands and, like James's parents, had come to the United States in search of a better life. Nellie's father started a business designing and building homes to serve the growing populace. The couple added one more new resident when their son, Jay, was born on June 3, 1924, in Grand Rapids, a former lumber center named for the rapids on the Grand River that flows through town. Years later, the city would turn out to be Jay's "right place" for starting his own business.

Devout Christians, the Van Andels belonged to the Christian Reformed Church, a denomination that emerged from the Protestant Reformation in sixteenth-century Europe dating back to John Calvin. As a reformer, Calvin married the idea of work with spirituality.

Rather than viewing work as a form of bondage, Calvin believed work brought pleasure and meaning to life. It was a God-given right to explore one's talents and skills and use them to their fullest potential, according to the Calvinist view. Meaningful work brought glory to God and prosperity and self-esteem to those who persevered. Jay's family believed in those principles and immersed their son in them as well. He attended a Christian school, played with the neighborhood children of other immigrant families with similar backgrounds, and went to church every Sunday. There were two services, and Jay recalled he had to wear his church clothes all day, which meant no playing football in between or roughhousing. "Two basic distinctive of Reformed churches were the emphasis on the sovereignty of God and the responsibility of man to live faithfully by God's word in every part of life," Jay wrote years later.[5] ". . . As I look back I'd have to say that all my political, economic, and entrepreneurial beliefs come from these two tenets of my religious upbringing."

The Van Andels also taught their children to look beyond their time in church and to practice Christian values such as honesty, generosity, and respect. Jay recalled that one day he found a dime in a back alley near his family's home. Money was scarce during the Depression, and a dime could make a big difference for a struggling family. Jay's mother insisted he knock on every door on the street to see if anyone had lost the 10 cents. No one claimed the coin and Jay was allowed to keep it. The real reward, he later said, was the lesson of going the extra mile to help someone else.[6]

James worked long hours to develop his auto sales business and in 1933 became partners with another Dutchman, John Flikkema. (The dealership they started, Van Andel & Flikkema, still sells Chryslers and Jeeps in Grand Rapids.) Much of James's personality and business philosophy filtered down to his son. "Sometimes my father could come across as gruff or standoffish, but those who knew him well found him a caring man, dedicated to his family and his community," Jay recalled.[7] Another major influence on Jay's development was his maternal grandfather. During the Depression he lost his housing construction business and came to live with the Van Andels. He and Jay took long walks around town and sometimes would stop at the public square where men gathered to discuss theology, speaking in Dutch. "Granddad could hold his own in a debate, and he earned the respect of anyone who heard him," Jay recalled.[8] The old man, who also had been an architect, woodworker, and an entrepreneur, made a huge impression on the boy. Jay later said his close relationship with his grandfather shaped his character and sparked his interest in learning how things were put together and made. Even when young, Jay liked to do things himself, his mother recalled. One of his early sentences, "Me do it," became a childhood motto.[9] Watching his father and grandfather instilled in Jay the notion of self-reliance and to keep working on a problem until he could find a solution.

Jay's first real taste of entrepreneurship came in 1939, also in the form of an automobile—not selling the vehicles, like his father, but providing a service. James gave his son a 1929 Model A Ford to drive to Grand Rapids Christian High School. Only one other student at the school drove a car, and the Model A had a rumble seat. Jay figured he could carry riders there and charge a quarter a week to help pay for gas, plus earn some spending money. One day a schoolmate asked Jay for a ride. "He lived just a couple of blocks away from me, so of course I was happy to take his quarter every week," Jay said.[10] The boy's name was Rich DeVos. They did not know it yet, but their friendship would lead to an adventurous and profitable partnership.

Richard Marvin DeVos

Richard Marvin DeVos was born on March 4, 1926, in Grand Rapids, Michigan, also to descendants of Dutch immigrants. His parents, Ethel and Simon DeVos, also had been financially strapped, especially after Simon lost his job during the Great Depression. They couldn't make the payments on their $6,000 home in Grand Rapids and were forced to rent it to tenants for the $25 monthly mortgage. The family moved into the attic of Rich's grandparents' house. Simon eked out a living sacking flour for a grocer and selling socks and men's underwear in a store on Saturdays. "From that day his advice was clear and simple," Rich recalled. " 'Own your own business, Rich,' he would say. 'It's the only way to be free.' "[11] Even though the family was poor, the DeVoses made sure their children grew up in a loving atmosphere. "We may have lacked for money at times, but we never lacked for love," Rich said.[12] His sister, Jan, recalled that her brother had a special talent—he was a great fudge maker and improviser. "He made lots of different kinds of fudge," she said. "He figured out a way to pass the fudge on a string to the babysitter in the next house."[13] Rich also was adept at sports and found creative ways to play them around the family home. One winter he flooded a vacant lot to create a skating rink. "I've always been proud of my brother and his ingenuity," Jan said.[14]

Rich's parents also taught their son important lessons about money and work. Ethel gave Rich a painted cast-iron bank with moving parts. "I could roll the coin down a little trough or place it in the bird's beak and press a lever that sent the coin tumbling through the slot," Rich recalled. After school once a month, he and his mother walked to the local branch of First Kent Bank to make a deposit into Rich's savings account. "I loved to watch the bank teller add up my deposit and write in my little red bank book," he added. "Then she signed the book and stamped it."[15] Rich's father rooted in his son the Calvinist value of hard work. Whenever Rich would say, "I can't," Simon would admonish him: "There's no such word as 'can't.'" "He was right!" Richard said years later. "Think about it: Is there a good use for the word 'can't'? Not one! 'I can't' is a self-defeating statement; 'I can' is a statement of confidence and power.'"[16] It became one of his life's guiding principles. But first he had to learn a few more lessons.

Rich's parents enrolled their 15-year-old son in a private religious school, Grand Rapids Christian High School. While Rich was a popular student, he took for granted the sacrifices his parents made to pay his private school tuition and was, at best, a mediocre student. "I spent a lot of time chasing girls and goofing off," Rich later admitted. "I'm the kind of person who has to apply himself to get good grades—and I didn't apply!"[17] He didn't flunk any class that year, but barely passed Latin only because he promised his teacher he'd never take it again.[18] Unhappy with Rich's grades, his father pulled him out of private school. If Rich wasn't going to apply himself and prepare for college, he should go to a free public school, learn a trade, and become an electrician, his father reasoned. Rich enrolled in public school and was "miserable that whole year," he recalled. "For the first time, I realized all that I had lost by goofing off in school."[19] He promised his father that he would take

odd jobs to earn the money to go back to private school. It proved
to be one of the best decisions he ever made because it was there, at
Grand Rapids Christian High, that Rich got to know Jay Van Andel
during the rides back and forth from school. "I can still picture everyone piling into Jay's car after school—packing the seats, overflowing
into the rumble seat and even standing on the running board of his
Model A Ford," Rich said.[20] Their conversations looked to the future
and laid the foundation for their careers.

The two became fast friends even though Rich was two years
younger than Jay and they were opposites in personality. Rich was dark-
haired, strikingly handsome, and gregarious. He often wore a toothy
grin and loved to talk—and he was good at it. Jay was more introverted
and quiet, lanky with wavy, sandy-colored hair, a dimpled chin, and
was a self-described "bookworm." "Back in high school he was one
of those students who could make straight As without ever opening
a book," Rich recalled years later. "He has a mind that just stores and
processes information like a computer. He can look at a problem, size
it up, lay out all the pros and cons, and give the facts to back up his point
of view. He's really amazing."[21] Rich and Jay complemented each other
then and throughout their lives. The two friends made "an unbeatable
pair at whatever we set our minds to doing," Jay said.[22] They both were
bound by shared similar Christian backgrounds, family influences,
and an ingrained Calvinist work ethic. Like Jay, Rich also had learned
a lot from his grandfather, whom he described as an "old-fashioned
'huckster,' a term, appropriately enough, that comes from an old Dutch
word that means 'to peddle.'"[23] Thanks to his grandfather, Rich was
about to become a "direct seller" before such a marketing term had
been coined. "My granddad drove to the farmer's market every day in
his old truck and bought vegetables, which he then sold door-to-door
to the people in our neighborhood," Rich recalled in his book *Hope from
My Heart: Ten Lessons for Life*. "Whatever was left over at the end of the
day I would sell."[24] He made only a few pennies on his first sale—a few
onions sold to neighbors—but he said he learned a million-dollar lesson:
"Don't let the fear of rejection stop you. Keep knocking on doors, keep
pitching until you make the sale. Be persistent and you'll be rewarded."[25]
Rich continued selling vegetables when his grandfather had some left
over for him. "It took persistence, but I loved it," he said.[26]

Rich worked at other entrepreneurial businesses when he was growing up. While in elementary school and junior high Rich mowed lawns, washed cars, and worked at a gas station to earn enough money to buy a bicycle. He started a paper delivery route and received 35 cents a week. In high school Rich worked in a men's clothing store after classes, and on weekends washed cars at a local gas station for 50 cents. "It was hard work, but I was making more money than I had ever dreamed and it was fun," Rich said. "The entrepreneurs I know have a positive attitude about work. They will tell you that sometimes 'work is just work,' but they will also tell you that—for them—most work is fun."[27] Despite money problems, Rich remembers his father as a positive, encouraging man. "He would always tell me, 'You're going to do great things,'" Rich recalled. "'You're going to do better than I've ever done. You're going to go farther than I've ever gone. You're going to see things I've never seen.'"[28]

The Pact: Someday, A Business Together

Jay and Rich made a pact: someday they would go into business together. The opportunity came sooner rather than later. Jay was 16 and Rich was 14 when they landed their first joint business venture. Jay's father needed help delivering two pickup trucks to a customer in Bozeman, Montana. "Of course, we jumped at the chance," Jay said. "Today, of course, no caring parent would ask such a thing, but the United States of 1940 was a safer place."[29] The boys watched their pennies carefully and would sleep on hay in the backs of the trucks to avoid paying for a motel room. "We didn't mind at all—it was an Adventure, we were men, and we could take it," Jay said.[30] The trucks had bald tires that went flat, and the teenagers patched them with a kit. But when a service station attendant wanted to charge a nickel to air the tires, they balked and spent an hour using their hand pump instead. "I think he believed we would give in and pay him the nickel, but he didn't count on our determination and willingness to work," Jay recalled.[31]

During his high school years, Rich said he already had a "fuzzy idea" that he was going to own his own business, but didn't know how to make that happen. Then a young man came to speak to the students about setting goals. He told the assembly that he had set 20 "almost impossible" goals himself, one of which was traveling around the world by the time he was 18. As Rich watched the slide show from the young man's trip, he was in awe. That night he said he began to write down goals and dreams. "From that day on, I had a focus and a vision for the future—and my life was never the same."[32]

By the time Jay graduated from high school in 1942, the world was at war. He entered the Army Air Force Reserve Corps at Calvin College and then enlisted as a private in the hopes of going to officer training school. By March the next year he was on the way to training camp in St. Petersburg, Florida, when his train derailed. Unhurt but rattled, Jay made it to the camp, which had been thrown together on the site of a former country club golf course and had no hot water, an open mess hall next to the latrines, and no decent medical care. Jay and many other GIs got sick there with what was later diagnosed as spinal meningitis. He spent a month in the camp's makeshift hospital, an experience that left him with a lifelong aversion to medical care and an interest in alternative methods of healing and disease prevention.[33]

The boy who had built model airplanes soon found himself in aviation cadet training at Seymour Johnson Field (now Seymour Johnson Air Force Base) at Goldsboro, North Carolina, southeast of Raleigh. Afterward, he went to Aircraft Armament Officers' School at Yale University, a year that changed his life. Jay worked harder than he ever had, often leaving his room after lights-out to study in the showers until 5 AM. The general who gave the send-off speech after graduation said something that stuck with Jay: "In war there is no excuse for failure."[34] In his life, there wasn't either. Soon after, Jay was training crews for the B-17 Flying Fortress and, later, the B-29 Superfortress, the main aircraft used in the U.S. military's firebombing campaign against Japan and the planes that carried the atomic bombs that were dropped on Hiroshima and Nagasaki.

Meanwhile, back home, Rich had served as class president during his senior year in high school. After he graduated, he enlisted in the Army and was stationed with a glider unit on the island of Tinian in the Pacific. He and Jay wrote to each other and kept up each other's morale. "Look, this is not our final chapter," Jay wrote in one letter.

"This is not what we're about. This is only a step along the way. This war will end at some point and we have to make the decision of what is it that we're going to be doing with our lives and be remembered for."[35] The two met whenever they were both on home soil. During one of those visits one night, the guys had dropped off some girls after a double date when Rich turned to his best friend. "Well, Jay, when this is all over, what are we going to do? Go back to college?" he asked.[36] That option didn't appeal to either one of them.

■ ■ ■

The more they talked, they knew what they wanted to do—form a partnership and go into business together. Neither one could envision working for anybody else. "I think there is something in the inner being of entrepreneurs that makes them want to be their own bosses," Jay explained.[37] They did not want to be followers and play it safe. They wanted to be leaders, entrepreneurs, risk takers, and they wanted the freedom to choose meaningful work. As Rich put it, "What I wanted— my goal—was to build and succeed in my own business. And I never had any doubt that I could do exactly that."[38] The two friends shook hands on it. They were men, they could take it, and they were ready for the next phase of their big adventure. "It was only a question of what kind of business we were going to get in," Rich later recalled, "not a question of whether we were going to get a job."[39]

Chapter 3

Taking Flight and Sailing Away

After World War II ended, airplanes became all the rage with the American public. Air power had helped the Allies win the war, and commercial aviation benefited from the research and development money poured into new technology. Germany and England had tested jet engines, and the Messerschmitt Me 262 made history as the first operational jet fighter. New airplanes, most of them based on American bombers, emerged for commercial air travel and the demand for civil air transportation exploded.

First Attempts

Jay and Rich hoped to capitalize on the trend. They both liked airplanes and had worked with them during the war, so they decided their first enterprise should be to build a business around them. A mutual friend, Jim Bosscher, suggested the three of them pool their money and buy an airplane. Rich was still in the Army, but he pitched in his share. Jay and Bosscher bought a two-seat Piper Cub in Detroit with a down payment of $700. "We didn't know the first thing about flying, so we had to hire a pilot to fly it from Detroit to Grand Rapids," Jay recalled. "In this way Rich became part owner of an airplane before he ever owned a car!"[1]

The next problem was how to pay for the plane. The partners decided to open a flying service. They named it Wolverine Air Service—a take on Michigan's nickname, "The Wolverine State." They offered flying instruction, rides, group transportations, and airplane sales and rentals. "If you can drive a car—you can fly a plane," read an advertisement for Wolverine. Never mind that none of the three partners themselves knew how to fly. They found two former military pilots who had flown bombers, and Bosscher, who had worked as an aircraft mechanic during the war, handled the mechanical work. When the planned new local airstrip ran out of money, the partners attached pontoons to the bottom of the Piper Cub and landed and took off from the Grand River—a bit of improvisation that worked until the airpark opened. "Try or cry, that's my slogan," Rich said years later about learning to take risks. "Either try or stop crying about it. Confidence will come in the *doing*."[2]

The fledgling air service put its office in an old chicken coop, as Rich described it, although Jay maintained it was a tool shed. A year into the operation, Bosscher sold the partners his share of the business so he could return to school. Meanwhile, Rich and Jay had discovered another new craze, drive-in restaurants, and decided to start one at the airstrip. They had $300 to invest, built a wooden structure, and opened the Riverside Drive-Inn Restaurant in 1947. It had no electricity at first and no water—the partners had to fill up jugs from nearby and carry them to the restaurant; Rich and Jay took turns flipping hamburgers and waiting on customers.

In its first year of operation, Wolverine Air Service did quite well. It flew 2 million passenger miles and earned $50,000. After several more years in business, the air service had 12 airplanes and 15 pilots. It operated a flight school, charter service, and aircraft repair service, and sold aircraft and gasoline. Wolverine also started putting together travel packages. It offered canoe rides on the river and arranged charter boat fishing excursions on Lake Superior. "A good entrepreneur never rests, so we were always trying to think of something else that we could provide customers at the air park," Jay said.[3] But the business wasn't without its troubles, giving its owners another lesson in resilience. Airplanes sometimes ran out of gas—"one summer, students landed the planes in fields twenty-five times," Jay recalled.[4] The wrong lubricating oil ruined several aircraft, and hail and wind damaged others. Still, "except for a few slight problems . . . Amway today might have been an airline," Jay quipped.[5]

Learning from Failure

Rich and Jay had been taking business classes on the GI Bill at Calvin College whenever they could. But the bill was about to run out, and once again the partners assessed their futures. Neither was ready to settle down. They were both single and still had adventure on their minds. The friends had vacationed in Mexico and Key West, but they wanted to take their time and explore the Caribbean and see South America. They thought the best way to do that was by sailboat, and, as usual, they didn't let lack of experience stop them. In the coastal town of South Norwalk, Connecticut, they bought a 38-foot wooden schooner named *Elizabeth*. During the war the boat had languished in dry dock, which—unbeknownst to the two novice sailors—had caused the hull to dry out and leak. "We didn't know the first thing about buying a boat," Rich admitted years later, "and if I'd known then what I know now, we'd have run, not walked, away. . . ."[6] The only thing worse than the boat was their sailing skills. "But we weren't about to let inexperience get in our way," Rich added.[7] Jay later said that learning to sail a boat was a lot like starting a business. "We didn't know any more about sailing than we did about flying airplanes when we launched the airplane business, but we jumped in anyway," he said. "We made a lot of mistakes, but we kept plugging away, and every day we learned something new."[8]

They set sail from North Carolina in January 1949 with ambitious, if sketchy, plans to cruise down the East Coast, then over to Cuba, the Dominican Republic, Puerto Rico, Venezuela, and around the Atlantic side of South America. The sailors relied on an instruction guide in one hand as they maneuvered the boat's tiller with the other one. It was a voyage of trial and error. "I can't tell you how many times our log book read 'Aground again!'" Rich recalled.[9] Navigation not being their strong suit, the sailors got lost in New Jersey and had to call the Coast Guard, which spent eight hours trying to find them. They weren't even in the Atlantic, but had taken a wrong turn on the Intercoastal Waterway and wound up in a bayou.

The *Elizabeth* leaked all the way to Florida, keeping the bilge pumps working hard. She made it to Cuba, where Jay and Rich had local fishermen recaulk the schooner's seams. They also hired a Cuban crewman before setting sail into the Bahamas Channel. "Unfortunately, the new caulking was worse than the old!" Rich said.[10] The Cuban had an infected tooth and was sick and not much help, either. As they hit rough seas, the ocean rushed in faster than they could pump it out. The boat was about 10 miles out to sea and 85 miles from a port when the cabin began to fill with water. The crew sent out an "SOS" by shooting a flare gun and blinking the sailor's universal call for help on their flashlights.

Luckily, the Bahamas Channel was a major shipping lane. At 2:30 AM an American freighter, the *Adabelle Lykes*, bound for Puerto Rico, spotted the distress signal and pulled alongside the broken boat. She was in such bad shape that it would have to be sunk so it wouldn't be a hazard for other ships in the channel. Jay and Rich had 10 minutes to gather their personal belongings and their remaining cash. Then the other ship's crew chopped a hole in the hull and the captain backed up and smashed his ship into the sailboat to break it up. The sailors watched sadly as the *Elizabeth* disappeared beneath the waves. "It was no Titanic moment," Rich said. "She just leaked and went down."[11]

The captain put Jay and Rich ashore in Puerto Rico. "Our friends and family thought, 'Well, their little adventure's over. They'll come home now.' But Jay and I hadn't come all that way just to turn back," Rich said. "Sure, we'd lost our boat, but we still had a lot of the world to see."[12] The friends still wanted to go to South America. They signed on as deckhands for a British tanker bound for the island of Curacao in the Dutch Antilles off the Venezuelan coast. Once there, they hopped aboard a prop plane to Caracas, Venezuela, then went to Colombia and caught a paddle-wheel steamer up the Magdalena River. Even then—long before the days of drug cartels, routine kidnappings, and murders—violence erupted daily. Communism was gaining popularity, anti-American sentiment was rising, and armed troops patrolled the shore to guard against attacks by bandits who would rob riverboats at night. When the river became too shallow for the boat to go any farther, Jay and Rich got off and caught a train to Medellin. In 1949 it wasn't the drug capital it is today. Instead, the travelers found a pretty city tucked into the cool Andes Mountains. They caught a plane to Cali and then boarded a narrow-gauge train to Buenaventura on the Pacific Coast, where they planned to take an ocean liner down the west coast of South America. Along the way they stopped in Ecuador, Peru, and Chile and talked about what they would do back in the United States. One possibility was importing merchandise they had seen on their travels. "There was no question in our minds that we would start some kind of business again," Jay said. "We weren't sure what it would be, but we had proven to ourselves that we could succeed together."[13]

After spending a month in Santiago, Jay and Rich flew to Buenos Aires, where socialist Juan Peron served as dictator and ran Argentina as a police state. Next on their itinerary were Uruaguay and Brazil. In Rio de Janeiro, on the beach at Copacabana, they came up with the name Ja-Ri—a shortened combination of their first names—for their new business once they got back to the States. Finally, the trip was coming to an end. From Rio, Jay and Rich traveled to Belem at the mouth of the Amazon River, flew to the Guyanas, hop-scotched across several Caribbean islands, including Haiti, and flew into Miami. They had been gone six months, had survived a brush with death at sea, explored a continent together, and had put together a plan for a new business. Rich said the adventure changed his life and way of thinking. "That trip reinforced one truth that Jay and I already knew: If you're not taking risks, you're not living," Rich said. "You've got to take risks and make your own opportunities. You've got to try new experiences and see what happens. It doesn't matter how old you are, or whether you're rich or poor. You have to leap into life and live the adventure."[14] For Jay, seeing the poverty and strong-arm dictatorships of other countries also had a lasting impact. He became a passionate advocate for free enterprise and found it "disheartening to see so many talented and bright people locked out of a chance to succeed."[15] He and Rich were eager to return to the United States and a system that encouraged initiative and where taking risks could lead to great rewards—eventually.

Changing Direction

Upon their return from South America, Jay and Rich didn't waste any time jumping into business together. They formed the Ja-Ri (pronounced "jay-ree") Corporation, an umbrella corporation for their various enterprises. They began importing carved mahogany goods they had seen in Haiti. Competition in the retail market was stiff, however, and the two partners didn't know much about selling to department stores and gift shops. The venture didn't last. They also pursued other avenues that looked like a good way to make money. They ran an ice cream cart business, which failed. With another mutual friend, they started the Grand Rapids Toy Company, which sold wooden rocking horses on which they held patents. The toy venture was a "disaster," Jay said in retrospect, because consumers at that time didn't want high-end, expensive toys.[16] It was a costly business mistake, but they bought back the stock of shareholders at the same price they paid for it so no one lost money—except them.

Jay and Rich had failed as sailors and they had a string of failures as entrepreneurs. They refused to believe failure was final, however. Years later, Rich had this to say about failure:

> You learn much more from failure than from instant success. So when you fail, you should learn everything you can from your failure. If you learn a billion-dollar lesson from a million-dollar flop, then it was well worth it—a cheap education.[17]

The partners kept trying to find something that would make money. They got into the wholesale and retail baked-goods business and sold door-to-door and by mail order. The company, Stone Mill Products, specialized in natural, organic breads and did well enough that Jay and Rich sold it for a profit in 1955. Collectively, all of the businesses that they were involved in taught them valuable lessons, but none of them developed into the big hit the partners longed to make.

Selling Nutrilite

While Jay and Rich had been away on their South American adventure, Jay's cousin Neil Maskaant had sold Jay's parents a dietary supplement called Nutrilite. The product was the idea of Carl F. Rehnborg, who, as a young adventurer himself, had lived in China in the years after World War I until the late 1920s. During his travels from Shanghai to outlying provinces, he noticed that poor, rural Chinese people who ate mostly vegetables and unrefined rice seemed healthier than people who could afford meat and refined foods. Rehnborg was interested in the Chinese culture's tradition of holistic medicine and philosophy of balance in all things. While in the United States, he had worked for Carnation and persuaded the milk company to form a subsidiary to sell canned milk in China. Osteoporosis, the debilitating, degenerative bone disease that is partly attributed to a lack of calcium, was common and Chinese people rarely drank milk. The Chinese didn't particularly care for the taste, and milk upset many stomachs. Rehnborg had seen Carnation research indicating that cows fed alfalfa and water produced the most milk and had shiny coats, so he concluded alfalfa must be a "super food." What was lacking in the diets of the people who had more money to spend on food was the nutrients found in plants, he concluded. Upon returning and settling in California, he began to experiment with a plant-based supplement. By 1939, he had a full-time vitamin business called Nutrilite Products Inc.

Jay's parents loved the product so much they persuaded their son to talk to his cousin about possibly selling it himself. Rehnborg has been credited not only as the father of plant-based food supplements, but also as the pioneer of multilevel marketing, the selling structure that Amway later adopted and refined. Nutrilite was sold directly to customers; you couldn't buy it in a store. Moreover, Rehnborg noticed that when he gave friends the vitamins, they didn't use them and offered him no feedback. But when they had to pay for the vitamins, the supplements took on more value and they suggested that their friends try the product, too. Rehnborg came up with the idea to pay a commission to his friends when they convinced someone else to buy the product. "Reference calls are the most valuable kind of advertising you can have," Rehnborg said.[18] His salespeople began to set up talks at clubs and organizations, and the business grew.

At first, Jay wasn't enthusiastic about the prospect of "pill peddling" but decided to listen to his cousin. When he found out Neil was making $1,000 a month selling Nutrilite, he got interested fast—especially when he learned that the company would pay commissions not only for direct sales, but also for products sold by distributors whom Jay would recruit and train. He promptly ordered two boxes and a sales kit. When he heard about the program, Rich was interested, too. They both agreed to become Nutrilite distributors, even though both at first had their doubts. "The qualms some people have at the thought of selling vitamins quickly disappears when the prospect of making a lot of money enters the picture," Jay observed.[19]

The partners also liked Nutrilite's decentralized organizational structure. They felt that companies with a rigid centralized corporate organization suppressed individual creativity and motivation. "Microcontrol of the individual worker by dozens of managers and committees and vice presidents can't help but crush creativity in the very areas where it is most needed," Jay said. "The thousands of brilliant people who leave megafirms each year to start their own businesses know about the stifling effects of a rigid corporate structure."[20] Because each distributor of Nutrilite had his or her own business, Jay and Rich believed, the company could take advantage of each person's creativity through direct selling. "What distinguished Nutrilite was the focus on individuals, not groups of employees," Jay said. "Individuals retained control over the way they ran their distributorship, because it was their distributorship, and no else's. . . . Upward mobility didn't depend on how well one was able to impress a manager or vice president; it depended only on personal achievement."[21] It also didn't depend on previous experience or a fancy resume. The Nutrilite central operation offered support and handled capital-intensive areas such as research and manufacturing, but it "maintained the independence of each person while rewarding cooperation and emulation."[22] The intent was that distributors could start their business—or end it—without the huge costs business start-ups often encounter raising funds and taking on debt.

When Jay and Rich sketched out the structure of the flow of business, it resembled a pyramid. "In this it was really no different from more traditional firms," Jay said. "In an ordinary firm, there is a small, well-paid group at the top composed of the chairman, president, vice presidents, and so on. Under these people is a larger group of managers, and under the managers is the largest group of all—the technicians, clerks, computer operators, secretaries, and laborers."[23] The federal government and the military are structured that way, he noted. "There's nothing sinister about the shape," Jay explained. Because it focused on individuals, "Nutrilite actually had a more fluid form in its marketing division than traditional corporations."[24] Jay and Rich were convinced the approach resulted in high-quality products and superior customer service. But as they later found with Amway, the decentralized approach had its own distinctive drawbacks when individual distributors got *too* creative and used aggressive sales tactics or recruiting efforts that went beyond the central organization's policies. "Renegade" distributors at Amway eventually would prompt government inquiries, forcing the company to rein them in and issue stronger guidelines and policies on recruiting and sales tactics and avoiding misrepresentation.

■ ■ ■

As they moved into a new phase with their Nutrilite business, perhaps the best thing that had come out of Jay and Rich's adventures and early ventures was their partnership based first on friendship, trust, and shared values. Rich summed it up this way:

> We understood each other because we had seen each other in non-business surroundings. We trusted one another because both of us had been taught honesty and faithfulness by Christian parents. When we entered into various business ventures in our youth, some were successful and some weren't, but I learned Jay's strengths and weaknesses and he learned mine.[25]

They also learned that they needed each other to succeed. "I doubt if there would be an Amway today if either one of us had tried to create it alone," Jay recalled.[26]

The two friends had been in the right place and at the right time when they met and decided to go into business together. They had been searching for the next piece of the puzzle—the right product, the next big thing, the entrepreneur's equivalent of a grand slam hit out of the ballpark. They were ready to take their Nutrilite business to the next level—or multiple levels.

Chapter 4

Sell Something Everybody Needs

Selling vitamins turned out to be a lot like Rich DeVos's early experience selling onions and other vegetables his grandfather had left over from the farmer's market—only more difficult. People needed to eat, but a lot of them didn't see the need to take nutritional supplements and thought they were a waste of money. Those who did want to buy vitamins could find them in retail outlets. Miles Laboratories' first vitamin product, the One-A-Day brand, released in 1940, became the first mass-market multivitamin success story.[1] It was cheap, too, compared with Nutrilite. A month's supply of the Nutrilite extra strength formulation could cost up to $20, which was a lot of money at the time.[2]

Learning the Ropes

The day after they bought their Nutrilite starter kits, Jay and Rich made their first sale of one box to a man who owned a grocery store in Ada, a town outside Grand Rapids. Despite that early encouraging sign, they didn't sell another box for two weeks and had no luck attracting others to their distributor organization. Friends whom they told about their new business "thought we were crazy," Jay said.[3] He and Rich began to wonder if they were, too—or at least if they had made a mistake. They grew so discouraged by the constant rejection that they considered doing the very thing they abhorred: quitting. However, they had learned from past mistakes that it wasn't worth expending time and effort on an enterprise that wasn't producing the results they wanted. They shifted their attention back to their other businesses.

Then Jay's cousin invited them to attend a Nutrilite distributor meeting in Chicago. The Ja-Ri partners agreed, figuring they either needed to find a reason to stay with Nutrilite or drop it. A hundred and fifty people turned out for the meeting, many more than Jay or Rich expected to see. Moreover, the people who attended were "all excited about selling vitamins, and many of them enjoying considerable success in their Nutrilite businesses," Jay recalled.[4] Some were doing so well they had quit their previous jobs to sell the supplement full time. One speaker after another related their success stories and shared strategies to boost sales. Jay and Rich soaked up the enthusiasm and information and left newly inspired. On the drive home from Chicago, they decided that maybe their problem was a lack of focus. They took a big gamble—they decided to drop everything else they were doing and concentrate all their energies on Nutrilite. "We were so excited by the time we reached Grand Rapids that we pulled over into a gas station on Hall Street and subjected the fellow behind the counter to a high-energy sales talk," Jay recalled. "He bought a box, probably more as a friendly gesture than out of a desire for better nutrition."[5] Whatever the reason, they had made a sale and were determined to make more.

As they had learned at the distributor meeting, testimonials from satisfied Nutrilite customers often convinced others to try the product. Jay and Rich started selling more boxes by using that strategy as well.

Next they set up a meeting in the basement of the restaurant at the Grand Rapids airport to try to convince others to become distributors. They hoped to attract 100 people. Only 8 came. And it was a very strange group—they came all together, sat and listened to Jay and Rich pitch the product, watched a film about it, and didn't ask a question or say a word. Then they all got up and left together. "Rich and I were flabbergasted," Jay said.[6] After the meeting, however, one of the attendees confessed they were all other Nutrilite salespeople who attended just to size up the new guys on the block—doubly discouraging because Jay and Rich then realized they had competition from other distributors in the area.

Love and Marriage

Nutrilite not only gave Jay a business, it also indirectly brought him love. His aunt was a housekeeper for the Hoekstra family in Grand Rapids and she also was one of his Nutrilite customers. When she suggested that Mrs. Hoekstra might want to buy some Nutrilite products, Jay stopped by there one morning in 1951. "I was met at the door by her beautiful blond-haired, blue-eyed daughter, Betty," Jay said. "Making a Nutrilite sale suddenly became a second reason for my visit! I probably botched my sales presentation, but Mrs. Hoekstra decided to buy a box of Nutrilite products anyway."[7] He asked Betty out and she agreed. After several months of dating, Jay knew he'd found the woman he wanted to marry. She accepted his proposal, and they married in August 1952. Their living room became the site of Nutrilite meetings, and the basement served as the office. Jay and Rich ran the fledgling business on a shoestring. They mended the ripped seats of their cheap chairs with duct tape and used the top of the washer and dryer as a staging area to ship products. Jay wrote sales manuals, ran them off on a mimeograph machine, and collated them on the Ping-Pong table. A year after Jay's wedding, Rich married a woman also of Dutch heritage, Helen Van Wesep. She acted as secretary since she knew how to type. Jay and Rich kept setting up sales meetings at the airport and pushing the product. Once they held a sales meeting in Lansing, the state capital, and advertised it on the radio and in the newspaper. Jay and Rich even stood on street corners and handed out brochures. The auditorium they had booked would hold 200 people. Despite their effort, "it was a disaster!" Rich recalled. "Only two people showed up. It's tough to make a powerhouse sales speech to an empty auditorium."[8] He and Jay couldn't afford a motel room, so they drove home in the middle of the night.

■ ■ ■

Despite continuing setbacks, the partners kept at it and slowly built a distributor network that generated a group sales volume of $85,000 in the first year. Jay was adept at putting together sales presentations, and Rich, a natural speaker who radiated confidence and enthusiasm, was good at pitching them. They lived by three rules for their business: believe in the product and use it, be determined to succeed, and stay personally involved. "We had to know what was going on to make good decisions about products and policies," Jay explained.[9] To stay in touch with employees and distributors in their network, they began holding monthly "Speak Up" meetings to address concerns before they festered into major problems—a practice that Amway has continued.

Eventually, Jay and Rich became the nation's most successful Nutrilite distributors. But just when business was looking up, they encountered trouble. It came not from their operation in Michigan but from California, where Nutrilite was based.

The Debate Begins over Structure

Carl Rehnborg, Nutrilite's inventor, had met a psychologist named William Casselberry at a Dale Carnegie sales course. The two became business associates. Casselberry headed up Nutrilite sales with a man named Lee Mytinger, who had previously sold, among other things, cemetery plots. Nutrilite split into two companies: Nutrilite Products Inc. handled the manufacturing, and Mytinger & Casselberry ran the distribution operation, which included Jay and Rich and the other distributors. One of their marketing tools was a book called *How to Get Well and Stay Well*. It attracted the attention not only of potential customers, but also of the U.S. Food and Drug Administration. Regulators had grown increasingly concerned about some vitamin manufacturers' flamboyant claims—claims that weren't backed by the current science. William W. Goodrich, who was the FDA's general counsel from 1939 to 1971, recalled in an oral history interview that the Mytinger & Casselberry incident made the FDA start scrutinizing the way vitamins were being sold directly to consumers. One-A-Day, for example, had product labeling and an insert in the box, which the FDA had gone over line by line and raised objections to when it felt some health claims were too broad.[10] But the direct-sales model was of special concern to the FDA because there was no control over the claims made by individual salespeople, except in published materials. "The adaptation of house-to-house direct selling sales combined with the pyramid-type method of distribution that was feeding that direct sales technique led to the first big confrontation we had with this problem," Goodrich recalled.[11]

The word *pyramid* often is used to describe an organizational structure common in many firms, with a chairman and/or president at the top and different levels of managers below them. (The military is structured this way, as is the federal government.) The pyramid structure becomes illegal, however—a so-called pyramid scheme—when certain specific activities take place related to recruiting. The Direct Selling Association, the nation's leading trade group for multilevel marketers, defines it this way:

> Pyramid schemes are illegal scams in which large numbers of people at the bottom of the pyramid pay money to a few people at the top. Each new participant pays for the chance to advance to the top and profit from payments of others who might join later.[12]

For example, if John gives $100 to a recruiter to join an organization on the bottom level, and then he enlists 10 more people to give $100 and moves up, John gets $900. It sounds good in principle, but the recruiting would have to continue forever for everyone in the pyramid to continue making money. "In order for everyone in a pyramid scheme to profit, there would have to be a never-ending supply of new participants," according to the DSA. Of course, the pyramid would collapse eventually because there is a limit to the number of people who can participate. It's all based on mathematics. "Pyramid schemes always fall apart because the payoff relies primarily on new recruits, and sooner or later, every scheme runs out of new members," the National Consumers League says.[13] Some pyramid schemes masquerade as multilevel marketing (MLM) by coming up with a line of products and claiming to be in the business of selling them to consumers. However, little or no effort is made to actually market the products. Instead, money is made in typical pyramid scheme fashion—from recruiting. "New participants are often encouraged to buy the products themselves, and the money is used to 'pay off' those at the top of the pyramid."[14] Often, the product being sold has questionable value to consumers or it was excessively marketed as a "miracle cure."

Goodrich didn't go so far as to call the Mytinger & Casselberry distribution organization a pyramid scheme, but he did say that their Nutrilite book went too far. It used

> . . . all the psychology techniques; that is, that everybody wants to be well, and you're sick, first, it hurts, and second, it costs you money. Therefore, you want to be well. And the way to get well and stay well is to feed your body right. And if you feed your body right, you take these vitamins and minerals. And if you do that, then you're not going to have these diseases. And if you have the diseases, the vitamins and minerals are going to restore the so-called balance in your body to where the disease can't exist in that kind of an environment. Well, you know the old spiel.[15]

The book included many testimonials. One page listed all the diseases that Nutrilite was supposed to address. "It was a book that didn't pull any punches," Goodrich said. "That is, it went on and told you that if you had epilepsy or if you had heart disease, this was for you."[16]

The FDA cited Mytinger & Casselberry for disseminating misleading information. The salesmen, in turn, hired a lawyer who recommended they rewrite the book. They pulled out the last section that contained the claims that triggered the FDA investigation and brought out a new edition, but the agency cited it again. In 1948 the FDA began to seize Nutrilite product shipments, setting in motion a long legal battle. Mytinger & Casselberry filed suit against the agency to enjoin it from confiscating Nutrilite and claiming they were proceeding in good faith and that the agency was harassing them.[17] The case went to trial and the FDA lost. Goodrich blamed the ruling on bias against the FDA by the judge, who issued a temporary restraining order against the agency. Then the case went on to district court, where the FDA lost again, and all the way to the Supreme Court—twice. The first time the FDA lawyers lost when they argued the district court had no jurisdiction. But the second time the Supreme Court reversed the lower court's decision. Still, the FDA pursued its case against Mytinger & Casselberry, contending that house-to-house sellers were making unsupportable claims about Nutrilite.

The consent decree that resulted from the dispute broke new ground. It led the FDA to establish guidelines for vitamin and mineral supplement claims. Nutrilite stayed in business, but Mytinger & Casselberry could no longer use testimonials to promote the vitamins. The case also was notable because it highlighted the problem of distributors who used sales techniques that pushed the envelope—a problem that has bedeviled Amway for decades. Moreover, it was the first but not the last time the government and multilevel marketers would lock horns over the way such direct-selling organizations do business. Goodrich said:

> What I learned in this case was the way people looked at vitamins somewhat differently from other products. We had a physician from Cincinnati Medical School who had written on this subject in the medical journals. His evaluation of it, which I think is right, was that Americans want to believe in tonics; they always have believed in tonics. And the vitamins should be considered a tonic and are considered as a tonic because they're nontoxic and they're readily available, and if people feel like they take them, they're doing them some good, whether or not they are, then they really weren't doing an awful lot of harm. And that has made it hard on us on regulating vitamins all the way through.[18]

In his memoir, Jay hinted that the FDA was uneasy about companies such as Nutrilite and tried to make trouble for them. He wrote:

> In the 1950s, no one quite knew what path the vitamin industry would take or how big it would become. Certainly the

medical profession was concerned that vitamins, which were of course nonprescription, would become a competitor to traditional medicine. The big pharmaceutical firms were none too pleased, either. To the FDA and the traditional medical-care industry, Nutrilite was a little fly in the ointment.[19]

Nutrilite continued its marketing campaign in publications such as *LIFE* and the *Saturday Evening Post* and by sponsoring a national radio show that featured singer Dennis Day. But the negative publicity and restriction on using testimonials hurt sales. "It's difficult to sell anything if you can't tell people that it works," Jay said.[20] To keep a revenue stream going, the company decided to bring out a line of cosmetics named after Carl Rehnborg's wife, Edith. That led to a dispute with Mytinger & Casselberry, which unveiled its own cosmetics products, competing to sell them through Nutrilite distributors. The falling-out led to a full-blown legal battle when Mytinger & Casselberry requested a court order to stop Rehnborg from selling cosmetics. Sales suffered for both companies, as distributors quit selling to see which side would win. Inside Nutrilite, managers began fighting for dominance, distrust ran rampant, and Rehnborg was in danger of losing his company.

Another Change in Direction

Back in Michigan, Jay and Rich watched the fight with growing alarm. Their Ja-Ri organization had 5,000 distributors, some of whom were talking about leaving. Nutrilite had alienated many by violating a cardinal principle of MLM called sponsorship—if someone is introduced into the business, or sponsored, by Bill, for example, then that person can't go buy products from another distributor; he has to buy them from Bill. Jay and Rich felt they needed to protect their distributors as Nutrilite managers began breaking lines of sponsorship. "Carl (Rehnborg), deeply attached to his product line and suffering under crushing regulatory pressure, was not as effective as he might have been in solving these problems," Jay said. "He was a visionary, he had a strong entrepreneurial drive, and he had a good product idea, but he was hindered by poor managers."[21] Jay stepped in and tried to help resolve the dispute between Rehnborg and Mytinger & Casselberry; Rehnborg even offered him the president's position at Nutrilite, but Jay turned it down. He couldn't accept the loss of independence. He said:

> It was important to Rich and to me to be self-employed, to set our own courses and make decisions that would truly be our own. Even in a high-level position at Nutrilite, I would be an employee, limited in my ability to do what I thought was best and at the mercy of someone else's decisions.[22]

In the summer of 1958 Ja-Ri held a key meeting of its distributors in Charlevoix, Michigan. Jay and Rich didn't want to drop Nutrilite, but they also wanted to reduce the group's reliance on it by developing a new product line. They also proposed creating a new direct-selling venture, calling it the American Way Association because both believed the American way of private ownership and free enterprise was the best way. The distributors were independent, of course, and could make their own decisions, but everyone at the meeting stayed with Jay and Rich. Before long, other Nutrilite distributors who had heard about Ja-Ri's new direction wanted to join them. At first, the partners refused because they didn't want to "raid" Nutrilite, but several years later they would allow distributors from other groups to join them and kept their lines of sponsorship intact.

The Grand Slam Hit

With the core of their new direct-selling venture established, Jay and Rich next set about figuring out what kind of product to sell. It was an important decision and one they discussed at length. After watching Nutrilite's battle with the FDA, the partners knew they didn't want to move into an industry that was highly regulated. They also didn't want to get involved in anything that had to be explained, that required a lot of training, or that required convincing the consumer that he or she needed it. "A Nutrilite sale required a one-hour presentation to convince the potential customer of their need for dietary supplements," Jay said. "Our new product line had to be something everyone knew they needed" and could be sold with a minimum of effort.[23]

What was something that everyone needed and used every day and always had to buy when it ran out? Something that they understood and recognized the need for immediately and that didn't require a lot of effort to sell? They kept kicking around ideas.

Then it hit them. Of course. It was so simple, so logical. Why hadn't they thought of it before?

Soap! They would sell soap.

Chapter 5

Unveiling "The Plan"

About the same time that Jay and Rich were launching their new direct-selling business in 1959, Fidel Castro was sworn in as prime minister of Cuba. Socialism, Communism, and Marxism were gaining footholds around the world. "A wave of pessimism swept over many Americans," Rich observed. "People said to me, 'Capitalism has failed. It is failing around the world.'"[1] Rich didn't believe it and neither did Jay. In their view, the capitalist system paid people's bills and made their lifestyles possible. It was "the American Way." In fact, that soon would be the name of their new company—Amway, a shortened version of "American Way." Rich explained that they settled on the name because "the American way of private ownership and free enterprise is the best way."[2]

Humble Beginnings

Rich and Jay also believed that soap and detergents would be the easiest products for training distributors. It was a matter of which one to use rather than whether to use one at all, and there was no pesky governmental regulation involved. They didn't have a manufacturing facility of their own, of course, so they scouted around for a product they could distribute. They found a liquid detergent called "Frisk," which was manufactured by Eckle Company, a small Detroit supplier, and one of the only biodegradable liquid detergents available, a feature they felt would distinguish it from other products. They renamed it "L.O.C. All-Purpose Cleaner" (L.O.C. being an acronym for "liquid organic compound"). The owner of the Frisk product, however, proved to be unreliable and inconsistent. "He sold us products first with red caps, but a later order would have yellow caps, and the next, blue," Rich recalled. "Sometimes the liquid was clear and other times yellow." One time, Jay and Rich received a shipment and the labels fell off the bottles. They found another supplier, only to have the original one sue them for a quarter of a million dollars, saying they'd stolen his formula.[3] The partners next acquired SA8, one of the first biodegradable powder detergents—*biodegradable* meaning it will break down and decompose into elements found in nature in a short time.[4] The term is often used to describe a product that is "environmentally friendly," which became more and more important to Jay and Rich when manufacturing future products. "Amway was probably the very first company of any size to market biodegradable detergents," Jay said.[5] L.O.C. also was a nonphosphate cleaner, which kept lakes and streams free from massive algae growth, and it was concentrated. A little bit went a long way, as the marketing slogan claimed. At the time they acquired the soap products, Jay and Rich did not want to depend on a third-party manufacturer, but they couldn't afford to make the product themselves. In 1960, though, they bought a 50 percent interest in the manufacturing company, changed its name to Amway Manufacturing Corporation, and moved its operations to Ada, near their homes.

Now that they had the beginnings of a product line, Jay and Rich set about determining how best to market it. Jay wrote the sales print advertising. He called it "The Amazing Frisk Story," a new and better cleaning agent that contained "the pure oils of fresh coconut meat, nitrogen from

the air we breathe and many of the same amines which are used in medicine today. Just a little goes a long way."[6] Frisk was sold in a five-gallon
can for $18. To sell the soap, Jay and Rich hatched out what they called
the "Amway Sales and Marketing Plan"; Amway insiders later shortened
it to, simply, "the Plan." It was designed to move the soap products and
Nutrilite through a network of distributors to retail customers. The partners met at Jay's house and laid down a big sheet of white butcher paper
on his kitchen floor to sketch out the details of the Plan: First, each distributor would be an independent business owner (IBO), not an Amway
employee. That person had an incentive to sell Amway products and
build a sales organization to sell even more. Jay explained the Plan this
way: "The more an individual sells, the more he makes, and the more
that individual's sales organization sells, the more he makes. No one
makes a dime unless products are sold."[7] The Plan of recruiting, sponsoring, and selling basically was the same as Nutrilite's had been.

Jay's cousin Neil Maaskant, who had introduced Jay and Rich to
Nutrilite, took the helm of Ja-Ri. Amway began as a new division of
the parent company. Jay and Rich decided to alternate titles; one year
Jay would be the chairman and Rich the president, and the next year it
would be reversed. In the early days of the fledgling company, the
partners still used Jay's basement as the office and Rich's as the warehouse. Jay's son Steve, who would succeeded him as Amway's chairman,
recalled those early years: "As kids, all we had to do to see the business
was go into the basement. I remember walking down in the basement
and the biggest part of my whole day was going down to see my dad's
assistant and she would make me a paper airplane."[8] Jay again wrote the
company's sales manuals, copied them on a mimeograph machine, and
collated them on the Ping-Pong table. Betty and Helen helped, too.
By November 1959, Amway had a handful of employees, a corporate
structure, and a new name—the Amway Sales Corporation. Its primary
role was to administer the Plan.

The Plan

Here's how the Plan worked: Distributors were encouraged to sell at
retail to persons they knew or were referred to rather than selling door-
to-door. Anyone wanting to become an authorized Amway distributor

had to be sponsored by another Amway distributor and fill out an application for the right to sell Amway products. A new Amway distributor
was not required to buy inventory, but was asked to purchase a $15.60
sales kit containing product information, sales aids, and literature. An
optional product kit, containing sample Amway products for demonstra-
tion, could be purchased for an additional $25.65. Amway said neither
the company nor sponsoring distributors made a profit on the sales kit.
If a distributor decided to leave the business, he or she could get a refund
on the price of the sales and product kits. The new salespeople sponsored
by an Amway distributor became part of that distributor's "personal
group," or "downline." They, in turn, could build their own personal
groups, building the personal group of the first sponsoring distributor.

Under the Plan, distributors earned income several ways. One way
was through the "basic discount," meaning the difference between
the price paid by the distributor for the product and the price charged
by the distributor at retail. Distributors did not make any profit selling
products to their sponsored distributors because they were sold at the same
price the sponsoring distributor paid. Most distributors averaged 30 percent of business volume as income.[9] Performance bonuses were based on a
point value, or PV, and business volume system assigned to every product,
and ranged from 3 to 25 percent. Point value is constant, but business volumes rise with inflation. As the number of PVs rose, so did the percent-
ages of sales paid out in the form of a bonus. A point value of 100 carried a
3 percent bonus, while 1,500 was 15 percent and 7,500 was 25 percent. At
7,500 — or about $8,500 sales per month—distributors could "go direct,"
breaking off from the personal group of their sponsor and dealing directly
with Amway. They received performance bonuses from Amway and were
responsible for redistributing bonuses to all distributors downline in their
personal group. Directs also were eligible for voting membership in the
Amway Distributors Association and they qualified for several bonuses—
the 3 percent direct distributor bonus, a sales training bonus (for any
directs who sponsored three other directs for any six months in a year),
and a profit-sharing bonus. Amway had about 3,000 direct distributors in
1972; by 1977, the number had grown to 4,000. Direct distributors had
to requalify every year based on the sales volume. Directs also had to buy
back any unused marketable products from a distributor who was not
moving inventory or wanted to leave the business.

Even with that requirement, making direct was the goal of many distributors because of the potential for rewards. And that was just the first level of achievement in the Amway distribution hierarchy. A distributor who made 7,500 PV in one month was called a Silver producer; a Gold direct maintained that PV for three months. From there, they go higher to levels named after precious stones: Ruby (15,000 PV in a month); Emerald (sponsors three Gold directs); and Diamonds (sponsors six Gold directs). When distributors reached one of these levels, they received a pin inset with the jewel—hence the description "pin levels" (see more about this in Chapter 8, "Diamonds, Rubies, Emeralds, and Pearls"). Other direct sellers, such as Tupperware, also have used pins as a way to reward distributors for reaching certain sales and sponsoring goals. Keeping in touch with its independent business owners became a big job and a high priority for Amway. It communicated with distributors with literature and with 10 or 15 sales rallies held each year. Thousands of distributors attended the meetings. High-volume distributors met with company officials in the afternoon, and IBOs and guests attended glitzy evening rallies that featured awards presentations, rousing speeches, entertainment, and personal testimonials of distributors who had made or surpassed their goals and were making good money. Celebrities often were brought in to make inspirational comments and cheer on the sellers. Direct distributors also held area meetings for their groups. In the late 1970s, about 5,000 distributor-operator meetings were held each week.[10] The meetings, usually held in a distributor's home, were aimed at training, motivating, and sponsoring.

Opportunity Meeting

Recruiting distributors—or "showing the Plan," as many called it— occurred at a separate "opportunity meeting," which each distributor was encouraged to hold at least once a week and to recruit individually rather than at mass meetings. The Amway Career Manual for distributors described how to recruit new distributors this way:

> Announce to your guests that you would like to tell them about an exciting opportunity to be in business for themselves

and to develop an income of as much as $1,000 per month. Explain that it is an opportunity that grows as they share it with others. Ask if they are as successful as they would like to be. If not, would they be interested in a chance to realize their dreams through a business of their own that they can build on a part-time basis—and, with such a modest initial expenditure? An opportunity does exist that will give them such a chance.[11]

The manual went on to advise distributors to give a short history of the company, describe products, distribute sales literature, and then ask some questions to discover the prospective distributors' goals: Did they want a new car, a new house, or a college education for their children? What kind of car would they like? How much extra money a month would they need for that new car (or house or college education for their children). Finally, the question that hooked many a prospective distributor: "Would you be interested if I could show you a way you can make your dreams come true?"[12]

The sales literature featured examples of how to build a personal group. Instead of a pyramid structure, the basic design was more like a flower, with a circle in the middle—representing the sponsor—and lines around it connected to other circles. "Drawing the circles," some called showing the Plan. The literature also showed an example of how to build toward a direct distributorship. For example, if you have a business volume (BV) of $500 of Amway products monthly, and the distributors you sponsor increase their sales and sponsor distributors of their own, contributing an additional $5,000 to your total business volume, you are now in the 21 percent performance bonus bracket (if you have at least 4,000 points in your monthly total point value). So you get your basic discount on your personal BV, plus 21 percent bonus on your personal PV, plus 21 percent and the percentage of performance bonus you get, earned by each of your distributors. You now earn $711.

That may have sounded good to some prospects, but a lot of uncertainties remained. Most new Amway distributors did not have any selling or business experience and had another full-time occupation, conducting their Amway business part time.[13] Turnover was high. About 75 percent of Amway distributors quit during their first year, and about 25 percent thereafter. The direct-selling industry in the 1950s was just getting started, and Jay and Rich had no successful examples to follow of businesses that were exactly like theirs. There were no case studies of direct-selling enterprises, no courses to take, no how-to seminars. "We didn't know if this new venture would be a success like the air service or a dud like the toy company," Jay later admitted. "We were pioneers, in a sense, and learning had to be done by trial and error."[14] As pioneers, the partners had to hit the road and train distributors while also giving them encouragement and rewarding them in nonmonetary ways with praise and celebration when a distributor landed a customer. Rich traveled coast to coast, speaking in major cities and drumming up more customers and distributors. He had a gift for motivating people and making them feel special. In 1965, Amway got its first plane, a twin-engine Piper Aztec. Two years later, Rich made an inspirational record called "Selling America." It would be the first in a long line of his taped motivational messages that spurred on Amway business owners.

On the Road

Harkening back to their experience with Nutrilite when it alienated distributors, Rich and Jay were determined to protect the lines of sponsorship when a distributor recruited and trained another person to sell Amway products. Maintaining control over those lines was essential, the partners believed. They put in place a code of "Rules of Conduct" of the Amway Sales Plan, published in 1963 and revised multiple times over the years, to try to prevent distributors from abusing their selling and recruiting privileges. Distributors were warned against misrepresenting the ease of making money from the Plan and quoting dollar incomes. In 1979, when the Federal Trade Commission (FTC) issued its final order on the question of whether Amway was an illegal pyramid scheme, it detailed the rules:[15]

- *Cross-group selling rule.* Amway distributors had to agree to sell at wholesale only to distributors they had sponsored and to buy only from their sponsor. The rule gave distributors an incentive to recruit others and to train and motivate them to sell products since the sponsor received income on the downline sales volume.

- *Retail store rule.* Amway distributors could not sell in retail stores or set up displays or booths at fairs, home shows, or other special events. Sales of Amway products in fund-raising drives also were restricted. The reason behind the rule was to give Amway distributors incentives to provide services to consumers—to go into their homes—demonstrate and explain the products and deliver them at the customer's convenience. Those kinds of services weren't available from a retail store and differentiated Amway, the company believed.

- *Customer protection rule.* Upon making a sale to a retail customer, an Amway distributor had an exclusive right to resell to that customer for the next 30 days. If it was a commercial account, the right was effective for 90 days. Whenever a distributor approached a new prospective customer, the salesperson had to ask the prospect if he or she already was buying products from an Amway distributor. If that was the case, the distributor could not sell to the customer and had to refer the customer to the regular distributor. The rule was carried over to Amway from the Nutrilite sales plan. Later, in 1972, Amway abolished the rule but said it was unethical to cut out another Amway distributor.

- *Advertising rule.* Only direct distributors could display the Amway name on the outside of their office, which was limited for wholesale only. Distributors had to get written approval from Amway to use outdoor advertising on billboards or signs and could not use the Amway name or logo on checks (except to describe themselves as Amway distributors), and any classified recruiting ads had to follow the exact wording of 17 formats Amway provided.

- *Price fixing.* Amway fixed the prices at which it sold its products to distributors and consumers. It also fixed the charge for freight collected by distributors. Amway's Career Manual for distributors explained wholesale prices this way:

> In Amway, a sponsor does not succeed unless his sponsored distributors succeed. He cannot make money by simply selling products to his sponsored distributors because he sells them for the same price he paid for them: the distributor cost. Instead, he makes money on the Performance Bonuses

they generate on their Business Volume, which in turn is based on their retail sales. . . ."[16]

Distributors who sold Amway products at wholesale prices to a retail customer faced possible termination.

Amway's first two cleaning products sold well—in the early 1960s, sales were more than $500,000—and became anchors of the product line. Distributors found that one of the keys to selling them was to offer testimonials, demonstrations, and suggestions for using the products in creative ways. Distributor Fred Hansen demonstrated L.O.C. at the Ohio State Fair in 1959 by asking a bystander for a handkerchief and then smearing it with grease, washing it with L.O.C., and returning the clean but wet cloth to its surprised owner. One enterprising distributor in North Carolina even showed a commercial fisherman how L.O.C. could get his nets clean.[17] The company also began what became an Amway tradition, holding sales events that became pep rallies, with speeches about pulling together and supporting each other on the team. Rich pumped up the distributors with rousing messages. "Soap. Why does Amway sell it? Simple," he said in one of his speeches. "Everybody needs soap. They use it up. Then they buy more. They don't need to get samples to understand soap, and they buy it without risk because it carries a money-back guarantee."[18]

Soap would remain a mainstay product for Amway, but Jay and Rich wanted to diversify and experimented with other products, such as home water-softening equipment and cookware. Some products were flops. During the Cold War years, with Americans concerned about the Soviet Union's possession of atomic bombs, Amway tried to sell bomb shelters and electric generators. The company had strayed from its original premise—sell something everyone needs and that is not too complicated to explain—and they did not sell many Cold War products. "Our Sales and Marketing Plan was not well suited at that time to products that required installation and maintenance expertise," Jay said. Products centered around the home became Amway's mainstay in those first years of business. An automobile polish called Silicon Glaze sold well. Jay and Rich came up with the formulation after testing various combinations of ingredients on Jay's car. "My car never did look the same after the experiments we performed on it," he said.[19]

Soap and Hope

The first years of business, while exciting, were not profitable ones for Amway. Michigan National Bank gave Amway a loan when other banks refused, and Monsanto Chemical, a key Amway supplier, continued to work with the company even when Amway had a net worth of only $10,000 and owed Monsanto Chemical $60,000. By 1960, Amway had outgrown Jay's and Rich's basements. The partners found an abandoned gas station in Ada and hired a contractor to put a door on a bathroom and to build some shelving. In the first full year of operating, Amway had gross sales of $500,000.[20]

As Amway continued to grow, the partners kept expanding the building, then built a 5,600-square-foot manufacturing facility. The partners also began to realize each other's strengths and how best to use them. They didn't sit down and say, "You do this and I'll do that." It was more of a natural division of tasks. Rich was the stronger motivational speaker and head of distributor relations. Jay had more of a knack with financial analysis and internal affairs. "Rich was the seller, and Jay kept his eyes on the books. They made a great pair," said the late President Gerald Ford, a long-time friend of Amway's founders.[21] Rich enjoyed making his "Selling America" motivational speeches to various groups and rallying the sales force, while Jay liked to see which products generated the most profits and how to fine-tune the business to make it as efficient and effective as possible. Jay was older, so he served as chairman. Rich was the president. Their board had two members. They agreed that business decisions needed a unanimous vote. Rich violated that agreement once. He wanted a bigger car and he bought a Packard as a company car without asking Jay. "I was driven by ego," Rich said years later. He apologized, but Jay shrugged it off. "I got my way, but I violated our own corporate policy of both of us agreeing on capital expenditures," Rich recalled.[22] He never did that again.

The 1960s were a decade of seeing what worked and what didn't, of camaraderie, of building a sales organization that gained more and

more experience, and of steady growth. Amway opened its first
international business in Canada in 1962, a natural step because the
company was close to the border and the markets were similar. Also
growing was the network of distributors who sold Amway products to
other distributors and so on down the line. Some surpassed Amway's
own forecasts, and new pin levels were added. In 1962, Amway
introduced its "Ruby direct" pin level. A year later, Jere and Eileen
Dutt became the first Diamond direct distributors, complete with a
new pin. In 1964, the company introduced one of its most enduring
products, Dish Drops dishwashing liquid. The Artistry prestige brand
of facial skin care and cosmetics, based on Nutrilite's Edith Rehnborg
line of cosmetics, debuted in 1968. That year, the company added a
"Triple Diamond" pin level. As the product line expanded, the company added more production lines, labs, and research centers. The Ada
headquarters seemed to be under construction all the time. By the end
of the decade, Amway's lines of sponsorship spread across the nation,
with more than 80,000 distributors. After 10 years of raising Amway
from infancy, Jay and Rich were excited about taking the company to
the next level.

That almost changed on the night of July 18, 1969. Jay was sitting
in his living room reading when he heard a boom outside. He rushed
to the window to look and saw an orange glow to the north. "My heart
pounded once, very hard, and my throat contracted in fear," Jay said."[23]
The glow came from the vicinity of Amway's factory. The phone rang,
and it was trouble—the east wing of the Amway plant had exploded.
(Rich, who had bought another boat despite his first disastrous experience with the *Elizabeth*, was out of town upstate in the lake country.)

By the time Jay arrived on the scene, 60-foot-tall flames engulfed
the building. Several hundred feet away sat tanks full of highly flammable
petroleum derivatives. Fire trucks already had arrived and were hooking
up hoses. Jay could see that the roof on the aerosol division of the factory
had collapsed. "The roar of burning gas was deafening," Jay said. When
some employees tried to enter an adjoining office building to get some
important files, Jay yelled, "Forget the papers. Get the people out!"[24] No
one was killed in the blast, but the explosion injured 17 people and did
more than half a million dollars in damage to the building. Jay set about
lining up new suppliers, making plans for a new aerosol building, and

finding jobs for the displaced employees. The accident convinced the partners that Amway needed its own fire department—and it's had one ever since.

■ ■ ■

After overcoming that setback, the next decade was a period of continued growth. Amway's number of active distributors rose to 300,000 in 1972.[25] Years later, Jay would look back and say that he and Rich made a good choice in kicking off Amway's product line with cleaning products. "For better or worse, Amway is today identified with soap more than any other product we sell," Jay said. "In picking something that was easy to sell, we made something of a breakthrough in direct selling. To this day, Amway has followed the principle of marketing products that have a broad appeal and are sold with a minimum of effort."[26]

Selling a combination of "soap and hope" had worked for Amway so far. The company also had bounced back from a potential disaster and put out one fire that threatened its existence. But by the mid-1970s another one was smoldering. And this time the heat came not from flames but from the federal government.

Chapter 6

Toppling the Pyramid

Direct marketing's most famous symbol may be the Tupperware party. Named for inventor and founder Earl Silas Tupper, Tupperware traces its roots to a vastly different product than its plastic containers.

The Method Catches On

During World War II, Tupper outfitted American troops with gas masks and other plastic items. After the war he decided to move into the consumer market and bought a used plastic molding machine and some polyethylene pellets from DuPont. Plastic in the 1940s, however, was not the ubiquitous, versatile, flexible material that's now part of everyday life and integral to products from computers to automobiles. Derived from crude oil, early plastic was "still primitive, being generally brittle, slimy and smelly."[1] Back then, Bakelite was the material often used to make radios, spoon handles, brushes, and assorted everyday items. Tupper set about transforming plastic into a more palatable material that was "resilient, solid, and grease-free, but also clean, clear, and translucent."[2] He also developed a patented seal, modeled on a paint can's inverted rim, that was water- and airtight. The seal—and the now-familiar "burp" of air before it locked—kept food from drying out, going stale, and losing flavor, or wilting, whether it was cookies cached away in the cupboard or leftovers stored in the refrigerator. Tupper named his first container the "Wonderbowl."[3]

In 1946, the inventor launched his line of Tupperware containers for sale in retail outlets. But consumers, still skeptical about plastic, weren't buying. They needed demonstrations to understand how the new-fangled products worked and to see that plastic food containers were hygienic and didn't smell.[4] Another company, Stanley Home Products, had used a network of sales representatives to introduce homemakers to its products at a party. Typically, the get-togethers were held at a home by a hostess, who invited her friends and family. This was a new twist on the traveling salesman who often traversed the cities and country-side, selling everything from encyclopedias to elixirs. The Fuller Brush Company sold cleaners, mops, and brushes that way, too, and had gone national. Tupper himself had hawked his family farm's poultry and produce door-to-door when he was growing up in New Hampshire. It made sense—why not sell Tupperware direct to consumers, too? Tupper switched gears, and the Tupperware home party was about to be born.

The timing was right for Tupperware to conquer the American consumer economically and socially. After World War II, the U.S. economy expanded and returning soldiers flooded the workforce. Wages were higher than ever, so middle-class families often found they could survive on one income. But as the birth rate soared and the consumer-driven economy took off, families began to need extra income as their standards of living rose and there were so many things to buy. Some women who had worked during the war also found they missed being a financial contributor to their households or maintaining some financial independence for themselves.

When Tupperware in 1951 removed its products from retail shelves and started only selling directly to consumers through independent sales representatives, many women saw an opportunity to work part time or as many hours as they wanted to, from home, without interfering with child-rearing or household duties. Tupper put a vibrant and forceful saleswoman named Brownie Wise in charge of home sales. Wise had been a top-selling Stanley Home Products dealer and manager before she joined Tupperware, which modeled its direct sales force on Stanley's. She was the one who convinced Tupper to switch from selling Tupperware through retailers and to focus on parties and one-on-one sales. Wise began building a network of women, mostly housewives looking for extra income and something to do, to sell Tupperware from their homes. She helped elevate the Tupperware party into a fun and profitable way to market products and Tupperware into the world's largest direct seller—although that title now belongs to Avon and then Alticor, Amway's parent company. Tupperware sales reps could build their own networks and those with high sales could receive rewards such as appliances. Even more importantly, Wise heaped recognition on the women who helped make Tupperware a national phenomenon.

The company held rallies, crowned and pinned top sellers, and boosted their sellers' confidence. Making a sell was as much about individual empowerment as moving the products. One early Tupperware seller, Mary Siriani, recalled that meetings were very "rah rah." "This is motivation time, rah, rah, let's really get up there," Siriani said. "Let's think of the next promotion, rise and shine, rooty toot toot, who are you going to recruit? All of this stuff. They were the razzamatazz."[5] As Wise told the "Tupperware ladies" long before the women's liberation movement hit the country, "You are your own treasure chest."[6] And they believed her. It gave them a sense of purpose and a feeling of freedom.

As the direct sales method caught fire, companies spun off other direct sales companies and entrepreneurs. Frank Stanley Beveridge, who had been a successful Fuller Brush salesman, started Stanley Home Products. Mary Kay Ash, who founded Mary Kay Cosmetics, and Mary Crowley, the founder of Home Interiors, cut their direct sales teeth at Stanley. The "party plan" method of selling spread as Tupperware inspired other successful companies. Over the years, other direct marketers borrowed from it and took several different approaches— PartyLite, Pampered Chef, and Longaberger Baskets, to name just a few. For example, Longaberger Baskets' founder, Dave Longaberger, had been a Fuller Brush salesman at one time and used sales associates to stage Longaberger "home shows." But, like Amway, Longaberger also gave associates a percentage of the commissions earned by other associates they recruited. Direct selling gained another gigantic plat-form later with the Internet, making it possible to sell products and recruit distributors around the world.

Expansion

Building an ever-larger army of distributors was critical to Amway's long-term growth. But as the company entered its second decade of business, Jay and Rich became concerned that some Amway distributors focused too much on recruiting and not enough on selling products. In 1970, they sent a warning to distributors, telling them they each had to make 10 customer retail sales each month. "You're not going to make it unless the guy below you makes it," they said.[7] Amway also tried to encourage retail sales by buying back—or having a top-line distributor buy back—unused products from lower-level distributors or those who wanted to get out of the business. Amway also paid a performance bonus to distributors who resold at least 70 percent of such products each month. That edict became known as the "70 percent rule."[8]

Despite the problem with some overzealous distributors, Jay and Rich remained optimistic about Amway's business prospects, and they were ready for their next adventure: overseas expansion. Amway's retail sales in the United States and Canada had been meteoric, skyrocketing from $4 million in 1963 to more than $100 million by the early 1970s. The company employed 1,500 people and had signed up 150,000 indepen-dent distributors. But the founders harbored even greater expectations. At Amway's international convention in 1972, Jay told the crowd: "It's time to get moving. There are millions of potential customers and distributors out there who need Amway. We've only tapped about one percent of the potential market."[9] The new annual sales goal was $250 million. And the next country the founders set their sights on lay far across the Pacific Ocean—Australia. They wanted to expand in an English-speaking country, and they also decided that Australia could be a good proving ground. Australia was far enough away that "if it will work way over there, then maybe it'll work elsewhere," as Rich put it.[10] It was a risk, but one the founders believed they had to take.

Amway launched its business in the land down under in 1971. Australia proved to be a learning experience for Jay and Rich, who had expected some resistance by consumers to the "American way" idea of free enterprise. They discovered, though, that Australians loved American consumer products. Amway at first tried to manufacture its merchandise for the Australian market inside the country, but found it could make the products at less cost back home in Ada and ship them. And Australians actually *preferred* that the products come from the United States. "They believed that if it came from America, it was superior," Rich said.[11] That wasn't the case in every country, Amway would learn as it began its march around the globe. Some international markets required it to adapt to foreign cultures and mind-sets. In hindsight, though, Amway's move into Australia went smoothly, and the market for its products grew quickly. By the end of the 1970s, Amway's sales on the continent had risen 70 percent.

The next market in Amway's sights lay across the Atlantic Ocean. More than 60 years after the Van Andel and DeVos families immigrated to the United States from Europe, their descendants returned not to flee financial hardship, but to find financial reward. England was the next country on Amway's international expansion list for several reasons: there was no language barrier, English law was similar to American law, and the country embraced many American products and looked to the States as a consumer powerhouse. It was a natural move and one that Jay and Rich, buoyed by their success in Australia, looked forward to making. Amway launched its business in the United Kingdom in 1973. Just as it was once said that the sun never set on the British empire when it had colonies around the world, Amway was just beginning to build a global empire where the sun never set on its business.

Pyramid Structures under Scrutiny

During the 1970s one-on-one marketing had become more common for vitamins, household products, and cosmetics—remember the familiar ding-dong, "Avon calling" commercials? But as legitimate multilevel marketing, or so-called network sales grew, so did illegal pyramid schemes. One of the most famous and basic pyramid schemes was the chain letter. It didn't offer a product or service, just a promise that if the recipient passed along the letter and sent a dollar or some other amount to the person at the top of the pyramid, the recipient eventually also would move from the bottom to the top and reap financial rewards, too. So many other abuses flourished that U.S. Senator Walter Mondale in 1974 targeted pyramid and Ponzi schemes as the country's biggest consumer fraud problem. Both use fraudulent methods to entice people to hand over their money, but there are some major differences. In a Ponzi scheme, such as the one New York financier Bernie Madoff used to defraud his clients, the promoter has no product to sell or commissions to recruit new members. The structure is named for Charles Ponzi, an ex-convict in South Boston who in 1919 came up with a nifty "investment" idea. He sold promissory notes payable that promised a 50 percent return in 45 to 90 days, collecting $15 million. Then he used the money from the new investors to pay off the first ones. When the scheme collapsed, thousands of people lost their investments. Madoff's Ponzi scheme also worked like a giant financial chain letter: the promoter, Madoff, collected money from clients, all of whom he promised a high rate of return on a short-term investment. But he, too, was just using the money from new recruits to pay obligations owed to longer-standing members in the program. It finally caught up with him, and the Madoff house of cards collapsed, as did the savings and investments of its participants. Pyramid schemes, however, purport to sell a product, but in reality depend on recruiting others to join the chain. Those at the top of the pyramid feed on those at the bottom. When there are no more people joining the pyramid at the bottom, it collapses. Mondale sponsored two bills to set standards and spell out differences between a legal multilevel marketer and a pyramid scheme. The bill passed the U.S. Senate twice but failed to make it into law.

Meanwhile, the Federal Trade Commission (FTC) had been on the lookout for pyramid and Ponzi schemes, too. One of its first cases related to multilevel marketing was against Koscot Interplanetary Inc. (Koscot being an acronym for "Kosmetics for the Communities of Tomorrow"). Koscot offered an opportunity for people to become "beauty advisers" and purchase cosmetics from a sponsor at a discount and sell them to customers door-to-door or through parties. When the advisers moved up a level to supervisor, they could purchase products from the company and sell them at a discount to beauty advisers and directly to consumers. The top level—director or distributor—offered even deeper discounts for purchasing products from the company, as well as sales commissions and bonuses for recruiting others. Prospective recruits attended an "opportunity meeting," watched movies, and heard speeches about the large sums of money they could make in a relatively short time by recruiting others into the Koscot program. The FTC determined that the company's incentive structure encouraged recruiting more than retail sales. The commission also concluded that Koscot was an illegal "entrepreneurial chain" because, like a chain letter, it

> contemplates an endless recruiting of participants since each person entering the program must bring in other distributors to achieve the represented earnings. The demand for prospective participants thus increases in geometric progression whereas the number of potential investors available in a given community or geographical area remains relatively constant.[12]

In other words, at some point the finite market in the geographic area would become saturated and the pyramid would collapse (remember, this is in the time period before the Internet became the global information web it is today). In the Koscot case, the FTC began to formulate a definition of an illegal pyramid scheme that would set future precedents: a ". . . multilevel merchandising program is organized and operated in such a manner that the realization of profit by any participant is predicated upon the exploitation of others who have virtually no chance of receiving a return on their investment and who had been induced to participate by misrepresentations as to potential earnings." Using multilevel marketers to peddle merchandise, the FTC said, "was and is an unfair act and practice, and was and is false, misleading and deceptive."[13] The commission found that

> a company which offers its distributors substantial rewards for recruiting other distributors, and charges them substantial amounts for this right, creates overwhelming barriers to the development of a sound retail distribution network and resultant meaningful retail sales opportunities for participants.[14]

A pyramid scheme that has periodically popped up from the East to West coasts is the Airplane Game. Thought to have originally been started in southern Florida, the game sold eight "seats" on a mythical airplane for $1,500 each. When all the seats were sold, the "pilot" received $12,000 and then the airplane split, creating two new planes. Then the two "copilots" of the first plane became pilots of the new ones. Mathematics, however, did not bear out the theory that everyone playing the game could become pilots. As participant Robert FitzPatrick detailed in his book *False Profits*, authorities in South Florida condemned the game as an illegal pyramid scheme after receiving numerous complaints. Then the state attorney general proclaimed that the game violated the state lottery law. Leaders were arrested and the organization disbanded, although it already was on the way to collapsing.[15]

The FTC also had received numerous complaints about Amway, including that some of its distributors made exaggerated claims about the wealth that one could attain by recruiting other independent business owners (IBOs). In 1975, the commission filed a complaint that accused Amway of running an illegal pyramid scheme, fixing prices, and controlling trade. If it lost the case, Amway could be shut down. "The FTC's charges were the first serious assault on Amway—they threatened the very existence of our corporation," Jay acknowledged in his memoir.[16]

The FTC's Definition of a Pyramid Scheme

Debra A. Valentine, former general counsel for the FTC, defined pyramid schemes this way:

> They promise consumers or investors large profits based primarily on recruiting others to join their program, not based

on profits from any real investment or real sale of goods to the public. Some schemes may purport to sell a product, but they often simply use the product to hide their pyramid structure.[17]

She went on to say that in addition to a lack of retail sales, "inventory loading" is another sign of a pyramid scheme. That happens when a company's incentive program forces recruits "to buy more products than they could ever sell, often at inflated prices," Valentine said. If that occurred throughout a company's distribution system, the people at the top of the pyramid would reap "substantial profits, even though little or no product moves to market," she explained. "The people at the bottom make excessive payments for inventory that simply accumulates in their basements." And although pyramid schemes claim that their products are "selling like hotcakes," the sales that take place happen between people inside the pyramid or to new recruits, not to consumers in the general public, she said.[18]

In a 1998 presentation to the International Monetary Fund's seminar on legal issues facing central banks, she gave an example of how a pyramid scheme operated in a so-called three-by-four matrix:

Level 1 $150 × 3 = $450

Level 2 $30 × 9 = $270

Level 3 $30 × 27 = $810

Level 4 $30 × 81 = $2,430

Valentine said:

Each investor pays $500 to the promoter and is told to build a "downline" by recruiting three new members, who then each should recruit three more members. . . . The investor is told that he will be paid $150 for each of the three new members whom he enlists at the first level. The investor is also promised a commission for each recruit at the next three levels. Thus, the investor should receive commissions for four levels of recruits below him, each of whom must recruit three more members— hence the name, a three-by-four matrix.

The prospect may seem easy and lucrative because the investor appears to be able to earn $3,960 on an initial investment of $500.

The promoter receives $500 for each new member and will pay $240 in commissions to earlier investors. That means he keeps more than half of the membership fee. If the scheme collapses after the fourth level, the promoter will have received $500 for the first investor with no commissions, $350 from the three at the next level, $320 from the nine at the next level, $290 from the 27 at the third level, and $260 from the 81 at the fourth level. "The simple math—$33,320 flowed down to the con artist—and all he did was attract one investor!" Valentine said. The investor who thought he was at the top of the pyramid now finds himself at the bottom and unable to attract new recruits. "He is not alone because mathematics shows that MOST investors will find themselves at the bottom of the pyramid when it collapses," Valentine continued. "The very structure of this matrix dictates that whenever the collapse occurs, seventy percent will be in the bottom level with no means to make a profit. They all will be out $500." Every pyramid or Ponzi scheme collapses because it "cannot expand beyond the size of the Earth's population," Valentine concluded. She went on to say that pyramid and Ponzi schemes often are confused with legitimate multi-level marketing programs. But unlike those illegal pyramids, multilevel marketers have a real product to sell, she noted. "More importantly, MLMs actually sell their product to members of the general public, without requiring these consumers to pay anything extra or to join the MLM system," she added. "MLMs may pay commissions to a long string of distributors, but these commissions are paid for real retail sales, not for new recruits."[19]

Amway clearly had merchandise sold under its own label to distributors and dealers throughout the United States. At the time, Amway had 1,500 direct distributors that purchased directly from Amway; other distributors generally purchased products directly from their sponsors. Amway's fiscal 1976 sales totaled about $169 million in the United States and $205 million worldwide. Soap and detergents accounted for 41.2 percent of Amway's 1974 sales, polishes and sanitation goods 20 percent, and toilet products 6.5 percent. Like Tupperware, Amway distributors sometimes also held parties to demonstrate products and to present the business opportunity to new recruits. But the FTC contended in its complaint that the Amway's Sales and Marketing Plan contained an "intolerable potential to deceive."

Hearings in the case began in May 1977. Attorneys representing Amway took a month to present their defense. Jay and Rich were called to testify at the trial. In one exchange during the testimony, an FTC lawyer asked Rich whether he ever said a distributor could make $1,000 a month or that some distributors made $50,000 a year.

Rich: "Yes, I've said that."

FTC: "Well, we have it on tape."

Rich: "That's no secret. We put the tape out. I'm not going to argue that point. What's the problem?"

FTC: "A lot of people never make that amount, you know."

Rich: "I understand. I never promised it to them."

FTC: "Well, let us show you some of the people who have been hurt by this."[20]

A parade of witnesses then testified that they couldn't get people to attend Amway meetings or buy products.

The legal proceedings dragged on for four years. In all, about 150 witnesses testified. The case generated almost 7,000 pages of transcripts and more than 1,000 exhibits, including transcripts of 23 tapes that made a pile "two or three feet high." The posttrial briefs and proposed findings totaled about 1,600 pages.[21]

■ ■ ■

As the FTC case moved forward, Amway went on with its business. The company decided to buy the Mutual Broadcasting Corporation in 1977. It included the Mutual Broadcasting System, which began operating in 1934 as an unusual cooperative venture among four radio stations—WOR in New York, WGN in Chicago, WLW in Cincinnati, and WXYZ in Detroit—as well as Mutual Sports and more than half of Mutual Reports. They shared the network's costs and their original programming. Among Mutual's popular shows were *The Lone Ranger, The Green Hornet, Amos & Andy,* and *The Shadow.* The network changed hands several times over the years and grew into the nation's largest radio network with 950 affiliate radio stations. Local stations could produce shows and have them distributed over the network. Amway acquired it from a privately held company. Jay said Amway bought the network to provide a "balanced" political viewpoint, but the timing, in the midst of the FTC investigation, raised more questions about its motives.[22] Mutual fell into financial trouble under Amway, though, and in 1985 Amway sold the network to Westwood One, a seller of radio shows and advertising packages, for $30 million in cash notes and stock.

In 1978, Amway also decided to get into the hotel business. One of the Amway founders' pet projects was revitalizing downtown Grand Rapids. Its own annual convention brought in 10,000 people a year, and hundreds more visited the corporate headquarters each week on business. They needed a place to stay, as did people attending meetings at the city's new convention center. Amway bought the historic Pantlind Hotel, which opened in 1916 and in the 1940s and 1950s was Grand Rapids' most elegant accommodation. Jay and Rich wanted to transform the structure back into a world-class hotel. The renovation took several years. In 1981 the Pantlind reopened as the Amway Grand Plaza Hotel, with almost 400 deluxe rooms and six restaurants and lounges. In the project's second phase, a new 29-story tower rose between the hotel and riverfront, with almost 300 deluxe rooms, as well as retail stores.

The Decision

Amway received its own revitalization of sorts on May 8, 1979, when the FTC handed down its decision and final order. It first ordered Amway, the Amway Distributors Association, and Rich and Jay to stop allocating customers among their distributors, fixing wholesale and retail prices for their products, taking retaliatory action against "recalcitrants," and spreading price-listing data that did not advise that sticking to the price was not obligatory. They also were prohibited from misrepresenting potential earnings and other relevant information to prospective distributors. But it was the first sentence in the government's final conclusion that became the single most important statement to Amway's future and that ignited the explosion of a new industry: "The Amway Sales and Marketing Plan is not a pyramid plan," the FTC said in its decision. It went on to say:

> In less than 20 years, the respondents have built a substantial manufacturing company and an efficient distribution system,

which has brought new products into the market, notably into the highly oligopolistic soap and detergents market. Consumers are benefited by this new source of supply, and have responded by remarkable brand loyalty to Amway products. The . . . vertical restraints by which Amway has achieved this entry— avoiding conventional retailing through grocery stores by direct selling—are reasonable. Respondents' restrains on price competition, however, must be prohibited.[23]

Amway would become a landmark case for the FTC because for the first time the government distinguished an illegal pyramid from a legitimate multilevel marketing program. "Since distributors were compensated both for selling products to consumers and to newly recruited distributors, there was some question as to whether this was a legitimate multilevel marketing program or an illegal pyramid scheme," Valentine said. The commission held that, although Amway had made false and misleading earnings claims when recruiting new distributors, the company's sales plan was not an illegal pyramid scheme because it did not charge an up-front "headhunting" or large investment fee from new recruits, nor did it promote "inventory loading" by requiring distributors to buy large volumes of nonreturnable inventory. Instead, Amway required distributors to buy only a relatively inexpensive sales kit. Moreover, Amway had three different policies to encourage distributors to actually sell the company's soaps, cleaners, and household products to real end users. First, Amway required distributors to buy back any unused and marketable products from their recruits upon request. Second, Amway required each distributor to sell at wholesale or retail at least 70 percent of its purchased inventory each month—the "70 percent rule" the founders had ordered in 1970. Finally, Amway required each sponsoring distributor to make at least one retail sale to each of 10 different customers each month, known as the "10 customer rule." The commission found that these three policies prevented distributors from buying or forcing others to buy unneeded inventory just to earn bonuses. Thus, Amway did not fit the Koscot definition. Amway participants were not purchasing the right to earn profits unrelated to the sale of products to consumers "by recruiting other participants, who themselves are interested in recruitment fees rather than the sale of products."[24]

The rules that Jay and Rich had imposed on distributors had helped them defeat the government's case. They said they condemned companies that had, like chain letters, enticed people to chase get-rich-quick schemes rather than the hard work that they both espoused. "These sorts of scams have done Amway a lot of damage because Amway is often confused with pyramid schemes," Jay said.[25] He pointed out that while Amway's organizational structure resembles a pyramid, so do most corporations, the military, or charitable organizations, he added. One of his cousins even was trapped in a pyramid scheme. But the negative publicity created the impression that all direct selling should be illegal. Amway launched a public relations campaign, taking out advertisements in hundreds of newspapers nationwide to educate people about illegal pyramid schemes and how to avoid them. Jay and Rich both made speeches to business and community organizations. But other network marketers and even some of Amway's own IBOs turned whistle-blowers and wrote books, articles, and blogs contending that Amway was, indeed, a pyramid scheme and that it exploited people's unrealistic dreams of big financial payoffs for little work. "As long as people love money more than anything, there will always be room for network marketing, especially if it's a well-financed scheme wrapped in a multibillion-dollar air of credibility and topped off with God, family, and country," writes former network marketer Patrick J. Smith in his book *The Dark Side of the Pyramid*. "Greed is the one secret that is hidden out in the open by a network marketing firms. How can rational people truly believe that if they invest one, two, eight, or even twenty hours per week in their (part-time) 'venture' that they will really become rich beyond their wildest dreams?"[26]

In the FTC's case against Amway, the company might have fit the description of an "entrepreneurial chain" except that Amway had a buy-back rule, the 10 customer rule, and the 70 percent rule. But the FTC's decision and order set a precedent for other multilevel marketers that then modeled their business on the "Amway rules," critics of the ruling say. "These exculpatory rules have now become boilerplate in the hundreds of pyramid offerings that have surfaced since 1979," contends New York attorney Bruce A. Craig, who served as an assistant attorney general for the State of Wisconsin for 30 years and litigated a number of pyramid cases, including Koscot and Amway in the early

1980s. In recent years, Craig has been urging the FTC to investigate whether Amway truly enforces its "rules," or whether distributors give it "token recognition" and don't broadly implement or enforce them. To deal with the pyramid issue, the FTC in 2006 proposed a new "Business Opportunity Rule" to cover business opportunities "commonly touted by fraudsters," such as those perpetrating pyramid schemes. The FTC had taken actions against such businesses using its Franchise Rule, but that rule had imposed a $500 minimum investment requirement. In contrast, the Business Opportunity Rule would apply to all businesses, including those with a smaller start-up cost. It also was designed to prohibit unfair or deceptive practices such as misrepresentations about the material terms of a business relationship, the use of shills, misrepresentations of endorsements or testimonials, failure to honor territorial protection guarantees, and failure to honor refunds.[27] Rebuttal comments poured in, many of them from people who themselves had been involved in a multilevel marketer or had a loved one who was. The direct sellers included Arbonne, Mary Kay, and Primerica, whose attorney was Timothy Muris.

As the FTC's proposed Business Opportunity Rule stalled, Craig wrote to David C. Vladeck, director of the FTC's Bureau of Consumer Protection, asking the commission to revisit the 1979 decision, which he said "erroneously concluded that Amway was not a pyramid scheme" because of the dealer rule provisions. "The ruling has effectively legitimized pyramids, now called MLMs, as all other pyramids immediately adopted the 'Amway rules,' " Craig told Vladeck. "While the Commission did bring some pyramid cases, they involved extended litigation, a confusing legal standard, and a requirement that it prove that the 'Amway rules' were not enforced. The unfortunate by-product of this litigation was the implication that other companies, such as Amway, were legal since they were not sued." The FTC never revisited the Amway decision to see if, in fact, it does have retail sales and a meaningful buy-back program, Craig added.

The 1979 ruling made billionaires of the Amway founders and funded a highly effective public relations and lobbying effort which, for the past 30 years, has entrenched the dubious principles of the Amway decision and influenced a significant number of legislators and other governmental officials both state and federal.[28]

The business opportunities rule has since been amended to exclude pyramids—"evidence of the influence of the pyramid lobby," as Craig put it.

The FTC's ruling that Amway's sales plan was lawful helped the company build credibility, especially abroad. However, its finding that the company used "false and misleading earnings claims" to recruit and that Amway and its distributor association illegally fixed wholesale and retail prices for its products made Jay and Rich take a look at the business from the regulator's viewpoint, however unreasonable they found it. "Again, the unique nature of the Amway organization resulted in problems with regulators unfamiliar with the way Amway worked," Jay said. "The 'restraint of trade' that was alleged to result from the modest set of rules we imposed on distributors was not an unusual charge either. The whole situation could have been resolved in a thirty-minute meeting if we had been dealing with reasonable people."[29] Much of the FTC's evidence was drawn from manuals and price lists and practices that Amway had discontinued before the trial, Jay added. In particular, the FTC relied on the 1963 rules of conduct manual that the company hadn't used since at least 1972 and the price-fixing practice had been stopped, he added.

Still, Amway had to change its pricing practices and the way it presented earnings potential to prospects. "Significantly, the commission did not find even one instance where a prospective distributor was misled by examples of how our Sales and Marketing Plan works," Rich said after the judgment. "Instead, the commission chose to base its conclusion on a purely theoretical legalistic standard called the capacity to deceive. That's quite a different matter. What the commission is saying is that somebody, someday, somewhere might possibly be misled."[30] Amway now discloses the average monthly income—$115—of active distributors on the business opportunity brochures handed out when distributors present the Sales and Marketing Plan to recruits. Jay said the company had to abide by the FTC's judgment, but he felt it was "another attack on the free enterprise system." The freedom to contract "is an essential part of a free market," Jay believed. "Without it, business is seriously hampered in its ability to make its customers, employees, and owners better off." If a condition of holding a distributorship was to sell products at a certain price, "no one is being defrauded, cheated or robbed, and the contract should be allowed to stand."[31] While Amway didn't like the ruling on price-fixing, it was satisfied the FTC saw the fairness of its policy restricting distributors from selling to retail stores.

Jay, though, said any charge that Amway was a pyramid scheme was "absurd" for several reasons: Amway did not require a substantial, non-refundable entry fee; it thrived on the sale of "high-quality" products; and true pyramid schemes saturated a market quickly, leading to the system's collapse.[32] Because each Amway distributor can establish a network community-wide or worldwide, he or she has "an enormous population within which to work," Jay pointed out.[33] If Amway were a pyramid scheme, why hadn't it collapsed?

Former IBOs, attorneys, and others, however, say that the pyramid does collapse, just at the bottom rungs as distributors get discouraged and quit. Robert FitzPatrick argued that multilevel marketers and pyramids structurally are the same because both rely on "an ever expanding chain of enrollment." Mathematically, the structure of multilevel marketers or illegal pyramids prevents them from expanding indefinitely, he added. "If growth continues according to plan, later recruits will inevitably lose their financial investments," he said. "Those who launch pyramids know the ruinous course these programs will follow yet effectively dupe others into enrolling. Therefore, early entrants win at the calculated loss of the later enrollees."[34]

Moving Forward

In the end, Jay and Rich came to view the FTC investigation as a teaching tool about dealing with the government. It also handed the company a defense when anyone accused it of being a pyramid scheme—no, the FTC had looked into the matter and decided that Amway was not one. Jay and Rich continued to believe that government officials just didn't understand multilevel marketing and would use their power to try to shut down the company with new regulations or litigation.

It was a stressful year for Amway and for Rich's health. Several years later, he began having what would become a string of heart problems. One morning, Rich felt unsteady. "I'd bump into door-frames as I exited doorways," he recalled. "Even when I'd set a straight course, I couldn't seem to stop from veering to the left side when I moved."[35] Helen insisted he call a doctor. Finally, he agreed. Tests showed Rich had suffered a precursor to a stroke or heart attack. He had to make some changes to his lifestyle, cutting back on cholesterol, getting more exercise, and eating healthier. He did not, however, cut back on his work helping Jay run Amway.

Three years later on the Fourth of July, Rich and his children, Dick, Dan, Cheri, and Doug, were on their 50-foot-racing sloop, *Windquest*, preparing to compete in the Queen's Cup overnight race across Lake Michigan. For a prerace event, the DeVoses planned to set sail from Grand Haven one evening. Rich was helping with changing the sail and taking down the spinnaker when a sharp pain stabbed him inside his chest. Not wanting to worry his children, Rich didn't say anything and went below deck to rest and try to get to feeling better. The next morning, though, the pain was so bad he couldn't pretend any longer. A plane picked him up in Milwaukee and flew him back to Grand Rapids.

Tests showed that Rich had a coronary blockage. A thoracic surgeon decided that Rich needed surgery. During the open-heart procedure, doctors found so much arterial damage that they had to bypass six arteries. "The surgery was a success, and the experience gave me a new appreciation of life and new reasons to hope," Rich said. "It also made me more aware of the passage of time."[36] He tried to relax more, take more time off, and spend more time with Helen and his family.

■ ■ ■

Despite the U.S. government's attacks on Amway, Jay and Rich still believed in the Plan, and so did a lot of other people who clung to the notion that Amway was their ticket—not only to the good life, but also to the Diamond life. Lawsuits and court cases would dog Amway for decades, but they did not prevent millions of people from becoming

IBOs and following a path that they hoped would lead to financial independence. For that to happen, the founders knew they would have to make some big changes and make sure the Plan wasn't undermined by distributors who didn't follow the company's policies. Trying to monitor and control the behavior of independent businesspeople flung all over the nation and the globe, however, would prove to be one of Amway's greatest challenges.

Chapter 7

Retooling the Machine

A year after the Federal Trade Commission (FTC) ruled that Amway was not a pyramid scheme, the company marked a major milestone: it jumped from being a multimillion-dollar business to a billion-dollar business. In 1980, sales hit $1.1 billion. Moreover, Amway was attracting some positive publicity for a change. *Readers Digest* ran a story in its August 1982 issue titled "Amway's Amazing 'Dutch Twins,'" referring to Rich and Jay. The company sponsored TV specials starring Bob Hope. The legendary comedian went on to become Amway's spokesman in a series of radio commercials. Distributors around the world were drawing attention, too. Peter Muller-Meerkatz, a university professor, and his wife, Eva, a business economist, of Germany had emerged as stars in Europe, signing 100 distributors by the end of their second month in business.[1]

77

Turning Point in Wisconsin

Despite the positive public relations buzz, Amway's troubles with the U.S. government continued. In 1982, Congress and the Internal Revenue Service investigated whether some Amway distributors were using their businesses as tax shelters and claiming large deductions for bogus or inflated expenses. A former IRS revenue agent had become an Amway distributor and, according to Jay, gave other distributors a "cleverly done but distorted and unreasonable interpretation of the tax law."[2] Amway cooperated with the IRS investigation, which cemented Jay's belief that the federal tax system needed an overhaul with a flat tax and no deductions. The federal government wasn't the only entity probing Amway, however. State governments had received complaints about the company, too, and attorneys general who focused on consumer protection were taking action.

One of the most aggressive states was Wisconsin. In July 1982, the State of Wisconsin filed a lawsuit against the company and Amway Direct Distributors who were doing business in a group called World Wide Diamond in Milwaukee County. Wisconsin Attorney General Bronson C. Follette, Assistant Attorney General Stephen J. Nicks, and Assistant Attorney General Bruce A. Craig brought the suit, which claimed that Amway had about 20,000 distributors in the state, 192 of which were directs. World Wide Diamond was holding meetings for new recruits twice a week, during which they were told that their incomes from their Amway businesses were "at a level significantly higher than what was earned." The distributors failed to distinguish between gross, adjusted gross, and net incomes, or to explain how long it took them to earn their incomes and the "significant business expenses" that resulted in losses or reduced incomes, according to case information. The "untrue, deceptive, and misleading statements" violated state law, the suit contended.[3] The attorney general's office collected earnings data from the tax returns of Amway distributors. In addition to the allegation of misrepresentation of individual income, a second allegation claimed the defendants also misrepresented potential income by stating or implying that an Amway distributor had a "reasonable chance, within three to nine months and working six to twelve hours a week, of earning in excess of $12,000 a year." According to the attorney general's office, group leaders also stated or implied that even higher incomes of up to $55,000 were possible in three to five years. In truth, the attorneys argued, the average annual adjusted gross income for Amway distributors in Wisconsin was $267, or 2.2 percent of the projected $12,000 income. Furthermore, from 1979 to 1980, less than 1 percent of all Wisconsin distributorships had an average adjusted gross income of more than $12,000, the lawsuit contended. And when it came to average annual net income after deducting business income, Wisconsin Amway distributors recorded a net loss of $918.

The suit's third allegation charged that the defendants used "unrealistic hypothetical examples" and, as evidence, presented a diagram given to Amway recruits that showed the circles of sponsorship and an example of how a distributor could earn a monthly gross income of $1,230 by sponsoring seven distributors who do 200 point value (PV) a month and who each sponsor seven distributors of their own. "YOU CAN ACHIEVE YOUR GOALS WHILE HELPING OTHERS!" the literature read. Then there was a note at the bottom: "Remember, these examples are illustrations only. Not every distributor will sponsor seven distributors. Some will sponsor more, some will sponsor less, depending upon time and effort spent building the business."[4] Jay later said that income from each Amway business depends on individual effort and whether people are working part time to bring in extra cash each month or full time. "Distributors in the early stages of building their businesses cannot expect to receive what the senior distributors upline from them are making," he explained. He knew of one who tried to start his Amway business by purchasing thousands of dollars of audiovisual equipment for his sales meetings—"maybe he thought that if he spent enough, he wouldn't have to work," Jay commented. He defended the literature passed out and the hypothetical examples as depicting the income that someone who was working very hard and had spent several years in the business "could" receive.[5]

The fourth allegation in the Wisconsin suit was failing to disclose the nature and identity of the Amway program, meaning that distributors were urged not to tell prospects that they were offering a business opportunity connected to Amway. According to the complaint, at an August 1980 presentation at the Holiday Inn in Oshkosh, for example, new distributors were told: "When you invite people, don't tell them much. The idea of products can turn some people off. Don't be a SAP, and mention Sales, Amway, and Products."[6] The state requested that Amway be enjoined from doing all of the allegedly "deceptive and misleading" activities described in the suit.

The Wisconsin attorney general obtained a consent judgment against Amway. It ordered a permanent injunction that required Amway distributors to disclose actual sales, income, and experiences when using hypothetical income examples. It also required the company's distributors to disclose the percentage of independent business owners (IBOs) who withdrew from the business to give a more realistic view of the risks involved. The Wisconsin suits further hammered Amway's image and constrained its business. Jay later insisted that Amway could not make the Plan "absolutely foolproof," nor could it oversee the claims that every distributor made. "We can't completely monitor, much less control, the behavior of millions of distributors to make sure that a few unscrupulous people aren't misrepresenting the Amway Plan or to keep people from making poor decisions with their businesses," Jay wrote in his memoir.[7] It underscored to him and Rich that government officials did not understand multilevel marketing (MLM), but could halt its operations with lawsuits and regulations. But it also served as a warning that some distributors were going too far in the claims they made to prospects and how they presented the Plan. As pointed out in the previous chapter, Assistant Attorney General Craig continued to raise questions about Amway and later urged the FTC to look into whether Amway was enforcing the rules that the commission used in its 1979 ruling to distinguish Amway from illegal pyramid schemes (see more in Chapter 14, "Amway Redux").

Avoiding Division and Friction in Canada

The most damaging government case, though, was yet to come. It ignited not in the United States, but across the border where Amway had launched its international business—in Canada. In November 1982, the Royal Canadian Mounted Police raided Amway Canada's headquarters and seized records and products. Amway was accused of defrauding Revenue Canada—that country's version of the IRS—of more than $28 million in customs duties. With penalties, the claim totaled $118 million in U.S. dollars. The revenue agency accused Amway of avoiding custom duties by undervaluing merchandise exported from the United States to Canadian distributors from 1974 to 1980. After Amway began operating in Canada in 1962, the company and Canadian customs officials had worked out a special agreement in August 1985 concerning how Amway would pay tariffs on imported items since it operated in a nontraditional way, shipping products through distributors. Canada's customs laws imposed tariffs on imported merchandise based on its fair market value in the country of origin. Jay said that Amway agreed to pay the same tariff that its competitors selling to stores paid, that it would have paid if it had bought the products from other manufacturers, or that it would have paid if it had sold the products to non–Amway outlets in the United States. "During this time, Canadian customs officials routinely audited the valuation methods Amway used for products if shipping to Amway of Canada," Jay said. "Each time, Canadian customs officials indicated their satisfaction with the arrangements, which met terms of the 1965 agreement."[8]

In early 1980, though, the agreement suddenly changed. Amway's tariffs on the same products mushroomed to four times the amount. An Amway executive believed fraudulent misrepresentations had occurred during the negotiations on the agreement and he recommended that Amway pay Revenue Canada the additional amount. "He even attempted to convince Rich and me that a fraud had been committed," Jay said.[9] They looked into the allegations, but refused to pay Revenue Canada the amount it said the company owed. Revenue Canada then issued its new ruling, which Jay and Rich said would basically stop Amway from shipping goods to Canada. Jay called Canada's action "heavy-handed" and suspected that the country's prime minister at the time, Pierre Trudeau, who favored social economics, didn't like Amway's brand of capitalism. He said Canada was out of step with the rest of the world. "Canada used a one-of-a-kind import valuation method employed by no other nation and had an antiquated, senseless set of import restrictions," Jay said. Amway's position was that transfer prices for the import of merchandise had been "strictly in keeping with those regarded as proper in the company's earlier agreements with Canadian custom authorities."[10] The company hired Vernon D. Acree, a retired U.S. commissioner of customs, to review the tariff arrangement. He found no evidence of concealment, cover-up, or fraud. Amway's argument was that the dispute boiled down to misunderstandings and bad advice. However, the Canadian government claimed that Amway had a policy to conceal and mislead and had submitted hundreds of false invoices and dummy price lists, and had established a dummy corporation in a deliberate attempt to defraud Revenue Canada.

Criminal indictments were handed down against Jay, Rich, and two vice presidents. When they did not respond to court orders that they appear at hearings, the government took steps to extradite them. Jay called that day "the climax of the worst ordeal Amway ever faced, and an unrivaled publicity nightmare."[11] Amway hired William W. Nicholson, who had been a member of President Gerald Ford's staff, to broker a settlement of the criminal charges. The Canadian government's attorneys offered a plea bargain: the court would dismiss the criminal indictments if the corporation would plead guilty to criminal fraud and pay the fine. Rich and Jay decided to end the stalemate. In November 1983, Amway Corporation and Amway of Canada Ltd. pleaded guilty to criminal fraud for tax evasion and paid a $25 million fine in Canadian dollars, the largest such fine ever imposed. Amway took out ads in *the Wall Street Journal, Washington Post, Detroit News,* and the *Grand Rapids Press* defending the company and contending it had a "very strong basis" for continuing to fight against the Canadian authorities, but that it was the best interest of Amway to agree to the Canadians' terms to avoid division and friction if the litigation had continued.

■ ■ ■

Amway's troubles with Canada didn't end with the criminal case, however. The Canadian government pursued a $125.4 million civil suit against the company, seeking unpaid customs duties, sales taxes, and the value of Amway products that crossed into Canada from 1974 to 1980, plus penalties. In September 1989, Amway paid $38.1 million to settle the charges in exchange for the Canadian government to drop its lawsuit. The long Revenue Canada dispute led to more negative publicity for Amway and cemented the company's distrust of the media, an attitude that persists. Some articles portrayed Amway as a cultic pyramid scheme, while others focused on the lavish lifestyles of entrenched big distributors and the high failure rate of new IBOs. Jay said the behavior of some "star distributors" was "taken out of context and ridiculed."[12] He complained that Amway "dropouts" with personal or financial problems were singled out and their problems blamed on Amway. Jay was particularly incensed at articles in the *Detroit Free Press* that described him as the "serious one of the two (founders), the angry one with the computer mind and alarming speeches about the destructive forces of a meddling 'central government.'" "I didn't realize I was such a troll," he commented dryly. His view was that Amway was being attacked because it was "an outstanding example of what free enterprise can do when allowed to work."[13] To counter the media coverage, Rich and Jay transformed an old boardroom into a crisis management center they called the "War Room." They hooked up telephones and fax machines and launched a "truth campaign." Jay wrote the copy for full-page ads placed in U.S. and Canadian newspapers. He was convinced the mainstream media was biased against network marketing firms because they traditionally didn't advertise in newspapers, magazines, and on TV.

"Revenue Canada and the state of Wisconsin took their toll—nothing before or since has hurt Amway so badly," Jay said in hindsight. The Canadian raid on Amway happened right before a segment about Amway aired on the highly rated CBS TV newsmagazine *60 Minutes*, which meant the program was able to only append that news at the end of the segment. (See a full discussion about the program in Chapter 8.) Considering the show's reputation for hard-hitting investigative journalism, Rich and Jay felt like the company came out quite well. They didn't like everything, but Jay said the broadcast was "fair, it was balanced, it was accurate, and we probably did ourselves good in the long run."[14] Friends offered their congratulations. Commentator Paul Harvey called Rich to tell him, "You guys did a great job. I'm proud of ya."[15] Many distributors, however, reacted to the program with anger and frustration. Rich agreed with some that the show's producers had taken little pieces of a big meeting out of context, such as when one distributor was caught on tape saying, "I'm going to have a ring for every finger." "You know, sometimes at a direct distributor meeting where we're on a talk about getting ahead in life and having some of the finer things in life, that sounds pretty good," Rich said. "But when it's on a national television screen, as though it represented all of us, and that all we think about is greed, or money, or rings, or cars, or buses, or whatever, then it doesn't look very good."[16]

Reversing the Damage

Their next appearance before the TV cameras didn't turn out so well for them. Talk show host Phil Donahue interviewed Rich in April that year. Jay had tried to talk Rich out of appearing, but Rich thought he could counter some of the negative media reports. He agreed to be on the show with the stipulation that he could give Amway's position in a one-on-one interview before the audience was allowed to participate. But Donahue showed a film clip of Amway's rallies and put Rich in the middle between current Amway distributors and former ones who had stories of personal and financial problems they blamed on the company. There was a lot of emotion, and the accusations flew. Some callers supported Amway. After the show aired, former First Lady Barbara Bush sent Rich a note that read "DeVos—10, Donahue—0!"[17]

After the *60 Minutes* show, the company was inundated with mail, both positive and negative toward the company. In one letter, the writer said, "I consider myself to be the victim of aggressive directs and their upline. I got caught in an ambitious and aggressive group." Another letter charged that directs leading his group were determined to reach their goal "at the expense of the distributors, come hell or high water. Their philosophy, 'Mortgage your home, cash in your insurance, get a bank loan and borrow from whosoever (sic) will loan you."[18] Then the sales organization's leaders told distributors at a meeting that certain things discussed there were to remain confidential and not mentioned outside the room. Rich spoke sternly to the directs on the tape. "Whoever was teaching that, and it was not some little new direct, was teaching an illegal, immoral, improper system," he said. "I can't tolerate it. You know, we've been talkin' to you for years that you don't buy a position in Amway, you earn it, and here, blatantly, being taught inside a meeting, and then being told don't tell anybody, are methods that go contrary to everything we've heard."[19]

At a Diamond Club meeting in Hawaii, Amway discussed how to cope with the tape business and whether the company should get into it.

Amway's leadership finally decided and announced in Hawaii that it was going to make some changes. Distributors would be able to get business volume on the tapes, but they couldn't make direct by selling tapes—they would have to make direct by selling the Amway line of products. Rich warned that unless the tapes are sold to support the Amway business, the tape business could be illegal and called a pyramid because the tapes weren't sold to consumers. Rich went on to say he was "vitally concerned about the image that this company is portraying. And I think we've got some bad actors in this business, and you know we have. And I am imploring all of you to do two things. Number one, clean up your act. And number two, if you know people who are continuing to do things improperly after all of this, then I want you to write us a note and just tell us who's doing it."[20]

New Rules of Conduct

In 1980, Amway had published a manifesto outlining the conduct for distributors. The Amway Distributors Association handed down 10 rules of conduct. It laid out guidelines for recruiting, for marketing support materials, and to project an image of Amway that wasn't all about materialism. But distributor excesses had continued. At times, Jay and Rich had to rein in distributors "who wanted to turn what was a business meeting into a religious crusade, and the distributors who insisted on using rallies only to show off their fine clothes and jewelry," Jay said.[21] Small distributors filed complaints and lawsuits against upline distributors, contending they had been pressured into spending hundreds or thousands of dollars to buy books and tapes and attend seminars, only to lose money and fail to grow their businesses. Rich and Jay knew they had to take action and crack down on distributor misconduct or face a mushrooming problem. So at the Diamond Club meeting, Rich again laid out the 10 points and asked the Diamonds to teach them to their groups. They were:

1. "I will unplug from any group, up or down, which is not in my line of sponsorship." No dealing in someone else's group or line of sponsorship.

2. "I will only use Amway-produced literature in the presentation of the Plan and will use only the figures Amway gives."

3. "I will not make my willingness to help a distributor conditioned on their purchasing my Tape of the Week or anything else I see, which is beyond the basic Amway-supplied material." There should be no conditions on servicing distributors, Rich said.

4. "If I offer tapes, books, and rallies, they will always be presented on a voluntary basis. No strings, no pressure, and no force."

5. "If I teach the curiosity approach, it will be in accordance with Rule 6, as passed out at the end of the meeting." In other words, distributors must tell prospects that they were coming to a business opportunity meeting, not a social event. And if they asked whether it was Amway, they had to tell the truth.

6. "I will not produce any literature or tapes about the Plan or the products." Only the company knows the points it needs to cover in all 50 states, plus satisfy the government, and phrase things exactly right, Rich said.

7. "I will not hide behind group names." If a distributor is signed on an Amway application form and has anyone sponsored who's linked to Amway, then "you are in Amway," Rich said.

8. "We will work together to build our businesses while creating an organization that truly cares about every distributor in it. We will talk about the big picture while making sure we do not diminish those who choose to do less or make them feel like losers."

9. "While recognizing the importance of financial goals, we will attempt to use tact, t–a–c–t, and dignity so as not to create an image of just money, money, money. Together we will create an organization which loves and cares for each distributor, regardless of level, and an organization which will be of service in our communities."

10. "I agree with the principle and will observe the rules relating to PV/BV transfers. We will do all we can to make no PV/BV is transferred to anyone who did not honestly buy it and who was complying with the 70 percent rule." Rich explained: "In other words, I need a pledge that you will not inventory load, that you will not push a bunch of stuff on somebody to win a pin or earn a trip; but they will, indeed, have not only bought the Amway products, but have, in turn, sold them so they got retail and money came back in."[22]

In closing, Rich urged distributors to "clean their hands." "Some of you have got to ask yourself whether you're really in the Amway business or whether you're in the tape business," Rich said. "You've got to ask yourself whether you're really in the rally business or in the Amway business. You must ask yourself if everything you're doing is to support your Amway business or is it really for a secondary motive." He appealed for distributors to keep their business in "balance" because "out of balance, it can destroy us."[23]

After the court cases and the fallout from distributors who were unhappy about the changes Amway imposed, the company saw it needed to seriously retool its business. The founders brought in Nicholson, who had negotiated the Canadian settlement, to reorganize Amway. He met with Rich and Jay in March 1984. Once again, they relied on their trusty butcher paper to hatch out a plan for bringing Amway's costs in line with revenues and to boost sales and profitability. Nicholson cleaned up the sales force and promised a new and better Amway, putting a lid on evangelism and cultism and emphasizing real sales training. Amway announced its first layoffs of 860 people; the cuts were carried out over a month and a half. Nicholson also devised product tie-ins with brand names. He arranged deals to allow Amway distributors to sell MCI long-distance phone service, Coca-Cola soft-drink dispensers, Firestone parts and services, and Tandy computers. Taking a page from Neiman-Marcus's famous Christmas catalog, Nicholson added luxury offerings to Amway's catalog, including a $72,000 gold ingot, a hovercraft, a hot air balloon, and a shipwreck's treasure unveiled by celebrity Zsa Zsa Gabor.[24] "That was the period where we were just trying to change attitudes, stretch the thought process, and have some fun with the company," Nicholson said. The goal was to change how people thought of Amway and to boost income and offer higher-priced items.[25] Nicholson, who had expected to work with Amway for only a few months on its turnaround strategy, ended up staying with the company and remains a consultant.

Still, Amway's legal troubles persisted. In May 1986, the FTC announced that Amway had agreed, under a consent decree filed in federal court, to pay a $100,000 civil penalty to settle FTC charges that it violated the commission's 1979 order prohibiting Amway from misrepresenting the amount of profit, earnings, or sales its distributors are likely to achieve. According to a complaint filed with the consent decree, Amway violated the 1979 order by "advertising earnings claims without including in it clear and conspicuous disclosures of the average earnings or sales of all distributors in any recent year or the percent of distributors who actually achieved the results claimed."[26] The ad appeared in newspapers around the nation in 1983 and offered distributorships and represented the earnings of distributors without the required disclosures of average income earned in a year, the FTC said. The consent decree and complaint were filed at the FTC's request by the Justice Department.

Retooling More than the Business

Meanwhile, Amway continued to expand overseas to Belgium, Switzerland, and Taiwan. Dick DeVos, Rich's eldest son, was put in charge of international operations. Then Amway became the object of another company's designs on international expansion. One day, Nicholson brought them the news that a major Japanese trading company wanted to acquire Amway. It was a tempting offer—Jay and Rich each would receive $1 billion in cash. Nicholson went to New York and was in discussions with the firm for several weeks. When it came time to make a final decision, though, the founders talked about it, then said, "No, Bill, we want to keep the whole thing."[27] They had sold businesses before when they weren't working out or to make a profit. But Jay and Rich weren't ready to quit. "We knew the Plan's potential, and we knew we could never, in good conscience, pick up our chips and go home," Jay said.[28] Besides, the international business was getting interesting. Amway opened for business in Thailand in 1987, and new distributors signed up by the thousands in the first week. For the first time in Amway's history, sales abroad surpassed sales in North America.

Amway was looking at a possible acquisition, too. In 1989, it teamed up with Minneapolis investor Irwin Jacobs to buy 10.3 percent of Avon's outstanding common shares and indicated in a Securities and Exchange Commission filing that it might seek control of its larger rival in person-to-person sales. On May 11, Amway offered $39 a share, or about $2 billion in cash, for Avon (Jacobs did not participate in the purchase offer). Analysts predicted a battle between the brash, evangelistic MLM giant and the much lower-key Avon with its image of the smiling "Avon Lady." The *Washington Post* even called it a "shotgun marriage between Oral Roberts and Betty Crocker."[29] But the battle was short-lived. Avon's board of directors said the company wasn't for sale under any circumstances and, a week after the overture was made, rejected Amway's bid. The language was hostile as well. Avon called Amway "an admitted criminal," a reference to its guilty plea in the Canadian case. Amway called Avon's statement "irresponsible." On May 18, Amway withdrew its offer, deciding not to become drawn into a hostile takeover.

■ ■ ■

Avon's comment certainly stung. Amway's leaders had learned from their experiences with Canada and Wisconsin in the 1980s and the FTC ruling that they needed to retool more than their business. They needed to turn around what they perceived as a fundamental misunderstanding of their business model. They would have to get involved in educating government officials and lobbying those who made decisions and who could shut down the company with court cases or regulations and taint the company's image. They would have to get more involved in politics.

But first Amway had to deal with the problem that went to the heart of its MLM model. Distributors, more than anything, represented the company and reflected its image. Some distributors stuck with the reforms that Jay and Rich instituted, but others didn't. In its 50th anniversary book, *A World of Opportunity*, Amway said that many "agreed to the code, but some rebelled and sales suffered."[30] The company never could fully control the profitable motivational tools businesses. Former distributors said Amway feared that taking strong action would drive away mega-distributors, which the company had grown to depend on with their huge sales forces and customer base. Amway had to create higher new levels and new pins for them. They had become so big and so powerful in their sales organizations that they weren't just leaders. They were kingpins.

Chapter 8

Diamonds, Rubies, Emeralds, and Pearls

To many outsiders, the world of Amway feels like a foreign country. It boasts its own royalty and crown jewels, its own language and subculture, and it requires a passport to cross the border. Becoming a card-carrying independent business owner (IBO) allows access inside the gates—to attend the meetings and rallies, to buy the "how-to" promotional materials, and to climb the Amway hierarchy by "pin levels." Each time IBOs attain a new level of achievement in the growth of their businesses, they are recognized during a major function with a special pin that's set with precious stones to celebrate their elevated status.

The pin levels also confer titles such as Diamond, Ruby, Emerald, Pearl, Silver Producer, and Crown Ambassador—Amway's highest, most prestigious pin level. A Crown Ambassador is a direct distributor who has sponsored 20 groups, each of which qualified at the top-performance bonus level for at least six months of Amway's fiscal year. Next in line in the pin levels are Diamonds. A Diamond direct distributor is someone who has sponsored six groups, each of which qualifies at the top-performance bonus level for six months or more of a fiscal year; a Double Diamond, 12 groups; an Executive Diamond, 9 groups; and a Triple Diamond, 15 groups. Lower on the totem pole are the Emerald level, which sponsors 3 groups, each of which qualified for the top-performance bonus level for at least six months of the fiscal year; the Pearl, which sponsors 3 groups, each of which qualifies at the 25 percent bonus level during the same month; the Silver producer, who has qualified for the top performance bonus level for at least one month; and a Ruby direct distributor, who has attained at least 15,000 personal group point value in one month.

Motivating distributors has become a business itself and a controversial one not only for Amway but also for the multilevel marketing (MLM) industry. As distributors' groups grew larger and larger within Amway, they became heads of selling organizations with thousands of members. They held their own rallies, wrote books, produced tapes and videos, and made a lot of money off their promotional materials, also called BSMs in the industry, short for business support materials. It should be pointed out that Amway does not profit from the sale of materials.

The Life of a Top Distributor

One of the best-known gatekeepers to the Amway world is Dexter R. Yager, Sr., arguably Amway's most famous distributor with a worldwide empire. Yager is part of an exclusive club of distributors who have attained the top level, Crown Ambassador. But he and his wife, Birdie, even surpassed Amway's predictions for its IBO's achievements, so Amway had to add a new level, the Founders Crown Ambassador pin, and a Founders Achievement Award, or FAA, points. In 1997, the Yagers were the first recipients of the Founders Distinguished Service Award, which recognizes leaders who develop 40 FAA points. Then-president Dick DeVos presented them with a bonus check for $1 million and pins on behalf of the "founding fathers," Rich DeVos and Jay Van Andel. By 1998, the Yagers hit 50 FAA points and kept going.

Two years later, Dexter and Birdie earned an unprecedented 55 FAA points and received a bonus check for $2.5 million, the largest such check ever presented in Amway history. Then, in 2006, Dexter and Birdie hit 60 FAA points. Only six people have met or achieved an equal or higher number of FAA points: Foo Howe Kean and Shu Chen of China, Max Schwarz and Mona May of Germany, and Barry Chi and Holly Chen of Taiwan. All are multimillionaires.

Dexter is both revered and reviled, treated like a king by admirers and referred to as a "kingpin"—one of a handful of business owners to reach the top of the Amway pyramid of distributors—by others.[1] *Network Marketing Lifestyle* magazine devoted a cover story to Dexter, calling him "the king of network marketing" and "the greatest networker in the world."[2] With his trimmed white beard, bald pate, and muscular build, he exudes a confident persona. Dexter posed for the magazine cover photograph in his racing boat, chunky gold rings on each finger, a bracelet that spelled out "DEX" in gold, and a gold necklace with a cross pendant dangling from his neck. Whenever a business owner achieves above a Diamond level, he or she scores a cover in *The Business Owner* magazine; the Yagers hold the distinction of having appeared on more covers than any other Amway IBOs. Dexter regards himself as much more than a distributor, however. He is a motivator, a self-described "master dreambuilder," "freedom crusader,"[3] and coauthor of books such as *Don't Let Anybody Steal Your Dream*, *Becoming Rich*, and *Millionaire Mentality*.[4] He encourages other people to dream big and they, too, can live the good life like he and Birdie have. "With the mastery of an artist, Dexter helps others paint their dreams in broad strokes, and encourages them to take action towards those dreams," his Web site states about him. "If it's a new car, I drive them by a car lot," Dexter says. "If it's a new home, I take them to a new housing development. It's not enough to think about it—you have to touch it, smell it, feel it, and experience it."[5] Dexter and Birdie's lavish lifestyle puts stars in the eyes of many beginning IBOs, who drool over the Rolls Royces, the jewelry, the sprawling estate, the boat, and the motorcycle they see on the couple's Web site and the slick magazine covers devoted to the MLM business. When Yager held a "Free Enterprise Day" in Charlotte, motels filled up months in advance. Buses of distributors trekked out to Yager's house to see the mansion, swimming pool, Rolls

Royces, and antique cars. The dream vacations and the celebrity—the Yagers have had their pictures snapped with presidents George H. W. Bush, Ronald Reagan, and Gerald Ford; General Norman Schwarzkopf; entertainer Bob Hope; and Olympic gymnast Mary Lou Retton—inspire other IBOs that someday they, too, can be rich and famous. "We have the choice of when we go on vacation and incredible options as to where we want to go," Dexter says. "All my life, people told me I'd never be accepted by anyone who had any class. We've known approximately six presidents of the United States, hundreds of entertainers, and all kinds of famous, successful people from all walks of life, simply because we started our own business and we didn't let anybody steal our dream."[6]

The Yagers' almost-rags-to-riches story inspires others to "earn their freedom,"[7] as Dexter puts it. Before he started his Amway business, he was making $95 a week (before taxes) as a car salesman and a brewery representative—a beer salesman, in other words. Birdie was a keypunch operator at a local U.S. Air Force base when they were living on an "alley" in Rome, New York. Then, in 1964, Dexter learned about Amway and became a distributor. He wanted to be a direct distributor and made his goal in 60 days. He stayed direct for three years, and the Yagers became Silver Producers. Dexter was able to leave his job and devote himself to the Amway business full time. After he quit his job, he got comfortable with his success and slowed down. Then Dexter got a new mental image. He started reading books on positive thinking. "These books put my mind into motion," Yager recalled. "When it settled, I had answers. I saw dreams as catalysts in our lives, guiding us to appropriate actions. I clearly saw the need for new dreams for Birdie and I (sic)."[8] For further inspiration, he would lie on the living room floor, listen to motivational tapes all night long, and duplicate them for his associates.

Yager rose so fast as an Amway business owner that when the CBS news program *60 Minutes* in 1982 was preparing a report about Amway, called "Soap and Hope," veteran newsman Mike Wallace set up a long interview with the Yagers at their estate outside Charlotte, North Carolina. *60 Minutes* had approached Amway before, requesting interviews for a program about the company. "We tried to put it off, we told them we didn't think we were a good subject for the show, but they said they were going to do a show, with or without us," Rich later explained in a taped message to direct distributors. "And we finally took it upon ourselves to say that if they're going to do it anyway, then we're not going to dodge it—even if it's a disaster, we're at least going to stand for what we believe, and if they don't put our thoughts on the tape, well, then that's up to them. But we're not got to run from it."[9] He and Jay were wary of Wallace's hard-hitting interview style, however, and decided they needed to be prepared. They tapped Walter Pfister, a former ABC vice president, to coach them. Jay recalled Pfister telling him, "If Amway people don't do their own talking, somebody else will do it for them. . . . My feeling is that if the company has nothing to hide . . . and has articulate spokespersons, then do it!"[10] Rich and Jay assigned their own cameraman to tape the interview, too, and tag along when the CBS crew toured the Ada facility, filming everything CBS did.

Amway had no control over the other people *60 Minutes* interviewed, of course. The news show took tape from Amway distributors all over the country, including Yager. At the time, Dexter owned five Rolls Royces, a Cadillac, a $350,000 motor coach, antique cars, a horse farm, and a tennis court. Wallace pointed out that Amway distributors came from hundreds of miles away to pay homage to the Yagers and gawk at the house and Rolls Royces. "They treat him almost like a god," Wallace said in his voiceover. Following are excerpts from the interview:

Wallace:	"You say that nobody has failed in Amway."
Yager:	"No, people quit."
Wallace:	"A lot of people quit."
Yager:	"A lot of people quit, a lot of people get in."
Wallace:	"Maybe three out of four quit in the course of a year."
Yager:	"I only know about my own facts. We've sponsored, Birdie and I, roughly about 50 people, and about 40 of them are still in. So those are the only facts that I can go on."
Wallace:	"But you know the statistics that you hear elsewhere, that maybe one in 80,000 people make more than just a minimum living out of Amway."
Yager:	"Those facts I don't know. I know that the facts are that the majority of the ones that I work with make it."
Wallace:	"And that has something to do with you, do you think?"

Yager: "That's 'cause I love 'em. That's 'cause I really love
                'em. They're like my kids."
Wallace: "And when you say the majority of the people that
                you sponsor make it . . ."
Yager: "Yes."
Wallace: "Make what?"
Yager: "Whatever they want out of the business. It's always
                the next goal, the next achievement."[11]

The Yagers' next goal is to pass their business—which has spilled
from North America to Latin America, Europe, and India—to their
three sons, Doyle, Jeff, and Steve, and continue the Yager dynasty.
Meanwhile, Dexter and Birdie travel the world as Amway ambassadors
and donors to charitable organizations, including an orphanage in Africa.
"Amway is a way of life," Birdie told Mike Wallace. "It's so complete
for me. It just makes me a complete person, I guess."[12] Interestingly,
though, the Yagers' Web site doesn't mention the word *Amway,* although
it provides links to www.iboai.com, the Independent Business Owners
Association International, which represents all IBOs affiliated with
Amway North America, and Quixtar. The couple's motivational tools
business has earned them much of their wealth and consists of the books,
seminars, and motivational tapes they first produced out of a converted
barn (a 400,000-square-foot facility outside of Charlotte) for distribution
of business materials to IBOs worldwide.[13]

In one of the books, *The Business Handbook: A Guide to Building Your
Own Successful Amway Business,* Dexter offers an insider's glimpse into
the inner workings of "The Plan." In it, Yager refers to direct sales as the
"oldest, most personal form of marketing," harkening to the days when
one person bartered goods or services with another, one on one.[14] His
handbook contains a glossary at the end for building a successful Amway
business.[15] It includes all the key words of Amway-speak—*frontline, upline,
downline,* and *crossline*—as well as definitions of words that distributors
have put their own spin on, such as *go-getter* (someone who shows the
plan at least 15 times and does 100 point value [PV] each month), *depth*
(the downline in ones's group and the "key to longevity in the network
marketing and distribution business"), and *burn* (the dream that becomes
all-consuming). The burn "compels you to achieve so much more than

you ever thought possible," Yager wrote. "As we have said many times, if the dream is big enough, the facts don't count. That kind of dream is truly a burn!"[16]

As the *60 Minutes* segment pointed out, Yager and other Amway jewel-level distributors sell people on the burn and the dream even more than they sell any product. The dream is that they, too, through Amway, can enjoy the Diamond life—and more. Even before Amway IBOs sell a single bottle of detergent or skin cream, they are urged to buy the books and magazines that feature their dream house, car, boat, vacation, second home, and whatever else they seek that money can buy. Attaining that goal, that dream, of becoming a Diamond, Ruby, Emerald, or Pearl, is as precious as, well, diamonds, rubies, emeralds, and pearls. The message is driven home time and time again that they can have anything they want from Amway as long as they stick with the Amway Plan. That, and if they also buy inspirational books, CDs, and DVDs, attend instructional seminars and rallies, and immerse themselves in the power of positive thinking. Yager's Amway business handbook also urges loyalty between sponsors and recruits. "Edify them," Yager wrote. "Be loyal to them. As you become an upline to your down-line, the positive seeds of loyalty and edification you plan (sic) in both directions will come back as a bountiful harvest of business growth and long-term relationships."[17]

■ ■ ■

Amway has had many other powerful mega-distributors, such as Bill and Peggy Britt, who started their business in 1969. Bill Britt had been a city manager and recalled that the night he went to see the Amway business plan for the first time, he had left his wallet in his car so he wouldn't be tempted. Now he's a global sales leader with major markets in North America, Europe, Latin America, Asia, Africa, and India. The Britts were Founders Crown Ambassadors 40 FAA in 2004. Jim Dornan was an aeronautical engineer, and his wife, Nancy, was a speech pathologist before they switched to Amway. They have two adult children who are now part of the business. In 2009, the Dornans became Founders Crown Ambassadors 50 FAA. Tim Foley was a star before he came to Amway—on the football field, that is. As a former defensive back for the Miami Dolphins, Foley spent 11 years in the

NFL and won two Super Bowl rings. He joined Amway in 1981 and has amassed a network in North America and Latin America, becoming a Founders Crown Ambassador in 2005. The other global sales leaders are spread across Europe, and in Japan, South Korea, Malaysia, Taiwan, and—the newest ones—in China.[18]

The Other Side

Behind the glitz, the money, and the celebrated lifestyles, though, jealousy and animosity can lurk as well. Like Amway itself, mega-distributors have been the target of numerous lawsuits brought by former IBOs who claim to have decimated their savings, ruined their marriages, and alienated family and friends because they spent so much money on motivational tools they were told they needed—and still they failed. For example, in 1994, Amway distributors John and Stacy Hanrahan were the lead plaintiffs in a class-action lawsuit they filed in U.S. District Court in Pennsylvania against Britt and Yager, their motivational sales organizations, and Amway. The suit contended that Britt and Yager "routinely and intentionally misrepresented" potential earnings to sales recruits, "coerced" them to buy motivational materials such as audio tapes and pay to attend rallies, and engaged in practices of "customer allocation and price fixing in connection with the sale of their motivational materials."[19] The Hanrahans also alleged that Amway was a pyramid scheme and that they and other IBOs lost money selling Amway products and that their income didn't cover the cost of their expenses of buying the tapes and attending the sales rallies. Amway and the code-fendants "vigorously denied" the allegations. In 1996, the defendants paid $375,000 into a cash fund to cover court costs and expenses for the plaintiffs and offered coupons for discounts on Amway products. "The proposed settlement is a compromise of disputed claims and is not to be taken as an indication of liability or that damages have been, or would be, found against any defendant," the settlement stated. Britt and Yager also agreed to put labels on their motivational materials informing IBOs that they were "optional" purchases. The settlement angered some other IBOs who didn't feel that Amway had gone far enough to rein in what they considered abuses in pressuring downline distributors to buy motivational materials from their upline. As one Web site devoted to bashing Amway put it, "Amway has had rules in place since long before the Hanrahan lawsuit, and it could not be more clear that these rules are unenforced and/or ineffective."[20]

Former IBOs have written their own books that allege the Amway distributor business and motivational tools businesses are deceptive. One of the first disaffected distributors to pen an exposé of Amway was Stephen Butterfield. He became fascinated with the Plan in the late 1970s while he was working as a college faculty member and grew weary of just scraping by. "I couldn't buy a house, an airline ticket or a good suit, I always drove a settle-for car, no other kind existed for me, and I got used to the taste of soybeans," Butterfield wrote in *Amway: The Cult of Free Enterprise*.[21] He wanted income security and felt the "desire to not be left out of the feast," as he put it.[22] Others on his campus were getting into Amway. "Somebody was going to make a percentage on every tube of toothpaste that passed through the groves of academe," he said.[23] Why not him? Butterfield attended the meetings and watched sponsors show the Plan and draw the diagrams. They showed how a prospect could build "legs" in a sales organization—so called because in the diagram, the prospect was at the center inside a circle, with lines drawn outward in every direction, with circles around each of the distributors recruited. The bigger the sales organization and the more circles, the greater the potential for bonuses. "You are entitled to a percentage on every tube of toothpaste and every vitamin pill sold anywhere in your entire network, and all the networks descending from it," Butterfield said.[24]

Once he learned the Plan, Butterfield was encouraged to attend seminars and rallies. Here's how he described them:

> Crowds begin filling the auditorium sometimes as much as an hour before the Rally, which usually kicks off at 8:15 with a mighty burst of applause. Distributors wear Amway jewelry and conspicuously squirt their mouths with Sweet Shot, an Amway aerosol breath-freshener in a pocket-size cartridge. Waves of reciprocal chanting sweep back and forth over the hall, one side shouting, 'Ain't it Great!' and the other answering 'Ain't it Though!' In a regional event, thousands flick their

Bics, or other brand–name propane lighters (Amway does not yet manufacture one) and whirl the flames in a circle to symbol-ize the mystical force of the Plan. In a dark hall, row upon row of little flames spiral in the air, to the beat of "Circles, Crazy Circles." Slogans and circles are flashed on a huge video screen at the front of the amphitheater, strobe-light style, in time to the music. The planners of the Rally borrow crowd-hypnosis techniques of this kind from the rock concert, but with a specific political objective. Rock musicians only want the crowd's money and applause; Amway leaders, in addition, want their loyalty, commitment and belief."[25]

Caught up in the excitement, Butterfield went to work. But it was frustrating. He said he showed the Plan 26 times without any results, despite having invested more than a hundred hours and $600. "I wanted a return," he said. "I did not blame my sponsor, my Direct or the Corporation; when I blamed anyone, it was the friends and family members who had turned it down. Why couldn't they see the 'genius' and 'beauty' of the Amway concept?"[26] He listened to more tapes and got counseling from his upline. He was so close, almost a direct. One month, he got a check for more than $1,500. He paid off debts and ate at gourmet restaurants. But Butterfield eventually grew tired of showing the Plan and living his life through the Amway business. He stopped booking meetings and looking for prospects. He walked away. "There is no question that if I had really been willing to do 'whatever it takes' for the rest of my life, I would have joined Dexter's Diamonds," Butterfield said.[27] But he came to see the business as a "disgusting, destructive process."[28] "'Positive attitude' has to mean something more human than belief in my ability to make a million dollars," Butterfield concluded:

> At some point I could take my eyes off the picture of the motor home taped on my refrigerator and actually look out of the kitchen window. . . . I might try talking to my neighbor about something besides an Exciting Business Opportunity. I could learn to trust my own intelligence and teach others to do likewise. I could begin the never-ending process of getting to know my mind. This is a positive attitude.[29]

Ruth Carter, author of *Amway Motivational Organizations: Behind the Smoke and Mirrors*, was considered a "core" distributor, meaning one who bought into the Amway network marketing concept completely. She was involved in the Amway business for 13 years. "I bought the products, I held meetings and sponsored people, I went to all the functions I was qualified to attend," Carter (the name is a pseudonym) recalled. "I spent a fortune on tapes, books, and other motivational and training materials."[30] Carter eventually became suspicious that sponsoring new Amway distributors was "just a front for the sale of motivational tools and functions."[31] According to Carter, her upline would tell her, "'The tools will help you grow in the business.'" Or, "'You can't afford to miss this major function. You'll set your business back behind from six months to a year if you don't go.'" Or "'You need to support your upline and buy books upline, not from the bookstore.'" Carter states that she even heard an upline tell another IBO, "'Why should you work at a job and buy someone else's wife a mink coat?'"[32] But Carter said she began to see that the mink coats weren't purchased with profits from selling Amway products, but from selling motivational tools—"tools which they tell you they only provide to help you in your business, because they 'love' you," Carter said.[33] Eventually, she left the business, set up a Web site, wrote a book, and started telling others about the "lies, the abuses, and the deceptions" that she had witnessed.[34]

In 1986, Eric Scheibeler, who was an Amway distributor, and his wife, Patty, were young, newly married, and planning their future together. Eric had found a job as an underwriter for a large insurance company, and Patty accepted a job with same company. They bought a home—a "dump," as Eric described it—and fixed it up. One of their neighbors, another married couple, had put pictures of their dream home and a Mercedes on their refrigerator door. They spoke of a "Diamond," an Amway top distributor, who was going to help them get wealthy. Another couple the Scheibelers knew had "gone direct"—whatever that was. Soon Eric and Patty found themselves sitting around their kitchen table as their friends laid out "the Plan" according to Amway.

Seeing a catalog with a huge selection of products and a book called *Profiles of Success* impressed Eric. "It depicted many, many couples who became wealthy in the business we had just been shown," he said.[35] The catalog had so many products that the Scheibelers were told they wouldn't have to sell anything and that they would be able to attend monthly seminars and receive ongoing training by people who had become wealthy through "the business." Eric was relieved. "Neither Patty nor I were salespeople," he said. "Apparently, our business would be just to purchase products we were already using from their special catalog at discount-store savings of 30 percent and then show the discount catalog to other potential 'members,' recruiting them to do the same," Scheibeler said. "It sounded good." Use your own products and teach others to do the same. Strangely enough, the word *Amway* was spoken once in the two-hour presentation, Eric recalled. Their friends gave Patty and Eric an information kit and arranged to come back in a few days to answer any questions and pick up the kit. When their Amway contacts returned, however, they didn't want to talk about the company. They asked the Scheibelers to compile a list of their dreams and goals. "Sure, we wanted to be debt-free, have a nice home in a safe neighborhood, drive newer and safer cars, vacation, help our parents, and be together," Eric said. "What did that have to do with how this business worked?" The Amway Diamonds lifestyle, they were told, promised unlimited family time and no set work schedule. The more you made, the less time it took. With no employees or overhead, there was no way to lose money. The Scheibelers were advised that Diamonds were making at least $250,000 a year in Amway. "I had always wanted to have my own business and this looked like the answer," Eric said. "I did not believe anyone was willing to work harder than I would in this business." He wanted to meet one of the millionaires who would mentor him. Soon, he got the chance.

With a few weeks, Eric and Patty met an Amway Double Diamond. He drove up in his Mercedes and wore a hand-tailored suit, expensive leather shoes, and jewelry. He was loaded with charisma, friendly and warm. Rather than delivering a hard-sell message, the Double Diamond talked about how hard he worked to succeed and how many people work and received less. "This really sounded like me," Eric said. All people really needed, the Double Diamond advised, was to get advice from people who had achieved success. Wealthy people could teach you how to become wealthy. After a quick review of the Amway sales and marketing plan, the Double Diamond flipped through *Profiles of Success,* which featured him, and told those gathered that "the business"—again,

Amway wasn't mentioned directly—had made him not only a millionaire, but a multimillionaire. The Scheibelers signed up to become Amway distributors.

Over the next months, they listened to tapes and looked at the materials in their sales kit. One of the tapes gave advice on how to invite others into the wholesaling business and how to deflect questions about Amway. If someone asked, "Is it Amway?" the literature suggested this response: "We get goods and services from over 2,000 different manufacturers. Are you looking for a particular product line or what?" If the person on the end of the line asked, "Is it legal?" the advised response was: "Do you think I'd call you about something that could hurt you or your family?"[36] Other tapes spoke of family, strong values, and patriotism. Eric and Patty didn't want to wear big diamonds, drive luxury cars, or live in a palatial home. They just wanted the freedom to be together and have the financial wherewithal to help the people they loved and build a future. Their sponsors mentioned that a seminar was coming up that could help them do just that. Dexter Yager was going to be speaking. Given his reputation as Amway's most famous and successful distributor, Eric and Patty couldn't wait to hear what he had to say. When they arrived at the location, however, they kept looking for the Amway seminar, only to learn that it was held under their sponsors' distributorship name, Walter Enterprises. "We quickly learned that saying Amway was taboo," Eric said. "This seemed unusual; it did not make much sense that this was a 'dirty word' among what seemed like a large group of Amway distributors."[37]

The Scheibelers walked into a large hall filled with men, most of whom were clean-shaven and wore suits, and women who wore conservative dresses. "It was a sharp-looking group," Eric said. "The energy in the room was contagious. We met a few people, and they all seemed friendly and upbeat. Someone walked onstage and began to warm up the group, pep-rally style. Many yelled with excitement. Again, this seemed odd, but we were intrigued, wondering what caused the near-evangelical fervor in the room."[38] The crowd went wild as the Double Diamonds took the stage to introduce Yager. Eric said he thought the plaster might vibrate loose from the ceiling. "We had never been to either a business or church meeting that had this level of emotion and excitement," he recalled. "These people had an absolute passion for life."

The Scheibelers picked up four distributors to sponsor, and the Double Diamond made arrangements to come to their home to do a meeting for them. Eric and Patty left the seminar feeling invigorated and fortunate to have met such great people.

As they began to learn about the business, however, Eric found the point value system misleading. He believed that it wasn't calculated dollar for dollar, as their sponsors indicated, but could take more than twice the sales volume to generate PV on the bonus schedule. Patty and Eric began building their business and went direct, becoming Silver producers. But they found it very difficult to keep so many people in their group active. "The turnover was overwhelming," Scheibeler said.[39] At some point, he and Patty surrendered their life to the business. They had little or no contact with anyone not connected with Amway, but their business was growing. They were Pearls on the way to becoming Emeralds and were building up to become Diamonds. Eric resigned from his full-time job at a large insurance company. The Scheibelers attended rallies with the Yagers and took trips paid for by Amway. But Eric recalled he was gone constantly. They weren't making big money, and they were in debt. The pressure to keep building the business strained their marriage. Their family life suffered. Eric said he came to see the abuses loyal Amway distributors endured. The Scheibelers came to view Amway as a "motivational cult," and they got out.[40]

The Price of Success

So who succeeds in the Amway business and why? Cofounders Rich DeVos and Jay Van Andel heard the repeated allegations that some distributors misrepresented the business's earnings potential, but they insisted that the company doesn't push Amway as a way to get rich quick and that they can't control what individual distributors might say.

"If you've ever listened to our presentation and done it as the Amway Corporation tells you, you will know that the work will be hard but the disappointments will be many, but if you're willing to pay the price, there's a chance for you to improve your lot in life," DeVos said in the *60 Minutes* Amway segment. "A chance. And that's all we've ever presented to people." An Amway distributor in Europe who spoke on condition of anonymity said that, in time, he came to realize that the vast majority of the people actively complaining about Amway on the Internet were all going to meetings run by particular groups of people. "I was going to meetings run by an entirely different group of people—i.e., different 'systems,'" the distributor said. "They weren't lying, they were fairly accurately reporting their experiences. It just wasn't my experience." Attending a seminar with 30,000 people can seem huge, he added. "But that 30,000 people represents only a small percentage of Amway IBOs," he continued. "You're just getting one tiny window into the huge Amway world. It really is way, way bigger than people think, and no one person's experience, or even a group's, can give you the whole picture."

Then who fails in the Amway business and why? DeVos echoed Yager's statement that no one actually fails. "They have chosen not to work this business as they were told to do," DeVos said. "And whenever we interview them and nail them right down and ask them how many nights they really gave up, how many meetings they really went to, you will find that those who complain haven't really paid the price to achieve in Amway," DeVos said.[41] But that price, like the cost of real diamonds, rubies, and emeralds, can be very high—too high for a lot of people who become part of the turnover and leave Amway behind.

A major weakness of the MLM model, some of Amway's own distributors contend, is that each IBO, as a representative of the company, reflects on Amway. Therefore, how Amway is perceived depends a great deal on the actions and behaviors of others. "Unfortunately, Amway has been guilty of not properly policing their field, including some top leadership, and this has caused massive reputation problems," the IBO in Europe commented. "It is clearly changing, but unfortunately, much of that had to be scared into them." The BERR case against Amway's operation in England is a good example of this. (BERR is England's Business Enterprise and Regulatory Reform agency; the case is presented in more detail in Chapter 14, "Amway Redux.")

■ ■ ■

The stories of Amway's top achievers around the world reveal one common trait. They didn't just follow advice, they took ownership of their businesses and made decisions for themselves. As one IBO put it,

"While top leaders will tell you about their loyalty to their mentors, when you dig deeper it's obvious the ones with long-term success aren't just followers. They are leaders as well." Some of the leaders, however, led their downlines into dangerous territory. How far were they willing to go to beat or bad-mouth the competition by spreading rumors? They were about to find out when two of the world's biggest consumer product companies clashed and took their battle all the way to the U.S. Supreme Court.

Chapter 9

Clash of the Soap Titans

I n 1837 two immigrants, William Procter and James Gamble, formed a business to make candles and soap. Like Amway's founding families, Procter and Gamble had emigrated from Europe to the United States to escape poverty and seek new opportunities. Procter left London after his woolens shop burned, and Gamble's family fled famine in Ireland. Both men ended up in Cincinnati, Ohio, nicknamed the "Porkopolis" for its hog-butchering industry. They had married sisters, and their mutual father-in-law convinced them to go into business together. Animal fat and wood ashes produced lye, a raw material used to make both soap and candles. Thus a new partnership, Procter & Gamble, was born. During the Civil War, Procter & Gamble received several contracts to supply candles and soap to soldiers in the Union Army.[1]

In Direct Competition

Gamble's son, James Norris Gamble, a trained chemist, in 1879 developed a formula for an inexpensive soap to compete with high-quality imported castile soap based on olive oil. Produced in cake form, the soap was designed mainly for washing clothes. The chemist became interested in using other raw materials for soap, including vegetable oils, which produced a lighter soap that floated. Eventually, Harley Procter, the founder's son, gave it a new name—Ivory Soap—based on a line from the Bible's Book of Psalms: "All thy garments smell of myrrh, and aloes, and cassia, out of the ivory palaces whereby they have made thee glad."[2] Ivory Soap made Procter & Gamble glad, too. The product and name, which identified the soap as pure and long lasting, became so successful that the company opened a new factory. When Procter & Gamble learned that the soap's key customers, mainly housewives, were shaving off slivers from the bars of soap to make it easier to use, they introduced another product, Ivory Soap Flakes, the precursor of modern powder detergents. That experience enticed Procter & Gamble to conduct more market research and launch a new concept: mass-marketed, consumer-driven brands. More soap products soon followed, including the Lenox brand. Procter & Gamble became so well known for soap that daytime radio serial programs such as *Ma Perkins,* which the company sponsored, were dubbed "soap operas." Later, in the 1950s, Procter & Gamble shifted its national advertising campaign to television soap operas such as *The Guiding Light.*

As the nation's first mass marketer of consumer products, Procter & Gamble discovered it needed a symbol on its packaging to identify the product as genuine. At first, the Star brand candles it produced bore a simple star logo. In the early 1850s, wharf hands who shipped the soap and candles began drawing the moon and stars on boxes. It began as a simple one-eyed crescent moon face, a popular design at the time, drawn inside a circle with stars. Later, the drawing became more ornate, featuring a Zeus-like man-in-the-moon with flowing beard looking over a field of 13 stars, which the company said represented the 13 American colonies. (In the 1920s, after the invention of the electric light bulb, Procter & Gamble discontinued making candles.)

Ironically for the company that named its best-known product based on a Bible verse, in the 1980s rumors began circulating that the Procter & Gamble logo was satanic and that Procter & Gamble used its profits to support the Church of Satan.[3] The calls and letters to the company asking about the rumors peaked in 1982 and 1985, and later in the 1990s.[4] Some religious groups perceived connections between the logo and the Bible's book of Revelation, specifically Revelation 12:1: "And there appeared a great wonder in heaven; a woman clothed with the sun, and the moon under her feet, and upon her head a crown of twelve stars." The stories typically claimed that Procter & Gamble's president discussed Satanism on the Phil Donahue nationally televised TV show and that the company's trademark was a satanic symbol. Neither allegations were true. The man-in-the-moon's flowing beard curled at the end, which some interpreted to look like upside-down "666," the so-called mark of the devil. Some saw in the curls of hair on the man's head the horns of a lamb that they interpreted to be the false prophet. Procter & Gamble, realizing it had a public relations nightmare on its hands, launched a public relations blitz. The company printed information pamphlets, lined up religious organizations, such as the Billy Graham Evangelistic Association, and leaders, such as the Rev. Jerry Falwell, to condemn the satanic worship rumors. Procter & Gamble also brought several lawsuits against individuals it believed were spreading them. Among those it sued were Amway distributors and Amway itself, which also had become closely identified with making soap and was one of Procter & Gamble's chief competitors. Procter & Gamble's Tide and Cheer laundry detergents competed with Amway's SA8 products, Crest competed with Amway's Glister, and Spic 'n Span and Top Job cleaning products competed with Amway's L.O.C. Multipurpose Cleaner.

Because many of Amway's distributors were active in their churches, it was alleged that some of them also heard the rumors, and even spread them, from the pulpit.[5] Amway said it helped Procter & Gamble squelch the rumors by publishing articles in *Amagram*, its monthly magazine sent to all distributors, and in its *Newsgram* monthly publication sent to all direct distributors. Amway said it also publicly denounced the rumor when the news media inquired about it, educated its distributors that the accusation was false, sent distributors copies of information packets that Procter & Gamble provided to the company, and asked distributors who had repeated the rumor to issue retractions.[6] Nevertheless, the devil worship claim persisted.

In early spring 1995, Procter & Gamble became increasingly alarmed that religious groups, college students, and Internet users were spreading false statements about its trademark and connections to Satanism in southern Florida and in Texas. In April, Roger Patton, an Amway distributor near Houston, had received a flier that repeated the Satanism rumor. Patton read the text of it into an electronic voice-mail system that Amway distributors used called AMVOX and sent it to an upline distributor. The message was received by Randy Haugen, an Amway Diamond in Ogden, Utah. Haugen had established a network of Amway distributors throughout Utah, Nevada, Texas, Mexico, and Canada. He served on the Amway Distributors Association Council, an advisory board to the corporation. He then forwarded the message to about 20 distributors, some of whom in turn forwarded it to more Amway distributors. It's not known exactly how many distributors received the message, but the AMVOX system was capable of reaching tens of thousands in the hierarchy of distributors.

In court documents, Amway claimed it did not know that the message had been sent until a distributor downline from Haugen called the company a few days later and asked about it. Amway said one of its employees called Haugen, told him the rumor was false, and urged that he issue a retraction. The employee also sent Haugen a copy of the information kit that Procter & Gamble had supplied to Amway to respond to the rumor. The next day, on April 26, Haugen sent out a new message over the voice-mail system to retract the rumor. It said in part:

> Hello, guys. This message is going out to all of Valerie and I's (sic) frontline and also to every Diamond in the organization. We had an AMVOX that came down that talked about Proctor (sic) and Gamble. . . . I'm going to read you a statement here and see if we can get this rumor, put it out, because I know a lot of you would like to know the truth. . . . Unfortunately, this familiar trademark has been subjected to prosperous, excuse me, preposterous, unfounded rumors since 1980–81. The rumors falsely allege that the trademark is the symbol of Satanism or devil worship. Typically, the story reports a

Proctor (sic) and Gamble executive discussed Satanism on a national televised talk show. Another story maintains that the trademark is a result of Procter and Gamble being taken over by the Monies (sic)—followers of Rev. Sun Myung Moon and his Unification Church. The rumors are, of course, totally false. Their trademark originated in 1851 as a symbol for their star branded candle. Later, it was designed to show a man in the moon looking over a field of thirteen stars commemorating the original American colonies. It represents only Procter and Gamble. So, if you hear any rumors saying anything to the effect that they are practicing Satanism and their symbols on their products are Satanic, then it is absolutely, 100 percent false. We don't want any bad rumors about any competitor or non-competitors on any company anywhere ever going out from us. So, if anybody you hear talking about this in the organization anywhere at all brings this up, it is absolutely not true. Not only is it not just substantiated, but it is not true, period. Amway Corporation does not endorse spreading false and malicious rumors against Proctor (sic) and Gamble or any other company. Please do your part, as independent distributors, by not spreading this rumor any farther or nipping it if you hear it from anybody else. . . .[7]

Amway said there was no evidence that the Satanism rumor was continuing to spread among its distributors and Haugen's "prompt retraction swiftly and effectively squelched the rumor."[8] According to court documents, Amway considered the matter closed.

Later, in early May 1995, however, Procter & Gamble heard about Haugen's AMVOX message with the rumor. It had noticed that calls from concerned consumers about the Satanism rumor had "spiked dramatically" after Haugen's message to the Amway voice-mail system.[9] In March, the company received 22 contacts from consumers concerned about the rumor; by May, the number had mushroomed to 200.[10] That August, Procter & Gamble filed suit against Haugen in U.S. District Court in Utah for spreading "false and malicious" statements connecting Procter & Gamble with Satanism. "We have been fighting this outrageous rumor for over fifteen years," James J. Johnson,

Procter & Gamble's senior vice president and general counsel, said in a prepared statement. The company estimated it had answered almost 200,000 calls and letters addressing the false rumors over that period of that time. "Throughout that time, people associated with Amway have played a role," Johnson continued. "Over the years we have had numerous incidents, beyond this lawsuit, linking the spread of the rumor to Amway distributors. Additionally, nearly half of the lawsuits we have filed in connection with this rumor have involved Amway distributors."[11] Procter & Gamble had filed 15 lawsuits, six against Amway distributors, since the early 1980s. Procter & Gamble's attorney went on to say that Amway used the devil worship rumor to encourage a boycott of Procter & Gamble products. After filing the suit, Procter & Gamble began the legal process of discovery. Amway was not named as a party until later in the case, but Procter & Gamble served it with a subpoena, seeking documents, including e-mail messages. Amway produced several hundred pages of documents, and Procter & Gamble attorneys took more than 1,000 pages of deposition testimony from 11 different Amway employees.

Amway, of course, took a different view of the proceedings. It charged that Procter & Gamble attempted to make Amway the public scapegoat for the Satanism rumor. In April 1996, Procter & Gamble filed a second amended complaint. This time it also alleged defamation, common law unfair competition, violations of the Utah Truth in Advertising Act, tortuous interference, negligent supervision and violations of the Lanham Act—the Trademark Act of 1946 that prohibited false description or representation of trademarks—and vicarious liability arising out of the Satanism rumor. Procter & Gamble later filed a fourth amended complaint with claims for product disparagement based on allegations that Amway had told consumers that Procter & Gamble's Crest toothpaste scratches teeth, and asserting fraud. The Utah court dismissed that complaint as untimely filed.

If at First P&G Does Not Succeed . . .

After losing in Utah, the consumer products giant wasn't giving up, however. In July 1997, Procter & Gamble sued Amway again, this time in the U.S. District Court for the Southeastern District in Texas in Houston, with another long list of allegations: unfair competition, negligent supervision, negligence, business disparagement, defamation, tortious interference with prospective business relations, vicarious liability, fraud, violations of the Lanham Act, and violations of the Texas Business and Commerce Code. The suit also alleged that Amway was a pyramid scheme: "The Amway enterprise is in reality an elaborate, illegal pyramid scheme," the suit read. It continued:

> Amway's objective is to entice consumers out of the retail marketplace by convincing them that purchasing Amway products will make them rich. Of those who invest the time, money, and personal sacrifice to become Amway distributors, only a select few even break even. Even fewer realized the profits touted by Amway in its sales pitch—and they do so by siphoning money from the victims at the bottom."[12]

Procter & Gamble named as defendants the Amway Distributors Association, Haugen, Patton, and some of Amway's other top distributors and organizations, all of whom were based in Utah or Texas. The suit also alleged violations of the federal Racketeer Influenced and Corrupt Organizations Act, known as RICO, based on Amway's alleged pyramid scheme. Passed in 1970 to combat organized crime, the RICO law gives winning plaintiffs triple damages, plus attorney fees. If the court found that Amway violated RICO, the company could suffer a devastating financial blow. Procter & Gamble sought $595 million in damages due to alleged lost sales from the devil worship rumors.

Procter & Gamble lined up an expert witness, G. Robert Blakely, a law professor at Notre Dame University widely considered to be one of the nation's authorities on the RICO act and the structure and function of organized crime groups. Blakely's report later was sealed and he refused to talk about it, saying he was under a gag order and that it should never have been made public.[13] But a copy of the sealed report found its way onto the Internet and was posted on the Amway Wiki Web site, www.amwaywiki.com, for anyone who wants to read it. Despite the Federal Trade Commission's 1979 landmark ruling that Amway did not operate an illegal pyramid scheme, Procter & Gamble alleged that it was just that. In the suit filed in Houston, Procter & Gamble charged that the Amway plan "primarily rewards distributors for recruiting new distributors, who will in turn be rewarded for recruiting new distributors, in a seemingly endless proliferation of 'downlines.'"[14] Procter & Gamble further accused Amway of being "elaborately disguised as a marketing network in which 'products' flow down in return for money flowing up. The existence of the 'products' creates the illusion of legitimacy and masks the purpose of the payments." Its complaint went on to state that:

> . . . no legitimate distribution network contains so many layers of middlemen, selling and reselling the same goods a dozen or more times, encouraging those below to keep the base of the pyramid expanding with new victims. And, the pressure to keep Amway's pyramid going with new recruits is enormous, because the Amway Pyramid is in a constant state of collapse and renew.

The suit also contended that Amway was not really in the business of marketing goods to the American public because, it alleged, 82 percent of all final sales of Amway products were made to its own distributors: "Hence, like every pyramid scheme, the Amway Pyramid is a closed system—the profits come not from the distribution of a good or service to those outside the pyramid, but from a redistribution of wealth among the layers within the pyramid." It spawned a second line of business, "selling motivational tapes," according to the suit.[15] As far as claims of unfair competition, Procter & Gamble also accused Amway of making disparaging remarks about Procter & Gamble products, including that "Tide laundry detergent would form 'sludge' that would clog drainpipes, all part of an effort to lure customers away from Procter & Gamble products and entice them to become part of Amway's distribution 'scheme.'"[16]

While Amway was mounting its defense, it became aware of an alleged secret relationship between Procter & Gamble and Sidney Schwartz, the author of a critical Amway Web site called "Amway: The Untold Story." Amway had filed its own lawsuit against Procter & Gamble in November 1998 "to protect Amway's successful, multinational business."[17] In it, Amway claimed that Procter & Gamble supported Schwartz with free legal services and consulting payments and that he, in turn, was spreading false or misleading information about Amway on the World Wide Web. "Amway prefers to meet its competitors in the open marketplace, not cloaked behind a mask of false and misleading attacks," the company said in a press release. "By collecting evidence about P&G's subsidy of false and misleading attacks on the Internet, Amway hopes to return to a level playing field with P&G and other manufacturers of household and personal care products."[18] A memo was sent to the Diamonds, warning about Schwartz's site. After Amway took legal action to shut down Schwartz, he voluntarily unplugged the site. Internet free-speech champions jumped into the fray, contending that Amway was trying to suppress free speech. A Web site of the same name continues operating today, but Schwartz is not affiliated with it.

■ ■ ■

In the Utah case, the Utah court in April 1999 entered a final judgment dismissing Procter & Gamble's claims. But a month later, the district court case in Houston was going to trial. Amway moved for summary judgment and the district court granted the motion, dismissing Procter & Gamble's Lanham Act claims on the basis of the so-called *res judicata* effect. It holds that when two lawsuits proceed simultaneously, the first judgment takes precedence so that a suit isn't brought against the same party for the same cause of action piecemeal rather than in succession before the proper courts. It also dismissed Procter & Gamble's remaining claims. In August 2000, the U.S. Tenth Circuit Court of Appeals in Denver agreed with lower court rulings that there was no evidence that the corporate parent was involved with the distributor's alleged wrongdoing since Amway distributors are not technically employees of the company. However, the appeals panel said the court should reconsider the other claims of Procter & Gamble, which they colorfully described as the "corporate butt of the Beelzebub canard," based on a state "tortious interference" law and a federal unfair competition statute.

In May 1999, after hearing two weeks of testimony, District Judge Vanessa Gilmore dismissed Procter & Gamble's lawsuit for lack of proof of malice. The federal judge in Houston threw out some of Procter & Gamble's claims and ruled for Amway in part of the case. Procter & Gamble appealed, and the three-judge U.S. Court of Appeals for the Fifth Circuit in New Orleans upheld part of the lower court ruling, but sent part of it back to the district court to reconsider Procter & Gamble's claims under the RICO law. It was the first time a federal appellate court permitted this type of claim. Amway moved to have the district case thrown out and said it was prepared to take the case all the way to the U.S. Supreme Court. There was no RICO violation, Amway contended, because the distributor believed the rumor to be true—hence, there was no fraud committed. Michael A. Mohr, who was vice president and general counsel of Alticor, Amway's parent company, told the *New York Times* that the speech was innocent and was about religion. "When you've got speech between individuals about a public figure"—referring to Procter & Gamble—"on a matter of public concern, I think the First Amendment applies," he said.[19] The appeals court, however, wrote in its order that a rumor gets no First Amendment protection if the "speakers' motives in spreading the Satanism rumor were economic."

In the fall of 2001, the Supreme Court heard the case based on the issue of the First Amendment and commercial speech. Amway hired Kenneth Starr, the former solicitor general who served as independent counsel during the Clinton administration and who investigated Clinton's Whitewater real estate investments and his affair with former White House intern Monica Lewinsky. Starr argued that the court should clarify its views on the First Amendment and commercial speech such as advertising, which, unlike other kinds of speech, is subject to government regulation. However, in October, the court, without making comment, declined to review the lower court's ruling.

Enough Is Enough

One more lawsuit continued to drag on. The U.S. District Court jury in Salt Lake City ruled in March 2007 that four former Amway distributors had, indeed, spread false rumors linking Procter & Gamble to Satanism to advance their own business. A jury awarded Procter & Gamble $19.25 million in the civil case. A federal judge previously had dismissed the lawsuit, and the U.S. Circuit Court of Appeals in Denver had agreed. The case was reinstated after further appeal. Randy Haugen said he was shocked by the jury verdict. "It's hard to imagine they'd pursue it this long, especially after all the retractions we put out," he said. "We are stunned. All of us."[20] The defendants appealed. The next month a U.S. District judge awarded almost $13 million in prejudgment interest to Procter & Gamble. The Amway distributors faced the possibility of postjudgment interest if their appeal failed. Procter & Gamble also cross-appealed, asking for treble damages.

Thirteen proved to be the Amway distributors' unlucky number. The 13-year epic battle between the soap titans finally ended in December 2008, when the defendants dropped their appeal. Haugen and his wife, Valorie, went on to become Black Diamonds at MonaVie, a multilevel marketing company that markets health juices based on the acai berry, found in the Amazon rain forest, and other nutritional products. The Haugens even made a documentary for MonaVie. Amway (or Quixtar, as Amway's North American operations would come to be known), in 2008 sued MonaVie in a Salt Lake City federal court. Its complaint alleged that MonaVie distributors competed unfairly by making false claims about the benefits of its health juice and using those false premises to raid Amway IBO organizations and steal thousands of independent distributors. The nasty legal disputes went back and forth for several years and finally were settled under confidential terms in November 2010.

■ ■ ■

All of the legal battles and regulatory hurdles that Amway had faced over the years had convinced its leaders that they had to become more proactive in dealing with the government and the courts. Any large corporation, of course, is the target of lawsuits—that's why they have their own legal departments and/or outside counsel. But Amway's reputation was at stake. Its name had been dragged through the mud many times and some of it had stuck.

Amway's leaders had learned from their experiences with Canada and Wisconsin in the 1980s and the FTC ruling that they needed to retool more than their business. They needed to turn around what they perceived as a fundamental misunderstanding of their business model. They would have to get involved in educating government officials and lobbying those who made decisions and who could shut down the company with court cases or regulations and taint the company's image. They would have to get more involved in politics.

Chapter 10

Friends in High Places

With Amway's money and its millions of distributors—a formidable bloc of conservative-leaning voters—came the power to win friends and influence people and politics in Michigan; Washington, D.C.; and beyond. Rich and Jay's Dutch Calvinist upbringing instilled in them a strong belief that Christian principles should be applied to politics and that government had a moral duty to stay out of certain areas, such as entrepreneurialism.

To Amway and its founders, creating jobs was the realm of the private sector, not the government. The company's tenets of free enterprise, limited government, and strong Christian ideals naturally dovetailed with those of conservative Republicans. Thus, in the 1970s, Amway began making large contributions to conservative groups, the Republican Party, and some individual political campaigns. Since then, few companies have forged closer ties to the Republican Party and right-wing causes than Amway. Its friends included former Republican presidents

119

Gerald Ford, Ronald Reagan, George H. W. Bush, and George W. Bush; former House Speaker Newt Gingrich; former U.S. Senator and presidential candidate Bob Dole; former Attorney General John Ashcroft; former House Majority Whip Tom DeLay—who was a former Amway distributor—and conservative Christian leader Jerry Falwell.

Getting Involved

Jay's foray into politics began at the local level when he served on the Ada Planning Commission in the 1960s. The commission had the power to annex property, expand the tax base, and bring jobs to the area. "As the fastest growing business in the state, Rich and I wanted to make sure that Amway was represented," Jay said.[1] He jumped from there to state politics, working with the Michigan State Chamber of Commerce—Jay was elected chairman of that organization in 1970—and then on the Michigan State Compensation Committee, which set salaries for legislators and other elected officials. He angered some of them by "refusing to pay them what they thought they were worth."[2] From there, Jay moved into active roles in the state Republican Party. He was named chairman of the Republican State Finance Committee and bankrolled some Republican candidates, although later he preferred to make donations through the party itself rather than to individuals or committees.

By 1972, business power brokers in Washington, D.C., had taken notice. Jay nabbed a seat on the national board of the U.S. Chamber of Commerce, the world's largest nonprofit lobbying group, and in 1979 became its chairman. That was the same year that the Federal Trade Commission had ruled Amway to be a legal multilevel marketer and not a pyramid scheme. Jay traveled the country as a spokesman for free enterprise and free trade, and against regulation that discouraged business. It was a natural step from there to the front lines of the national Republican Party. In 1980, Ronald Reagan was running for president. Rich and Jay were admirers of his conservative agenda. Ford arranged for them to meet Reagan in Los Angeles when the former actor was campaigning there. During the discussion, they encouraged Reagan to consider Bush Sr. for his running mate and Alexander Haig for secretary of state, both of whom he ended up choosing for those positions.[3] After the Carter administration, which Jay believed had mistakenly focused on spending rather than investment to drive the economy, the Amway founders saw in Reagan a chance for tax reform, limited government, less regulation, and a more investment-friendly climate for business. Rich and Jay bought pro-Reagan ads at their own expense and ran them in newspapers around the United States.

After Reagan was elected, Jay met with him occasionally in the Oval Office. Although they saw eye to eye on many issues, Jay didn't always agree with Reagan. When some of the president's staff favored a tax increase to cut the deficit, Reagan called the U.S. Chamber to get its input. Jay, who was the head of the chamber's executive committee at the time, refused to support the hike. The president called him from Air Force One, and the two had a long conversation, but neither one would give up his position. "I think it pained Reagan to push for higher taxes, but he had to go by what he thought was best for the economy at the time, and so did I," Jay said.[4] Later, in 1985, Jay testified before a House Ways and Means subcommittee supporting Reagan's proposal to reform the federal income tax system. It still didn't go far enough for Jay, who favored a deduction-free, flat tax rate and an end to "Gestapo-like IRS tactics."[5] But he viewed Reagan's tax policies as moves in the right direction.

Giving to the GOP

During that period when the Cold War quietly simmered, former Russian KGB agents, high-ranking Soviet military officials, and other high-placed Soviets defected to the United States. To assist the defectors in building new lives, Jay helped found the nonpartisan research institution Jamestown Foundation in 1984. After the Cold War ended, the group refocused on providing information and analysis to policy makers about China, Russia, and Eurasia. Meanwhile, Rich also had become active in the national Republican Party, serving as finance chairman of the Republican National Committee during the first two years of the Reagan administration. Amway already had other political insiders in place in the Reagan and later the Bush Sr. White House. One of them was presidential historian and philanthropist Doug Wead, the man credited with coining the term *compassionate conservative*. Wead co-wrote *Reagan: In Pursuit of the Presidency—1980* (with Bill Wead, 1980), *The Courage of a Conservative: James G. Watt* (1985)—Reagan's Secretary of the Interior until Watt was forced to step down in 1983 after he told a distasteful ethnic joke—and a "first families" trilogy about presidents' children, mothers and fathers, and siblings. The author also had worked with Amway mega-distributor Dexter Yager, cowriting his books *Don't Let Anybody Steal Your Dream* (1978) and later *Millionaire Mentality* (1993). Wead has studied network marketing since 1974 and built an Amway Diamond business within four years. He went on to become special assistant to former President George H. W. Bush and helped organize his presidential campaign. While he was in the White House, his networking business was put into a blind management trust. Wead continued as an aide to the younger President Bush and later drew parallels between politics and network marketing:

> In polling we learned that if you poll 100 people, you get a little direction, but if you really want to know what's going to happen within about 3 percent, you need about 1,550. If you do that or at random, you can tell almost within 3 percent exactly what's going to happen or where the public is going to go on an issue. And what I learned in networking is it's about the same. When you reach a level where you've [got] about 1,500 people who are plugged into a system, who are listening to the tapes and coming to the functions, you know how it works.[6]

Wead stayed in the Amway business for 30 years, then left in 2009 to join XanGo LLC, a health and wellness products multilevel marketer, as a full-time consultant.

Jay remained close to Reagan and was even considered to be ambassador to the Caribbean, at the U.S. Embassy in Barbados, in 1988. He turned it down—regretfully, he said, because he had always wanted to be an ambassador and loved the Caribbean, but didn't feel he had the time with his duties corunning Amway. When George H. W. Bush took office, he tapped Jay to be the commissioner general and ambassador to the Genoa Expo, the World's Fair in Genoa, Italy. Held in 1992, the fair celebrated the 500th anniversary of Christopher Columbus's journey to the New World. Jay received the rank of ambassador and the title of "Your Excellency," but the position required him to be overseas for only several months instead of several years. John Gartland, Amway's Washington lobbyist, worked with Jay as deputy commissioner general and lived in Italy to work with the bureaucracy. Amway was a major sponsor of the U.S. Pavilion at the Expo.

Jay remained close to President Bush and his wife, Barbara, and later their son, George W. (Betsy DeVos received the status of "Pioneer" after she raised $100,000 for the Bush-Cheney campaign.) Jay was a "confidant of several of the world's great heads of state," the late commentator Paul Harvey wrote in a foreword to Jay's memoir. "He might well have been elected or appointed to any public office of his choosing. Nobody ever loved his country more, but Jay's 'choosing' was Amway."[7]

Jay and Rich's political involvement mostly played out behind the scenes as they used their wealth to influence politics. From the 1990s to this day, money has flowed from Amway's founding families to the nation's capital and into Republican coffers. The DeVos family remains close to the Republican National Committee and ranks as a top contributor to Republican congressional campaigns, GOP candidates, and conservative causes. Among the candidates Rich DeVos—who identified his occupation as a "door-to-door salesman" in a contribution report to the Federal Election Commission[8]—has given money to are John Ashcroft, Wead, George W. Bush, the late North Carolina Senator Jesse Helms, former Texas Senator Phil Gramm, presidential candidate John McCain, former U.S. Senator Rick Santorum, and former New York Mayor Rudolph Guiliani. The Washington, D.C.–based Center for Responsive Politics estimates that Amway and Alticor have given more than $8.7 million to Republicans since 1989, about half of it in "soft money" to individuals and organizations. Of the 135 companies on the list of top all-time donors, Amway was the only one to give 100 percent of its contributions to Republicans.[9] The Center for Public Integrity, a public interest watchdog organization, also ranked Jay number 100 on its "Club 100" list of 100 Americans who contributed more than $100,000 to state political parties. Fifteen of the Club 100 members were Michigan residents, and of them, Jay gave the most to the state party in a series of donations totaling $400,000.[10]

Crown Ambassador distributors Birdie and Dexter Yager and their Internet Services Corporation also have given more than $269,000 to Republicans.[11]

Rich Passes the Baton

Meanwhile, big changes were afoot within Amway that would shake up the company's own internal and external politics. In the summer of 1992, Rich suffered a stroke. For the first time, he began to wonder if he should continue as president of Amway with the daily stress of running a large company. After his earlier heart trouble and bypass surgery, Rich had changed his lifestyle, was eating healthier than he ever had, was exercising regularly, and trying to keep a lid on stress. Still, that December, he woke up at 4 AM with such severe chest pains that Rich knew he was having a heart attack. He was rushed by ambulance to the emergency room in Grand Rapids. When he arrived, his heart had almost stopped beating. He heard a nurse say, "There's no pulse." Then he passed out.[12] When he regained consciousness, doctors didn't know whether Rich would survive. They discussed with the DeVos family an experimental and risky procedure that was being performed at the Cleveland Clinic. Rich wanted to do it and expected to live through the night. The doctors weren't so sure. The next day, doctors performed the surgery. It required three bypasses. Rich got home in time for Christmas, but then developed an almost-fatal staph infection in his chest. He had to be sliced open three more times. Doctors cut out so much muscle that Rich's chest had to be rebuilt by a plastic surgeon. The ordeal left him weak and wondering if his "time was up."[13] The next year, the day before he left the hospital, Rich resigned his position at Amway and passed his baton to his eldest son, Dick, who became president of Alticor. Dick had been groomed for the succession and in 1974, he had joined Amway, doing a variety of jobs—packing, loading trucks, driving trucks, and working in marketing, accounting, and research. Dick spearheaded Amway's international push as the head of its international division. When he took over, Amway operated in 11 countries, but only 10 percent of its revenues came from foreign sales. Under his watch, Amway expanded into Asia, including China, and half of the company's revenues began coming from overseas markets. As its international business picked up, Amway remained active politically. More than ever, what happened on Capitol Hill affected it directly.

■ ■ ■

After he retired, Rich stepped up his political involvement. In 1994, Amway spent $2.5 million to launch a television studio at the Republican party's Washington headquarters. Two years later, Amway drew the media spotlight again when it donated $1.3 million to the San Diego Convention & Visitors Bureau to provide "unfiltered" coverage of the Republican National Convention on televangelist Pat Robertson's cable Family Channel. The Democratic National Committee argued that Amway was trying to get around a federal ban on corporations buying TV time for political parties.[14] "We think of it more as a public service," Rich told *BusinessWeek*.[15]

At the GOP convention, Amway kept up its high profile by chartering an 83-foot yacht to entertain delegates and VIP guests.[16] The ultimate expression of political patronage, though, came in 1997 when Rich and Helen each wrote checks totaling $1 million to the RNC.[17] There was no doubt that on the national political scene, Amway had secured a seat at the table, which also included the prison ministry of Charles Colson, the former Watergate felon who is now a Christian prison evangelist. Colson, not coincidentally, wrote the foreword to *How to Be Like Rich DeVos*. He and Rich met in 1975 when Colson spoke at a Gospel Films banquet in Michigan. Colson was familiar with Amway after having bought the company's products from his limousine driver, who was an independent distributor, when Colson worked in the Nixon White House.[18] There were other political connections, such as one between Betsy's family and the Bushes. Her brother, Erik Prince, a former Navy SEAL and regular contributor to the RNC, founded the controversial Blackwater private security firm—later renamed Xe Services LLC—that raked in lucrative contracts after the U.S. invasion of Afghanistan and the U.S. occupation of Iraq. In 2009, it lost its license from the State Department to guard diplomats at the U.S. Embassy in Baghdad after 17 Iraqi civilians died in a shooting two years before. (Prince has since moved to Abu Dhabi.)

Jay Passes the Baton

After Rich stepped down, Jay also began thinking about retiring. In 1988, his wife, Betty, had begun losing her memory, an early sign of what would turn out to be Alzheimer's disease. Around the same time, Jay began to notice problems with using his hands. Tests confirmed he had Parkinson's disease. All of Jay and Betty's children had been involved in Amway, but Jay could pick only one to succeed him. He chose his son Steve, who looked remarkably like his father—tall and lanky with a long face and fair coloring. But the two were quite different. "Steve is not a carbon copy of me," Jay said. 'He has never seen the need to fashion his approach to management after my own. He has his own style and his own methods, and they seem to work very well in combination with . . . Dick."[19]

At age 71, Jay announced his retirement as chairman of Amway in September 1995 and passed the job on to his son. Unlike Dick, Steve had joined Amway after college and stayed there. "For the sake of continuity, Rich and I believe that it's extremely important to perpetuate the philosophies and ideas that have been built into this company," Jay wrote in the company's newsletter. "We believe that the members of our families can bring that into play better than anyone else."[20] The founders had been lifelong friends and well-matched partners. Would Steve and Dick be? Understandably, long-time Amway employees were concerned about the transition and whether the company could continue thriving under new leadership. For a while, the successors heard comments such as "That's the way we've always done it," or "I don't think your father would have done it that way."[21] Steve pointed out that he and Dick had known each other their entire lives. "We've learned business together as well as lived business together," he said. The two spent a lot of time together when they were growing the business in Asia. "We've had a personal relationship that goes back to the fact that we grew up next door to each other," Dick said.[22] Like their fathers, the two sons were different but complementary in personality, with Dick the more gregarious of the two and Steve the more reserved, analytical one.

After retiring, Jay focused on expanding the family's legacy. Dating from his early bad experience in the Army, Jay never did trust mainstream health care. But his wife's condition, his advancing illness, and Rich's serious heart problems convinced him that more must be done for such debilitating diseases. He and Betty founded the Van Andel Institute in 1996 to contribute to hospitals, schools, and other charities, and to fund cutting-edge medical research. The institute put together a team of world-class scientists, including Nobel laureates, and began researching the causes of Alzheimer's, Parkinson's, cancer, and other diseases. Van Andel also continued funding Republican candidates and causes. He supported Bob Dole in 1995 and contributed $2 million to the Progress for America fund, the conservative organization that ran negative television ads attacking Senator John Kerry's record on national security during the 2004 presidential campaign.

Amway's Influence

As the DeVos and Van Andel families' influence continued to spread in conservative circles, Rich became the consummate insider, taken inside the fold as a member of the Council for National Policy, which the *New York Times* described as "a little-known club of a few hundred of the most powerful conservatives in the country."[23] An aura of secrecy surrounded the organization. The membership list remained confidential. Meetings were closed to the media and held at undisclosed locations. Its Web site gives little information about the council except to say that it promotes limited government, traditional values, and a strong national defense. Jay also was involved in conservative organizations as a long-time trustee of the Heritage Foundation and the Hudson Institute, both conservative think tanks founded on principles of free enterprise, limited government, individual freedom, traditional American values, and a strong national defense. Hudson's founder, futurist Herman Kahn, described its philosophy as "contrarianism," uninfluenced by money or ideology.[24] Another Hudson trustee, Emmanuel A. Kampouris, retired chairman and chief executive officer of American Standard Companies, Inc., also served on Alticor's board. Like his father, Steve Van Andel took the public policy route and chaired the U.S. Chamber in 2001 and 2002. During his stint, he visited 11 nations and met with heads of state. One of them was President Jiang Zemin of China. By that time, China had banned direct sales and Steve's meeting proved crucial to convince the Chinese that direct selling was a legal and viable business.[25] (Amway's expansion into China is covered in Chapter 12, "The Biggest Market Ever.")

As Amway continued expanding overseas, international trade became a significant issue, in addition to the company's concerns about taxation. Amway hired an army of lobbyists to make its voice heard in the din of debates over business-related bills. For the first nine months of 2010, the Center for Responsive Politics estimated that Amway and Alticor spent $220,000 on lobbying, hired 27 lobbyists, and mentioned 424 bills. Among the legislation Amway lobbyists pushed for in 2010 were the China Fair Trade Act, tax bills, health care, patent reform, and dietary supplement safety.[26] Former or current Amway distributors also have served in the U.S. House; they're referred to informally as the "Amway Caucus." All have been Republicans: Jon Christensen of Nebraska, Dick Chrysler of Michigan, John Ensign of Nevada, Sue Myrick of North Carolina, and Richard Pombo of California. *Mother Jones* magazine reported that Amway and its salespeople may have contributed nearly half of the $669,525 in Myrick's campaign coffer.[27] A review of Federal Election Commission records shows that Myrick received contributions from Amway mega-distributors and Diamonds from all over the United States: Dexter and Birdie Yager and their children, Bill and Peggy Britt, Bill and Margaret Florence, Don and Nancy Wilson, and, of course, Rich. Myrick since has distanced her connections with the company. Her biography on her congressional Web site cites her public relations firm and her stint as mayor of Charlotte as her previous experience in business and public service. But there's no mention of Amway.[28]

■ ■ ■

Amway's political contributions led critics to charge that the company was buying influence and cited a comment made by Dick's wife, Betsy, to the Capitol Hill insider publication *Roll Call*. It was widely quoted, but often not in its entirety:

"I have decided, however, to stop taking offense at the suggestion that we are buying influence. Now I simply concede the point. They are right. We do expect some things in return," Betsy said. The last half of her comments were: "We expect to foster a conservative governing philosophy consisting of limited government and respect for traditional American virtues. We expect a return on our investment; we expect a good and honest government. Furthermore, we expect the Republican Party to use the money to promote these policies, and yes, to win elections. People like us must surely be stopped."[29]

Betsy's family also had deep Republican connections, donating hundreds of thousands of dollars to Republican candidates and conservative and Christian causes.

What did Amway get for its political connections? For one thing, in 1997, the same year that Rich and Helen made the $1 million contribution to the RNC, then–House Speaker Newt Gingrich and Senate Majority Whip Trent Lott inserted a provision into the tax bill to lessen the tax load for several companies, including Amway, and make it easier for shareholders to invest in Asian affiliates. It didn't hurt that Amway's lobbyist, Roger Mentz, was a former U.S. Treasury official. According to the *Wall Street Journal* and the Center for Public Integrity, Mentz persuaded the Treasury Department to announce that it did not oppose the tax bill clause for Amway and other companies, which collectively benefited them by $14 million.[30] More significant than any single piece of legislation, however, was Amway's rising status as a behind-the-scenes political powerhouse when it came to free trade issues. It would prove invaluable as Amway spread around the globe, and especially to the Far East.

Chapter 11

West Meets East

In 1989, the most visible symbol of the Cold War, the wall that had divided East and West Germany, came tumbling down. Amid the celebrating and realization that a new world order was dawning, East Germans poured across the newly opened border.

A band of capitalists rushed in the other direction, flocking to the former Communist country to take early advantage of a promising new market. Among them was a handful of Amway distributors aiming to spread the word about the company and recruit budding new entrepreneurs in the eastern zone. Even comedian and former *Tonight Show* host Jay Leno took note of the Amway brigade in his monologue: "If you think they had trouble getting rid of the Communists . . ." he said, trailing off and drawing laughs. Rich DeVos took the joke as a compliment, "a tribute to the tenacity of Amway people worldwide."[1] The humor publication *The Onion* also took a jab, "reporting" under a contrived Moscow dateline: "The struggling nation of Russia took a major step toward getting out of debt and achieving financial independence

Monday, when it became an official Amway distributor. 'I can't express how wonderful it feels to finally be in control of our destiny,' Russian president Vladimir Putin said. 'To be able to start up our company in our spare time with only a small up-front investment is an incredible opportunity.'" The president of nearby Tajikistan—once an Amway distributor, according to *The Onion*'s lampoon—warned that his nation got into deep debt with Amway and was in danger of alienating its neighbors with its sales pitches: "I'm just glad Iran didn't call for a jihad on Tajikistan, what with the way we were constantly bugging them to buy toothpaste from us," *The Onion* quoted.[2]

All joking aside, Rich and Jay weren't interested only in selling products in the Eastern bloc. They also were on a mission to export capitalism, to liberate a whole new generation of entrepreneurs, and help people overcome poverty and despair. "People in East Germany, Hungary, Poland, Czechoslovakia, and China, like people everywhere, want deeper satisfaction as well," Rich said. "The freedom to become complete and whole persons. The freedom to become what God intends all of us to be. The freedom of mind and imagination that can only exist in a truly democratic society. The freedom not just to scrape by, but to find genuine satisfaction in life."[3] The message struck a collective chord in many people who had lived in Marxist-socialist countries or who had struggled against crushing poverty and for the first time had the power to control their own lives. By the mid-1990s, Amway had recruited more than 100,000 distributors in the former East Germany, 40,000 in Hungary, and thousands more in Poland. Rich took the company's growth in former Communist countries as a sign that free enterprise worked. "People want to live in a nation where they are free to try new solutions, to trade without restrictions, to compete in a free marketplace, to choose careers, and to own their own businesses," he said. "They are tired of empty shelves and broken promises. They want the things we have, things we take for granted."[4]

Breaking into former Communist countries may have been the ultimate symbol that Amway had, indeed, taken its brand of aggressive capitalism where no entrepreneur had trod before, but the company had been building its international business and pushing into markets with language and cultural barriers and differences for the previous two decades. After moving into its first international market, Canada, in 1962, Amway expanded to 18 countries in Europe, Latin America, and Asia from 1971 to 1987. English-speaking countries with free-market economies and at least basically similar cultures such as Australia and the United Kingdom were obvious targets. But Amway next set up operations in Hong Kong, Germany, Malaysia, France, and the Netherlands. In the 1980s, Amway added Taiwan and Thailand to its international operations. Jay explained the company's philosophy of where to expand next by saying it looked for countries with a "substantial middle class, with the purchasing power for our products. The countries also had to be politically stable, without high tax rates."[5] But some potentially lucrative markets existed in countries with vastly different cultures and ways of doing business. "I think the key is to be open to change and be willing to adapt," advised William S. Pinckney, managing director and CEO of Amway India.[6]

That was especially true in Asia and eastern Europe as Western ways of doing business collided with cultures that looked at buying, selling, and business relationships differently, not to mention regulation and laws that changed from country to country and even state to state. One business model did not fit all. Amway found itself realigning the wheels over and over again so the sales engine could move forward.

Yen and Yang

When Amway decided to enter Japan in 1979, it faced a culture with deeply ingrained attitudes about work, employment, and a "notoriously difficult retail distribution system," as *Forbes* magazine put it.[7] Generations of workers had grown up with expectations of working for one company for life. Major companies in Japan traditionally subsidized housing for their employees and provided perks such as child care, recreation facilities, resorts, and free classes, and even arranged marriages. Few people struck out on their own in a culture that thrived on conformity and the corporation-as-caretaker mentality. But Amway's message of financial freedom resonated with housewives, who saw a culturally acceptable way to earn money, and with corporate workers who were dissatisfied with the rigid, routine grind of lifetime employment and willing to give up security for the opportunity to work for themselves. Kaoru Nakajima was one of those "salarymen" who toiled in a company for eight years, then became an Amway distributor in 1982. He rose to one of its global sales leaders with his photo and bio splashed in Amway publications. "Now I am my own boss. Now I am free." Nakajima said. "Now I am selling products that make me proud. Now I am helping people in five different countries to own their own businesses. When I see so many people getting more abundant lives, I feel really excited. This is no job to me. It is more like play."[8] *Forbes* took note of Amway's success in Japan in a story headlined "Soap and Hope in Tokyo." "It's secret? Selling a dream in a dreamless society," the article concluded.[9]

By the mid-1990s, Nakajima was among 1 million Amway distributors in Japan, and revenues in Japan had more than doubled.[10] In 1994, Amway Japan held a two-day motivational sales event at the 50,000-seat Tokyo Dome. The stadium was packed with distributors and new recruits, most of them wearing business suits. Singer Diana Ross performed some of her solo hits, like "Touch Me in the Morning," and a medley of classics by the Supremes. Former President George Herbert Walker Bush spoke of the end of the Cold War and the triumph of capitalism.[11] The Land of the Rising Sun also had become the land of Amway's rising sales. By 1996, Amway Japan Ltd. was the company's most successful overseas subsidiary, with sales of 212 billion yen, or about $1.9 billion, accounting for 30 percent of Amway's worldwide business. Japanese consumers showed a willingness to pay for quality and convenience, loved luxury brands, and were greatly influenced by their friends' experiences with products. Word-of-mouth recommendations had allowed Amway to operate for 10 years in Japan without doing any advertising.

But in the spring of 1997, Amway Japan experienced its first performance decline. A *Harvard Business Review* case study found that the market was in flux as distributors' motivations fluctuated, dissatisfaction with Amway products grew, and the company had difficulty controlling the distributor network. By fiscal 1999, things weren't much better. Net sales slid more than 25 percent, Amway's core distributor force of 1.1 million fell almost 4 percent, and the number of people applying to become new distributors declined significantly.

Dick DeVos blamed the poor performance on weak consumer demand, especially for high-ticket houseware items such as water and air treatment systems and cookware, the impact of negative publicity, and more competition from other direct-selling companies in Japan. As the value of the yen against the U.S. dollar declined, gross margins also suffered because of higher imported product prices. Sales of Artistry cosmetics fell, as did nutritional supplements and home care products such as soap.

Other uncertainties remain in the "new normal" of Japan's long economic downturn as consumers become more interested in reduced costs than convenience. A growing segment of consumers are staying at home, a trend nicknamed *sugomori,* which translates to "chicks in the nest." "Consumers in Japan have always had really high standards," said John Parker, president of Amway Japan. He assessed Japanese consumers this way:

> ". . . I think we've seen their focus become even sharper in this economic environment. So brand has become important—and has always been important in Japan—but has taken on some nuances in this climate. For Amway and, I think, for many other companies online, Japan has been a leader." Because of high Internet penetration, Parker said, the Japanese consumer is "very sophisticated when it comes to using online tools and using them to share their opinions with others. For a business like ours, we can really leverage that word-of-mouth. Consumers today, they don't want to be told about a brand or a product; they want to discover it. In fact, there's a certain amount of cachet for a consumer that discovers a cool product or maybe a new or unknown brand and then shares it with others. And the digital form allows that to happen in a way that's so much faster than has ever happened in the past."[12]

Dick DeVos, Rich's eldest son, had been named to oversee international operations in the 1980s at a time when global sales amounted to only about 10 percent of Amway's total revenues.[13] At first, Dick wasn't given much power to expand. The company was concerned about legal and regulatory barriers abroad. The key would be adapting to each country's government, culture, regulations, and laws. Dick believed that Amway could do just that. He asked his father and Jay to consider expanding to more prospective markets abroad. At first, they were reluctant, but Dick made a convincing argument, and the founders agreed. In hindsight, it would be one of the best business decisions they ever made because by the 1990s, the Asian market looked particularly attractive for two reasons: immense consumer buying power with some of the world's most populous and consumer-driven economies, and cultures with traditional close ties among family, friends, and neighbors. The idea of starting a business without having to pay for expensive office space and utilities and invest in a lot of inventory also was enormously appealing to many people who had lived in very structured societies and saw a window to become entrepreneurs. The work ethic also was similar to the Calvinist view that had driven Amway's founders to succeed. "Direct-selling executives find the entrepreneurial spirit strong within the region," observed Nicole Woolsey Biggart, a University of California at Davis management and sociology professor, "In essence, they see the Confucian ethic serving as an ideological support for economic activity much as the Protestant ethic did here. Finally, direct-selling companies are discovering that all these nations have extended family networks that make recruiting and selling particularly easy."[14]

Countering Critics in Korea

Recruiting may have been easy because Asian cultures tended to place a lot of faith in relationships with families and friends, but some of the countries still proved to be very difficult markets to enter. Laws varied and were quite different from those in the United States. When Amway set up an affiliate in South Korea in May 1991, for example, it ran into perception and cultural problems. In 1993, its manager in Korea, David Ussery, was briefly imprisoned after being charged with violating a law by not properly training distributors. He was found guilty, and Amway was fined $100,000. Then, in March 1997, the company came under attack by consumer groups and environmental activists who claimed Amway's leading detergent, Dish Drops, was not environmentally friendly as the company claimed.

They also contended that Amway overcharged Korean consumers for soap and that it improperly used relationships between friends and neighbors to sell its products. The accusations hurt; at the time, Korea was Amway's third-largest market. The campaign against Amway damaged its reputation in the country. Critics formed an Anti-Amway Committee that created so much vitriol the company experienced a 64 percent drop in its business in South Korea as sales plunged and half of its distributors stopped selling Amway products. The former general secretary of the South Korean National Council of Consumer Protection Organizations, You Jin Hee, went as far to say that Amway was "not a moral company. They have the wrong attitude in marketing their products."[15] The Korea Soap and Detergent Association, a trade group, began running advertisements that claimed Amway contributed to South Korea's trade deficit because it imported about $125 million of goods into South Korea in 1996. That amounted to less than 1 percent of the country's total imports, and Amway denied the claims. Amway refused to acquiesce to the Anti-Amway Committee's demand for an apology. Advocacy groups urged consumers to boycott Dish Drops. They even hung anti-Amway hung banners at bus terminals and train stations and passed out pamphlets with the headline: "Amway! Wrong Way! Go Away!"[16]

Amway viewed the attack as a competitive issue because Dish Drops had been so successful in South Korea, capturing 10 to 15 percent of the dish detergent market. The company countered with its own advertising campaign to defend itself against the attacks and filed a complaint against the Korea Soap and Detergent Association with the country's Fair Trade Commission. The group, in turn, filed a counter-complaint. Amway took steps to improve distributor training and stayed in the Korean market and introduced more new products. It took years to overcome the negative publicity, but Korea eventually evolved into one of Amway's strongest businesses and still is among the countries that Amway counts as its most successful overseas affiliates.

Good Morning, Vietnam

It was a different story when Amway entered Vietnam, another country that the United States had occupied during wartime. Now a one-party socialist republic dominated by the Community party, Vietnam, like China, faced the prospect of falling behind the rest of the world economically if it clung to old ways and political ideology and did not pursue economic development and a more open economy. When the former central, government-controlled economy allowed foreign business to move in, Amway made its entry in February 2008.

One morning, thousands of people converged on Phu Tho Stadium in Ho Chi Minh City—formerly called Saigon, the capital of Vietnam— to learn how to become Amway entrepreneurs. They included people such as Nguyen Thi That, a worker at an investment counseling office in Ho Chi Minh City who wanted to earn extra money part time. Phan Thi Thanh, a translator for an American company, flew from Hanoi to attend the rally. "It's a really good opportunity for me," she said, adding that she hopes to recruit others in Hanoi to join her distributor organization.[17] Amway saw a really good opportunity for itself, too, in Vietnam where the median age is only 27, and women—who represent that vast majority of Amway's customers—outnumber men. At the meeting in Ho Chi Minh City, the hopeful entrepreneurs learned how to become distributors for Amway's nutritional supplements, cosmetics, and personal and home care products to be manufactured at a new factory in Vietnam. A day earlier Amway held a meeting with more than 1,000 distributors in the ballroom of the Hotel Equatorial to brief them on Vietnamese laws concerning distributors and the importance of not exaggerating or misrepresenting anything when selling one-to-one to customers. At the stadium, thousands of Vietnamese lined up to buy Amway starter kits. Only two hours after the doors opened, 18,000 kits had been sold for 187,000 dong, or about $12, to people who wanted to start their own businesses.

Moving into Malaysia

The scene has been repeated all over Asia, including in some predominantly Muslim countries. In June 2008, Amway held a national convention at Putra Indoor Stadium in Bukit Jalil, Kuala Lumpur, Malaysia. The crowd that jammed the stadium, including Muslim women with their heads covered, wore Amway T-shirts that read, "Life Is Good.

Live It!" The people in the stadium jumped up and down, waving light sticks, as if they were watching a championship game. Doug DeVos made an appearance as the "face" of Amway.

The spectacle showed just how far Amway had come in adapting to foreign markets. Gone were the Christian-leaning messages. In a country where Islam was the dominant religion, Amway toned down the evangelical rhetoric and revved up the pulsating pop music and the excitement of entrepreneurial freedom. Amway entered Malaysia in 1976. Six years later, Foo Howe Kean left his previous jobs in the trading and hotel industries to join Amway soon after graduating from college. "My main objective in starting a business was to obtain financial rewards and freedom," he explained.[18] He and his wife, Shu Chen, have grown their business beyond Malaysia to Taiwan, China, Thailand, the Philippines, Hong Kong, Vietnam, and Indonesia. After hearing his personal story, others in Malaysia were eager to emulate him.

Entrepreneurs in India

In the 1990s, Amway spread deeper into Central America, Latin America, and Asia. One of its biggest international markets next to China was India, which Amway launched in May 1998. It became another case in which a business model that worked in one country didn't translate to another.

For example, in Australia, Amway set up one warehouse that delivered nationwide. Amway planned to do something similar in India. It set up five offices in major cities with the expectation that 20 percent of its distributors would pick up products there and the rest would order online and take home deliveries. In 2010, the opposite was true— about 80 percent picked up from the centers. Indian consumers liked to visit stores, touch, and look at the products. Now Amway has 130 offices and 55 warehouses. "I think if there is one big learning, it is to adapt rather than impose a model from the outside," William S. Pinckney, managing director and CEO of Amway India, explained. "India can put all your assumptions under a scanner."[19] Indian consumers also wanted multiple sizes of products—large, medium, small, and samples. Amway also began marketing "great value" products. "It's the only market where we have coconut oil," Pinckney added. "We realized that it will be easier selling some of these products and then start migrating people to other products."[20] Unlike in Japan, where consumers tended to be online savvy and commonly used computers to order products, Amway had to set up a "low-key" e-commerce site in India. That business is growing, but it's still a tiny slice.

When Amway arrived in the country, many middle-class Indians, especially housewives with few marketable skills but broad social networks, jumped at the chance to make more money. Amway rallies, even though in smaller cities, were sold out. By 2001, Amway had signed up almost 500,000 distributors in India, about half of them women. Many of the distributors are under 40 years old, which brings up another reason international sales are so important to Amway's continued business—demographics. Indian consumers may have smaller disposable incomes than those in Western countries, but as Steve Van Andel pointed out in Chapter 1, there are large numbers of them in very populous cities and people tend to have large social networks of friends and relatives. How many of those distributors in India actually make profits is a point of contention. So far, no Indian has made it into the ranks of Amway's global sales leaders. Those with markets in India, as of 2010, were North American mega-distributors Bill and Peggy Britt, Jim and Nancy Dornan, and Dexter and Birdie Yager.[21] Several news stories raised questions about Amway's higher prices for products such as protein powder, eye cream, and toothpaste. In one, "Amway: Selling Dreams in India," published in 2003 in the *Athens News*, several distributors claimed they have built small networks but aren't making any money because they have bought educational materials or have attended meetings to hear speakers. Others complain they are spending so much time trying to build their networks and sell products that they don't have much time for their families. "My wife is not happy," one man was quoted as saying.[22]

The Indian culture presented some unusual challenges for a Western company. In 2006, police probing multilevel marketing activities in the southern Indian state of Andhra Pradesh investigated an Amway distributor who had filed a dowry harassment case against her husband. Nine Amway offices were sealed by the police after the husband complained to authorities that his wife and her sister and brother-in-law, both of whom also were Amway distributors, "forced" him to recruit others into a "money circulation scheme." The husband was seeking revenge against his wife for the dowry harassment charge, an Amway spokesman told reporters. The Amway wholly owned subsidiary went to court, which ruled that provisions of the Prize Chits and Money Circulation Schemes Act of 1978 banning pyramid schemes did not apply to Amway. Its Indian dealers were allowed to resume business.[23] Another cultural difference concerns how employers give employees feedback. Professional criticism might be viewed as a personal attack. Indian culture puts friendship above professional work, and many employees see companies as an extension of their families, so it takes a soft touch by a manager and spending time with employees to build a relationship, as Pinckney said.[24]

Despite the cultural hurdles, India rose to become one of Amway's top 10 markets by 2008, with business there growing 25 percent in 2009. Amway currently ranks as the country's leading FMCG (Fast Moving Consumer Goods) company in India, with 115 products in its portfolio, two thirds of them in the nutrition and cosmetics categories. Pinckney continues to see huge potential in the Indian economy.[25] In September 2010, Amway announced plans to set up a second manufacturing facility in the country, in addition to a third-party vendor arrangement in Baddi.[26] About 90 percent of Amway's products sold in India are sourced there. "This was tough," Pinckney said. "But one thing is clear: Having a manufacturing facility here allowed us to do things quickly. If I was importing, it would take nine months to bring a product here. If I am manufacturing here, I can turn it around in six-seven weeks."[27] Amway also discovered that the tax structure changed from state to state, and it kept on changing. "There is a recognition of the fact that if you can make it here you can make it anywhere in the world," as Pinckney said. "Business challenges, regulatory environment, competitive intensity— I don't think any other country in the world is as intense as India."[28]

Yearning for Earnings in Eastern Europe

As the former Soviet Union's rule crumbled in eastern Europe in 1989 and 1990, Amway set up business in Poland. Workers protesting their poor working conditions had created a sweeping political movement and a trade union—Solidarity—that brought down the Communist government and elected the union's charismatic leader, Lech Walesa, president.

As more countries opened their borders and their economies to the capitalism their governments once condemned, Amway wasted no time getting set up in those markets as well: the Czech Republic and Slovakia in 1994, Slovenia in 1995, and Romania in 1997, Croatia in 2001, and Ukraine in 2003. In 2008, sales in the Czech Republic totaled about $454 million and one couple—Roman and Gita Hassmannovi—made Executive Diamond and the cover of the *Amagram* magazine there. In Slovenia, seven distributors achieved Diamond status by 2008. Romania's bloody revolution against Communism in 1989 led to the execution by firing squad of its ruling couple, Nicolae and Elena Ceausescu. After Amway arrived on the business scene in 1997, it took three years before sales posted solid growth. About 500,000 authorized distributors have signed up, and the number of privileged clients— those who join Amway to buy products, not to sell them—runs in the thousands and rising. But the strategies that worked in, say, Germany do not carry over to Romania. "We are working at European level (sic) and countries are very different; there is no similar profile for the customer," George Popescu, manager of Amway Romania, said in an interview with a business publication. "It is very likely that a certain launch won't have the same effects in Romania and Germany, but due to differences between the size of these two markets, it is more important for the company to have a more positive effect in Germany."[29]

Even so, Amway rose to become one of the top five companies on the cosmetics market by 2008, with its Artistry brand entering the luxury segment and launching new products every year.

To Russia with Love . . . and Money

But it was Russia, where Amway launched its business in 2005, that became one of its biggest, most important markets. Entrepreneurialism exploded there after the end of the Soviet republic. The first year in operation, Amway rang up more than $100 million in sales in

Russia—its highest first-year total for any market. The next year the figure doubled, and Amway counted more than 300,000 distributors. Again, Amway had to change its previous business models to adapt to the Russian market and accepted business practices. It opened product selection centers where Amway independent entrepreneurs, as they were called there, could buy Amway products and receive training about them. By 2008, Amway's sales in Russia topped $600 million, and the number of distributors grew to more than 1 million. One of them, Natalya Yena, was named a Crown Ambassador in 2008, while four couples rose to Triple Diamonds, and dozens of others—with names such as Mikhail, Tatiana, Olga, Igor, Sergey, and Vladimir—attained Diamond levels after only a few years in business.

Amway set about creating a high profile in eastern Europe by sponsoring sporting events such as the "Chestnut Run" in Kiev, Ukraine, where green shirts branded with "Amway" and "Nutrilite" logos were all over the streets of Ukraine's capital. Its products and programs won awards, such as a "Favorite of Success" rating among home cleaning products in a Ukraine competition called Favorite of Experts 2007. Amway won an award for corporate social responsibility in Russia in 2008 for its works with UNICEF and creating a "favorable environment" for the life and work of disabled people.[30]

■ ■ ■

The company founded in a small Midwestern suburb by the children of Dutch immigrants had amassed millions of distributors in North and South America, Europe, Asia, Australia, and Africa. But the one market that would rewrite Amway's destiny and boost its bottom line also was one of the toughest to crack. It would become a textbook case on how to attack a market that was so different in so many ways and break through cultural, language, and governmental barriers. It was the biggest market in the world and every major industry wanted a piece of it—China.

Chapter 12

The Biggest Market Ever

In 1992, Rich DeVos was attending a meeting in Hong Kong when a distributor there expressed worries about China taking over his country. "Well, I guess if they can come in here, we can go in there," Rich remarked. In hindsight, he realized it was an impulsive comment, "not thinking that that would be complicated or anything. We will just start to sponsor people over there and move on in." He talked to Eva Cheng, a woman of Chinese descent who had joined Amway in 1977 and ran the business in Hong Kong. "You go in and I'll take the business there," Cheng encouraged Rich. "Well, OK, we've got a deal," he replied. "You are Chinese and you know the Chinese. . . ."[1]

Enter Eva Cheng

A native of Hong Kong, Cheng graduated from Hong Kong University in 1975 with a bachelor of arts degree and an MBA. Tall, striking, intelligent, and determined, Cheng at first worked as a government official. Then she spotted an advertisement for a secretary at Amway and decided business might be a better career for her. She liked the idea of working for an American company, even though at the time direct selling was not well known in Hong Kong. Within three years after joining Amway, Cheng was named president of Amway Hong Kong after her boss left. At the time, there were only four employees. Managers from Ada "looked around—there was a receptionist, a part-time bookkeeper, and a warehouseman—and they asked me to take over," she recalled.[2] Amway's sales in Hong Kong were lagging and Cheng set about boosting them. She opened Amway's first store there in 1979 and hired workers to do cooking demonstrations; she washed the dishes in the bathroom. By the mid-1980s Cheng had taken over the market in Taiwan and by the 1990s she had grown the Amway business into the largest direct seller in Hong Kong.

Cheng often told Amway's headquarters it should enter the market into mainland China, which was beginning to open its previously closed doors to foreign investment and enterprises. "If Hong Kong is a pond, then Taiwan is a lake, and mainland China is the sea," Cheng liked to say.[3] Once Rich gave the go-ahead to proceed, Amway began preparing for its launch upon that sea. It formed a new company, Amway Asia Pacific, Ltd., and registered as a company in China in 1992. In December 1993, it sold stock to the public to finance the expansion. Then, it was ready to make its move into its biggest market ever, the world's most populous nation with more than 1 billion people. China's new middle class was expected to double by 2012. Its economy had been growing at a 7 to 14 percent annual clip. Moreover, many Chinese were eager to become entrepreneurs and consumers wanted American products. "There was a huge perception that a product made in the United States or overseas was good," Gan Chee Eng, vice president and chief marketing officer of Amway China, said.[4]

Paving the Way for Direct Sellers

Entering the Chinese market, however, proved to be much more difficult than simply sponsoring new distributors and tapping into entrepreneurial hopes. The Communist government was opening the country to global markets and foreign investment, but it was moving slowly and cautiously. The transition from a planned to a market economy had its share of bumps, and China's new Open Door Policy still imposed stringent business regulations. Moreover, Chinese officials were very distrustful of direct selling after hundreds of pyramid schemes had defrauded people of their savings. Direct sellers all were called the *chuan xiao*—which included pyramid schemes—so shady operators and legitimate multilevel marketers got painted with the same brush. "The rampage and chaos caused by pyramidal frauds past and present have left too big and too deep a scar in the country," Cheng observed.[5] Other business hurdles also loomed. The government would not allow Amway to import its products, so the company built a modern automated factory in Guangzhou, a major foreign trade port with a development zone. (Interestingly, with its new manufacturing plant, Amway had come full circle in its history since Carl Rehnborg, Nutrilite's founder, had studied the health effects of nutrition and diet there.)[6] Amway China opened for business in April 1995, first marketing cleaners—L.O.C. multipurpose cleaner, SA8 laundry detergent, Dish Drops dishwashing liquid, Zoom spray cleaner concentrate, and See Spray glass cleaner—and then personal care products. The company had invested $100 million in the Chinese market, and by 1997, it had built a network of 80,000 distributors, many of whom sold products door-to-door full time. That first year, Amway racked up $178 million in sales in China.

But the multilevel marketing (MLM) model remained under the wary, watchful eyes of government officials. It didn't help that direct-selling scandals continued. In the late 1990s, riots broke out when several pyramid schemes collapsed and some salespeople at the lowest levels lost their life savings. Fraud, corruption, and the manipulation of sales recruits caused the government to take a harder line on direct sellers and multilevel marketers. "Some of them recruit people in a deceptive way, like you can become super-rich in a month," Chen Defa, chairman of the Chinese Academy of Direct Selling Management, told the *New York Times*.[7] Disadvantaged or poorly educated young women with dreams of becoming entrepreneurs and escaping their situations became a target for fly-by-night sales schemes. So many abuses flourished that the Chinese government in Beijing grew increasingly worried about business models like Amway's that relied on leveraging personal connections or relationships. It also feared the massing of large networks of people outside its control. The independent nature of direct sales, not to mention throngs of independent business owners (IBOs) in a group fervor centered around capitalism, was a unfamiliar concept to those in power. "The idea of products being sold by independent salespeople on a person-to-person basis, not using wholesalers and not advertising, was strange and mysterious," Cheng said. "Add to this the fact that direct sellers were promoting their products and services through home parties, training meetings, spreading financial independence and personal success, getting large crowds excited . . . all these are very new and 'foreign' to government officials indeed." In 1996, the government applied four principles for direct selling businesses: allow them to exist, limit their growth, supervise closely, and pilot-test them carefully. "Unfortunately, the life span of pilot testing was short," Cheng recalled.[8]

Without clear regulations, the government could not manage the industry. So many pyramid scams had defrauded people that the Chinese government in 1998 made a drastic decision: it banned all direct selling, including by Amway. Cheng was watching the news on television when the ban was announced. "We could sense the storm coming, but we had never anticipated that an outright ban could be imposed," she said.[9] The State Council, China's cabinet, even referred to MLMs as fostering "evil cults, secret societies and superstitious and lawless activities."[10] The State Council's directive also pointed out that China's market was very young, government officials did not have enough experience, consumers were too immature and could not defend themselves, and that China was not ready for direct selling yet. Cheng called Rich at 2 A.M. to tell him what had happened. "What can Amway do for you?" he asked her. "We'll go on."[11]

The ban was devastating for direct-selling enterprises. A lot of people predicted doom for Amway. Cheng announced to her employees that, after more than 40 years of direct marketing, Amway was going to have to change its business model in China. She tried to quell any suspicions about Amway by ordering its product pickup centers to stay open late and to give refunds to any consumers who wanted their money back. "Instead of crying and moaning and screaming and yelling, we called on our 30,000 actives salespeople and 1,200 employees to stay calm, cooperative, and rational," Cheng recalled.[12] Then Amway and other direct-selling companies went to the government for help. Cheng met with a high-ranking government official to appeal the directive and ask that legitimate foreign investment be protected. Three months later, the government proposed a solution. One of the problems with Chinese regulations for Amway was that they viewed direct selling as a marketing method with "nonfixed" locations—no physical store, in other words. So the company broke with tradition and began opening what the Chinese call "shops plus salesmen" where customers could walk in and buy products. By 2007, it had 189 shops in 156 cities. The stores meant overhead and a big increase in operating costs, but Cheng said it was worth it because it increased the company's transparency and boosted its reputation. Licensed companies under the "shop plus salesmen" model could use direct-selling agents, but compensation could only come from their direct sales, not recruiting. Making a profit from group income was forbidden. The Amway Plan had taken a major detour in China. Rich called the changes a "revolution" in the history of Amway.[13]

Even after the ban, pyramid scams continued and the government kept cracking down with more regulations on companies that used independent sales people. Amway China had to revise its sales and marketing plans four times from 1998 to 2005 as regulations changed. It voluntarily stopped recruiting new salespeople and downsized its sales team five times. "Never confuse administrative victories with genuine business accomplishments," Cheng said. "Be prepared for new surprises but never feel disheartened." Because she was Chinese herself, Cheng understood the way people think and react. While the Western culture was "action-oriented," the Eastern culture was more cautious. It "thinks thrice before action and therefore, has a tendency to complicate simple matters," Cheng said. The only way to grow in chaotic times, she believed, was to "ride cultural cross-currents in a calm, rational and sensible manner."[14]

Those cultural crosscurrents continued to buffet direct sellers. In September 2005, the Chinese government issued its Direct Selling Regulation and Pyramid Prohibition Regulation, shocking global direct sellers with their strict provisions. They showed that Beijing continued to be very concerned about direct selling. Obtaining a direct-selling license in China required a $10 million initial investment, $2.5 million minimum bond, and compensation for salespeople not to exceed 30 percent of personal sales. Trainers had to be university graduates and on the company's payroll. No team-based bonuses were allowed. Before a license could even be granted, the government said it would consider national security, public order, and social benefit. Cheng viewed the regulation as a "major step forward," given China's obsession with social stability and alarm over pyramid frauds and the economic and social problems they had caused.

Growth of an Industry

In 2006, after heavy lobbying from Amway and other American companies, China lifted its direct-selling ban. Direct selling since has grown into an $8 billion industry, with companies such as Mary Kay, Avon, Herbalife, and other direct sellers operating in China.

Avon, for example, was granted a direct-selling license by China's Ministry of Commerce in late February 2006. That year, Amway's Chinese business exploded. Revenues shot to more than $1.5 billion and Amway ranked number 41 on the Ministry of Commerce's Largest Foreign Invested Companies. The company was on the list of Fortune China's Most Admired Multi-National Companies four times and on China Business News Network's List of top 10 Most Influential Multinationals. Sales in China kept growing—to $2.5 billion in 2008 and $3 billion in 2009.

Amway's best-selling products in China are Nutrilite protein powder, which can be added to soups and juices, and Artistry skin creams and cosmetics. National Public Radio correspondent Rob Gifford discovered just how far Amway had spread throughout the country when he was on assignment in the Gobi Desert. Two men in suits and ties approached him in the city of Zhangye and identified themselves as the local representatives of "An Li," Chinese for "Amway." One of the men told Gifford that he previously had worked in a factory. The other one said he had been employed in the office of a state-owned railroad. Their mentor, they said, had been with Amway for three years and was making $2,000 to $3,000 a month. Gifford accompanied the men to an Amway office sales meeting. "I have absorbed the earnestness of the evening," Gifford recollected in his book *China Road: A Journey into the Future of a Rising Power.* He described China as a changing nation of "slowly empowered individuals."[15]

With Amway's success in China, Cheng's profile rose as well. She also took over management of Amway in Thailand, Malaysia, Singapore, Indonesia, Brunei, and the Philippines and is chief executive of Amway Greater China and Southeast Asia. Cheng is one of seven people on Amway's executive team. *Forbes* in 2008 and 2009 named Cheng to its list of the world's most powerful women.[16]

In November 2007, Amway hit a milestone in China, celebrating 10 years of operation there. The entire Amway family was on hand for the formal evening affair. Cheng wore traditional Chinese dress. Amway presented checks to top distributors, the Chinese acrobatics team performed, and the evening ended with a fireworks display as only China can do them. In 2006, China top distributors Charlie Lee Kim Soon and Linda Ng Kwee Choo rose to Founders Crown Ambassadors and are treated like superstars at Amway rallies. "I'm a lucky woman," Linda said. "It's not soap, it's hope."[17]

There's no assurance, of course, that the Chinese government won't impose more regulations or rescind approvals of direct-sales businesses such as Amway's. Meanwhile, pyramid schemes have continued to proliferate in China. In one month alone, between mid-July and mid-August in 2007, Chinese authorities uncovered 600 pyramid schemes involving 1.7 billion yuan, or about $224 million at the time. They arrested people in 14 provinces and cities.[18] That same August, police said they broke up the country's largest alleged online pyramid scheme involving 170,000 people and 1.36 yuan, or about $180 million. Called the Swiss Mutual Fund, the scheme called for each investor to pay 8,000 yuan (about US$1,052), with the promise that they would receive 400,000 yuan (about US$52,000) in 30 months. After authorities began investigating, they discovered the fund hadn't been registered as required with the China Security Regulatory Commission, the Ministry of Civil Affairs, or the People's Bank of China. In November 2007, a riot broke out in Shenyang after 10,000 people marched on the provincial government offices, demanding their money back from an elaborate pyramid scheme that bought dead ants that were to be turned into health products. The businessman behind the fraud later was arrested.[19]

In April 2010, the 15 direct-sales companies approved to do business in China—including Amway, Mary Kay Cosmetics, Avon, and Herbalife—signed a "self-discipline pact," promising to promote the "healthy development" of direct-selling enterprises and to provide "high-quality" direct-selling services.[20] But it may take years for the Chinese government to welcome legitimate direct sellers with trust and open arms. "I'm in no position to speculate, but my experience tells me that we need a long-term view when operating in China," Cheng says.

■ ■ ■

After more than 12 years of operating in China, Amway had to learn to "take every sudden twist and turn calmly, to be respectful of local tradition and customers, to be compliant of relevant laws and regulations, and to undertake modifications in our sales approaches so as to promote harmony and fusion with the Chinese culture," Cheng said. To outsiders, the process seemed long and slow. But in a country with a recorded history of more than 5,000 years, a decade is, as Cheng said, "just a moment in China's river of time."[21]

Chapter 13

New Heart, New Identity

In 1996, Rich DeVos's heart problems worsened. Doctors told him he would die unless he underwent a heart transplant. Rich asked some questions about the procedure, then simply said, "Okay, let's do it."[1] But it wasn't quite that simple. There was a shortage of heart donors in the United States. Rich also had a rare A–B blood type, he was 70 years old, he had been through two bypass surgeries in the past, and he was in poor health. The odds of finding the right match in time were slim even if a doctor agreed to take his case given his age and the other factors. The hunt led to London, where Professor Sir Magdi Yacoub, a thoracic and cardiovascular surgeon who had researched transplants, talked candidly with Rich. The physical trauma of the surgery was grueling enough, but surviving such a major operation also depended on the patient's will and passion to live, the doctor told him. Rich convinced Dr. Yacoub that he had the grit and desire to persevere through the difficult surgery and recovery period. The doctor agreed to take his case.

Learning by Inspiration

Under British law, Rich couldn't receive a donor heart there if a British subject also was a match. He also had to stay near the hospital in case a donor heart became available. That meant relocating to London. When Charles W. Colson phoned his friend on January 1, 1997, to wish him a happy new year, Rich didn't know whether he had a year ahead of him. He told Colson he was leaving for England and that he and Helen were moving temporarily into a London hotel suite. "His voice was melancholy, and I don't think he expected to come home alive," Colson recalled. "I wondered if I would ever see him again on this Earth. Before I hung up, I reminded him, 'Christians never say good-bye, so let's just say *au revoir*—until we meet again.' "[2]

Five months passed with no donor heart becoming available. The DeVos's children, Dick, Dan, Cheri, and Doug, and their families visited Rich and Helen in London and tried to keep up their parents' spirits, but the situation was beginning to look bleak. Rich grew weaker every day. Then they heard some promising news. A woman required a lung transplant and, because lung transplants work best when paired with their original heart, her healthy heart would be available—and she had the same A-B blood type as Rich. But she, too, was waiting for a donor of a heart *and* lungs. What were the odds of that happening? Then the call the DeVos family been waiting for finally came. A young man was killed in an auto accident. Incredibly, he had the A-B blood type, too, and his heart and lungs became available for the woman. The DeVos's rushed to Harefield Hospital in Middlesex. As Rich was wheeled toward the operating room with the chances of survival against him, he felt exhausted and apprehensive, yet relieved, hopeful, and resigned at the same time. "Up until that moment, I had called the shots for the challenges in my life," Rich said. "I usually set the course. Sink or swim, the responsibility had most often been mine. But this time, I most certainly was not in control."[3]

■ ■ ■

The five-hour transplant operation to remove his dying heart and replace it with a healthy one was successful. The recovery, though, was the worst part. "A heart transplant is a harrowing experience, but the aftermath is more difficult than what precedes it: the pain, the drug-induced nightmares, the half-conscious hallucinations, the fear of infection, the fear of my body rejecting the new organ," Rich said. "I had survived, but there was no feeling of euphoria. I couldn't get oriented. For a time, I lost my usual optimism and sense of humor."[4] Rich was shuffling down the hospital hall one day, trying to regain his strength and get used to his new heart, when he came across a woman who asked if he'd had a transplant. When he said that he had, she asked the date of his surgery. He told her, and she smiled and exclaimed, "You have my heart!"[5] Rich believed a miracle had occurred—he had come face to face with the woman who had given him another chance at life. And they were *both* alive. When Colson visited Rich in his London hotel suite soon after the operation, it was like his friend was born again. "He was like a new man—like Lazarus called forth from the grave by the voice of Jesus himself," Colson said. "All of his old strength, determination, and optimism were fully restored. Added to that was a new depth of insight into the meaning of life."[6]

Controversy, though, often followed Amway and its wealthy founders, and Rich's transplant operation was no exception. Questions arose about how he had jumped ahead of 650 patients on the United Kingdom's waiting list for the operation, which at the time cost 60,000 British pounds. Some medical experts told the British media that it was "unlikely" a Briton of the same age would have received a new heart. But others said Rich received the donor heart because of the rare blood type involved. "It had nothing to do with money," Rich insisted.[7] Later, he said the operation and recovery changed his perspective about living and deepened his faith. "You cannot go through the experience of a heart transplant—and survive physically, psychologically, and spiritually—without a deep examination, or re-examination, of what is important in life."[8] He had to take antirejection medications every day and began to think about the fear of rejection and how it keeps people from trying to experience new things, to succeed, and to win. That realization later led Rich to write another book, *Hope from My Heart: Ten Lessons for Life*.

Renewing the Business

Several months after the operation, Rich returned to Grand Rapids, which held a homecoming celebration. His body had not rejected his new heart, and doctors were optimistic that the possibility of that happening had passed. And as Rich returned, he found that the company he had given life to was about to undergo a rebirth of its own.

Over the years, the once-nimble, entrepreneurial business had grown large and unwieldy. "Our very size evolved into slowness," Dick observed. "We added layers and became risk-averse."[9] Indeed, as the turn of a new century approached, Amway found itself at a financial crossroads. One unexpected side effect of its aggressive expansion into Asia was lower instead of higher revenues. The strong U.S. dollar and weak Asian economy conspired to push fiscal 1998 global sales down 18 percent, to $5.7 billion from $7 billion the year before. To cut costs and bring them in line with plunging revenues, the company offered voluntary early retirement for up to 900 U.S. workers and made other workforce reductions.[10] It also began looking for inefficiencies in its global business structure and eliminated duplications where several businesses essentially were doing the same thing in some parts of the world. In November 1999, the company also decided to privatize Amway Japan and Amway Asia Pacific, which were partly publicly owned. Amway offered $635 million to buy back the stock.

Another change was taking place, one that went to the very heart of Amway's identity in North America. The dot-com boom had exploded and e-commerce was the business buzzword. The Internet stock craze took flight and retailers flocked to the Internet to market their products. But Amway wasn't a typical retailer. It didn't have any retail outlets to begin with and its customers were used to placing orders with an independent business owner (IBO) rather than visiting a brick-and-mortar store. The Internet offered a natural and powerful new tool for IBOs and put a modern spin on the Amway model. "If you weren't part of that (I)nternet revolution, you were certainly looked at as kind of old school, and our ability to be competitive with the marketplace of new business owners was dropping off very quickly because our model just did not fit with the current environment," Steve Van Andel said. "The way to signal bringing technology in was to change the name of the company."[11] On September 1, 1999, Amway launched a Web site to support IBOs in the United States, Canada, Puerto Rico, and other territories and independent island nations in the Pacific and Atlantic oceans and the Caribbean Sea. Alticor became the holding company, and the North American operations of Amway were renamed Quixtar.com, a high-tech-sounding name pronounced "quick star." With a computer and modem, Quixtar IBOs could launch their own Web-based businesses. Quixtar called its news business model "I-commerce," representing the convergence of the Internet, the individual, a full-service infrastructure, and an independent business ownership plan. Retail customers could pay an annual fee of $19.95 in return for buying products at preferred pricing and "clients" could shop www.Quixtar.com without a charge, but purchased products at full retail prices. Members and clients had to register with a Quixtar IBO, of course. Customers also could buy Amway products and shop at more than 80 online "partner stores," including OmahaSteaks.com, KBtoys.com, TrueValue.com, and OfficeMax.com. As a portal to the other sites, Quixtar gave referring IBOs a percentage of the retail partner sales as a commission. Again, recruiting others to join Quixtar, at a cost of $39 for each new prospect, meant sponsoring IBOs received a cut of the downline business as well, plus leadership bonuses on top of the commissions. The business model let consumers order health and beauty products online instead of through the "person-to-person interaction that is the hallmark of Amway sales," as the trade Internet publication BrandChannel.com put it.[12] Quixtar was the first fully supported Web site within Amway's global business for IBOs' business functions and customer ordering. In addition to complementing Amway's online strategy, the Quixtar moniker served another purpose: it allowed Alticor to create a fresh, new identity for the United States and Canada. Quixtar operated independently from the Amway brand.

Quixtar got off to a fast start as Amway IBOs in North America moved their businesses online. Its first 100 days produced $100 million in sales, and its first year in business generated revenues of $448 million by IBOs and an additional $70 million at partner stores. In 2000, the National Retail Federation's *STORES* magazine ranked Quixtar seventh among e-commerce companies based on sales. The rankings, from first to sixth, were eBay, Amazon.com, Dell, buy.com, Egghead.com, and Gateway.[13] By 2002, Quixtar ranked sixth on the Internet research firm comScore Networks' list of the top 25 e-tailers and had amassed a network of more than 250,000 IBOs.[14] Moreover, Quixtar converted visitors to buyers at higher rates than did more established retail sites such as Staples.com, Amazon.com, and BarnesandNoble.com.[15]

In its first four years, the company's IBOs produced $3.1 billion in sales for Quixtar and more than $250 million for partner stores. Distributors collectively earned $998 million bonuses and incentives.[16] Health, beauty, and sports nutrition products created the most online buzz and sales, with Quixtar ranked first in market share in health and beauty. Its 20.5 percent market share compared with 12.2 percent for Drugstore.com, 5.7 percent for Merck–Medco.com, 4.5 percent for Avon, and 4.1 percent for MaryKay.com.[17] And that was without any advertising. "We've put our money into their [IBOs'] pockets rather than banner ads or other advertising—things that have cost a whole lot of money for other companies," said Ken McDonald, Quixtar's managing director.[18] Another built-in marketing tool on the Internet was the so-called "word of modem," or personal endorsement network, as consumers referred friends to favorite Web sites. Another innovation it issued to drive revenues was a feature called Ditto Delivery, an automatic, monthly replenishment program that automatically sent customers items such as vitamins or shampoo based on their predetermined needs. By mid-2002, the program accounted for more than 20 percent of the company's sales, a share that continued growing.[19]

That year marked another turning point. Dick DeVos, who was 46 at the time, decided to go back into business for himself. He retired as president of Alticor in 2002 to devote more time to his private venture, the Windquest Group, a maker of storage and closet organizers. He also still harbored political aspirations, and he and his wife, Betsy, had become more and more involved with the state Republican Party. Dick's younger brother, Doug, 37, was named president of Quixtar and Alticor when Dick retired in August of that year. In 2001, Doug changed Amway's financial reporting practices and began reporting actual sales to distributors rather than estimated retail sales by distributors to their customers. The product line also switched its emphasis from soap to health and beauty products. Today, Amway is mostly a health and beauty business. Artistry is one of the world's five largest selling prestige brands, with the largest markets in the United States, South Korea, Japan, China, and Thailand.

Renewing the Brand

At first, distributors could choose to be affiliated with Amway or Quixtar. But in January 2003, Amway moved all of its distributors to Quixtar. According to some litigants, using the word *Amway* was discouraged even in the Quixtar business.[20] The repositioning of the brand was designed to further distance Alticor from the negative publicity surrounding Amway. "Even the Amway distributors themselves cringe when a prospect asks them, 'Is this Amway?'" former Amway "Silver"-level distributor Patrick J. Smith (a pseudonym) wrote in *The Dark Side of the Pyramid*. "When your own network of distributors intuitively understands that they have to mitigate the negative baggage associated with a brand, then it is time for a change," he added.[21] A former Quixtar IBO in Texas said she felt that she was misleading prospective clients when she called friends and acquaintances to come hear about a business opportunity. "They would ask, 'Is it Amway?' and I would say, 'No, it's Quixtar.' But by the end of the meeting some of them would get mad and tell me they felt misled because it clearly *was* Amway. I didn't understand why we had to be so secretive."[22] Eventually, disillusioned, she dropped out of Quixtar.

The media soon picked up that Quixtar was the reincarnation of the former Amway. In June 2003, the newsmagazine *Dateline NBC* informed Doug DeVos, Quixtar's president, that it was preparing an investigative story about Quixtar, its distributors, and its marketing practices.[23] Two *Dateline* producers had registered as Quixtar IBOs and began attending rallies and meetings with a hidden camera. At one Quixtar rally in a crowded coliseum, a recruiter told *Dateline* producer Tim Sandler that just by working 10 to 15 hours a week, he could generate $250,000 in income. Quixtar prospects were encouraged to attend seminars and buy motivational books and tapes and read 15 to 30 minutes a day."[24]

Dateline also attended a "Spring Leadership Weekend" in Greenville, South Carolina. Before the rally, people had been sleeping outside like fans lining up for tickets at a rock concert. About 15,000 people packed the arena and watched a choreographed show. They were urged by successful Quixtar distributors onstage to dream big like they did. They also shared their own personal success stories. Amway star distributor Bill

Britt related to the crowd that he got into Quixtar for five reasons: "Good reasons. The first one was money. The second reason I got in was for money. In fact, that's what all five reasons were."[25] Bo Short, a former high-level distributor who later left Quixtar to start his own multilevel marketing business, told *Dateline* that mega-distributors make most of their money selling motivational materials, not soaps or cosmetics. "And it's a business that is completely separate from Quixtar, a hidden business that most recruits don't realize exists," Short said. Only a privileged few get to sell motivational materials—about 20 high-level distributors who are part of the exclusive club. Rank-and-file distributors can't sell motivational materials themselves, but are told to buy them in order to succeed, he said.[26]

"Why are the recruits told to listen to the tapes and read the books over and over and over again?" Chris Hansen asked Short.

"Because it creates a dependency and it creates a habit that keeps you bound to that business," Short replied.[27]

In July 2003, Ken McDonald, Quixtar's managing director, wrote to *Dateline* that Quixtar had rules governing what IBOs could say about how much money someone could make in a Quixtar business. The earnings representation of a quarter of a million dollars was "highly unlikely" during the time frame the recruiter cited and would also be a violation of Quixtar's rules, McDonald said.[28] He declined to provide on-air comments, but offered to give information to help *Dateline* understand Quixtar's business.[29] In a letter to *Dateline* that September, McDonald added the company did not "count heads" or project IBO earnings potential. He wrote:

> Our business requires little investment and little risk, which means that because this business is accessible to so many people, there will always be those who find they have little commitment and decide to opt out very quickly. Thus, it is unfair to attempt to project earnings potential for a Quixtar-powered business that includes all those who don't make a serious attempt to build such a business. Like our free market economy, we simply provide a framework in which individuals must make their own way. No median or mean figure will enlighten your audience about what is possible with a business powered by Quixtar.[30]

The *Dateline* segment, titled "In Pursuit of the Almighty Dollar," aired in May 2004. Quixtar immediately set up a Web site to respond to the story's allegations. It noted that the company provided written responses to *Dateline*'s questions and explained that it did not grant an interview because it believed its perspective would be taken out of context to support *Dateline*'s story line. The company also questioned *Dateline*'s "deceit" in registering producers as Quixtar IBOs. Quixtar went on to say that the story did not meet the benchmark of fair or balanced journalism because the program interviewed a few disgruntled IBOs and did not talk to Quixtar IBOs who were happy with their businesses. Once again, the company believed it had received unfair treatment at the hands of a biased news media.

Some of the criticism came from Quixtar's own IBOs. "It's the business practices of many IBOs that gave Amway, then Quixtar, its bad name," one distributor said. "The bad practices followed from Amway to Quixtar. And they will follow right back again unless something is done, and it has to be big time.[31] Another IBO offered this view:

> The people who lied about tool profits, were pushy with tools, and belligerent if you didn't buy tools with Amway are the same people, and used the same tactics, with Quixtar. The name change back to Amway MUST also fix this issue, or the combination of the name change and continuing hidden tool profits (which are becoming better known on the Internet every day) will bring it down, in my opinion.[32]

The Alticor reorganization produced some other effects on business. It created the Access Business Group, the unit that manufactures bottles, designs packaging and labels, oversees distribution, and engages in contract manufacturing, making products for other companies— shampoo, baby oil, detergents, cosmetics, and window cleaners—that then put their own labels on them. In another departure from tradition, three new members—none of them part of the DeVos or Van Andel families—joined the board to bring in their expertise in finance, corporate governance, and marketing. They were James McClung, a former senior vice president of chemical manufacturer FMC Corporation; Judson Green, who led Disney's resorts and theme parks; and Emmanuel

Kampouris, who served as chairman of American Standard Companies, an air-conditioning, bath, and kitchen products maker, and who knew Jay from the Hudson Institute.

■ ■ ■

There was another passage that marked the company's new identity. Jay's wife, Betty, died in 2003 at the family's home in the Caribbean. Parkinson's disease also continued to bedevil Jay. Less than a year after his wife's death, Jay joined her on December 7, 2004. He died at home in Ada. Now it was up to Steve, Doug, and especially Rich—the heart of the company with a new heart himself—to carry Amway into the future.

Chapter 14

Amway Redux

The year 2007 was pivotal for Amway/Quixtar at home and abroad. Once again, controversy dogged the company and questions arose about the way Amway/Quixtar IBOs marketed the business. One of its biggest legal challenges came in one of its oldest international markets, the United Kingdom. The top earner there, Trevor Lowe, had been an Amway distributor for 26 years, rising to Diamond level. Amway had immersed itself in the United Kingdom's culture, making gifts to charity, hiring popular television personalities to present recruitment videos, and paying two Conservative members of Parliament to act as consultants to Amway U.K. Some years earlier, former Prime Minister Tony Blair even recorded a video "message of support" for the United Kingdom's direct-selling association.[1] The United Kingdom was an important market for Amway because it represented the gateway to Europe.

However, the British government's Business Enterprise and Regulatory Reform agency, or BERR, had been investigating claims that Amway

U.K.'s agents exaggerated that IBOs could receive substantial financial rewards by selling Amway products and earning bonuses for recruiting other distributors, and misled people into purchasing books, videos, tickets to meetings, and other materials that were said to be vital in starting an Amway business. BERR's investigation concluded that only 10 percent of Amway's IBOs in Britain even made a profit—and those were the ones who had been business owners the longest—while 90 percent lost money after paying their registration fee. Only 101 IBOs, including Lowe, shared 75 percent of the business, the BERR probe found. It all sounded very familiar to claims Amway had faced in the States and the allegations made by some Quixtar IBOs in the *Dateline NBC* investigative story aired two years earlier—that the distributors selling the motivational tools and business support materials made the bulk of the money in the business on the backs of IBOs, who were told they needed to buy the materials to build their businesses.

United Kingdom's BERR Case

In April 2007, the Secretary of State for BERR presented a petition to "wind up," or shut down, Amway's U.K. operation, contending that its business model was "inherently objectionable." The Amway system functioned as an unlawful lottery, the government claimed, because bonus payments made to IBOs were unpredictable and made on chance, depending whether those who were recruited purchased products. Also, the business was an unlawful trading scheme, the secretary of state claimed, because IBOs were "induced" to make a joining and renewal payment in the belief they would receive payments or other benefits from introducing new people to the Amway business.[2] That November, the Chancery Division, which oversees legal business matters, began hearing arguments in the case. Queen's Counsel Mark Cunningham and barrister Andrew Westwood, representing the BERR secretary of state, argued that Amway's promises of "unachievable" wealth violated British company law, that most of Amway's products were overpriced, and that IBOs were encouraged to buy materials about how to grow their businesses.[3] Images of luxury cars, boats, and foreign holidays heightened the message that wealth was within reach by starting an Amway business. "The prospect of substantial rewards and easy money has been at all times, and remains, illusionary," Cunningham said. Only a "very narrow group" made any money, he added. Cunningham termed the company's modus operandi of encouraging agents to recruit family, friends, and colleagues a "pernicious" scheme that targeted the "gullible," "deluded," and "vulnerable" to join in pursuing an "unachievable" dream. "The reality of being an IBO is that a substantial majority make minimal financial returns," Cunningham concluded. "Our case is founded on the selling of the dream on one hand and the loss of minimal financial return on the other."[4] He presented records showing that it took at least 14 years for an IBO to make it into the top 20 Amway earners and that only 37 distributors made more than 25,000 British pounds sterling a year (amounting to just under $40,000 at the January 2011 exchange rate).

Amway's barristers told the court that the company was working hard to address the complaints and that it had substantially changed its business model in the United Kingdom. Amway "reinvented the U.K. business almost from the ground up," as Steve Van Andel and Doug DeVos phrased it in a note to global directors in November 2007.[5] Amway suspended the sale of business support materials, imposed a moratorium on sponsorships, and terminated or sanctioned IBOs it determined were making unreasonable claims. The executives also said the company had "taken a strong stance with the sales organizations, including refusing to renew the contracts of some leaders who would not endorse our reforms." They included Diamonds Jerry Scriven, Dave Butler, and Pat Gregory. Scriven and Gregory founded International Business Systems, whose activities were not approved by Amway U.K. More than 7,000 Amway Business Owners who had been affiliated with IBS chose to follow the company's reforms. To show off the new Amway U.K. model, the company held an expo event that attracted more than 4,000 people.

In May 2008, after hearing the arguments and considering the changes that Amway had made in its U.K. business, Justice Norris declined to shut down the operation. "I consider a winding up order to be disproportionate," the judge ruled. "The secretary of state's investigation and the presentation of this petition are a sufficient

salutary lesson to Amway and a clear warning to its peers that if the
risks inherent in the multi-level model are not rigorously controlled,
then serious and expensive consequences follow."[6] He went on to say
that Amway had failed to supervise and control the representations and
promotional material used by its IBOs when they recruited others.
However, the judge dismissed the public interest petition and declined
to have Amway U.K. "compulsorily wound up in bankruptcy" because
the new business model voluntarily offered by Amway U.K. during the
proceedings amounted to material and radical changes. In a note from
Steve and Doug to all global employees, the top executives interpreted the ruling as "validation" for the direct-selling business model.
"But this is not a pop-the-champagne victory," they warned in an
electronic message sent to global employees. "This is a reminder that
the marketplace and regulators hold us to the highest standards. We
have an obligation to meet those standards—and we intend to do so."[7]
The judge found Amway's "radical changes" in the way it markets to
be "fully formulated, comprehensive, open and transparent, and capable
of effective and ongoing implementation without the supervision of
the Secretary of State or the Court." Amway took issue with the government's numbers and disagreed with some of the judge's conclusions.
But "we hear the message," Steve and Doug said.[8]

■ ■ ■

After the ruling, the BERR secretary of state asked to appeal the decision,
saying the judge had fundamentally misunderstood his jurisdiction.
If he considered the old business model unacceptable, the judge had
no choice but to wind up Amway, the secretary of state argued. The
three judges sitting on Britain's Court of Appeal heard the evidence
presented by government investigators. In January 2009, the justices
unanimously upheld Justice Norris's ruling. Amway's fault, "serious
as it undoubtedly was, was essentially a failure to control rather than
deliberate wrongdoing or dishonesty," the appellate judges held in the
decision. The company had admitted its fault and "its management had
engaged with the secretary of state in seeking solutions to the problem,"
the court added. "It had not been discouraged in doing so, and the
judge found its proposals for change met the test which the secretary
of state had imposed on it."[9]

A Shot of Innovation

Beyond the litigation in the United Kingdom, Amway had bigger problems: it was running out of lucrative world markets. The strategy of growth through geographic expansion had worked up to a point. But Amway/Quixtar's own sales forecasts predicted less-than-stellar increases for the next five years. Global sales since 2000 had been sporadic: $5.1 billion that year, $4.1 billion in 2001, $4.5 billion in 2002, a nice jump to $6.2 billion in 2004, and slightly more in 2005, at $6.4 billion. In 2006, though, sales fell to $6.3 billion. Steve and Doug were worried that if they didn't do something to rev up sales and act soon, they'd be forced to react in the future. "We said we have to do something to change the trajectory," Doug recalled. The business was "stuck."[10] About 80 percent of the world already had access to Amway. How could it continue growing well into the future?

To be sure, the business had strengths: a large and committed sales force, a recognized brand, a research-and-development arm, manufacturing plants, success in global markets. But there was a generational disconnect. Times and attitudes were very different than when Jay and Rich started the company. "They actually lived the dream," Doug remarked. "The difference is, I don't have that (spirit) in the same way. I respect it, I love it . . . but I went to school to be a manager." Steve agreed. "To me, regardless of personality, that is just a totally different dynamic to operating the business than it was early on," he said.[11] Doug reflected on the lessons he and Steve had learned from their fathers. "It was always them together, and when they had a challenge in business it was always, 'We're never going to blame each other, and we're never going to say, "I told you so." So they taught us to work together in a spirit of partnership that stands the test of time. . . . If anything goes wrong we're going to fix it together, and even if we disagree, we're going to work through it together."[12]

What was lacking in Amway/Quixtar, the co-CEOs concluded, was a culture that encouraged innovation. The company had relied for too long on a predictable product line and a business driven by distributors instead of consumer demand. The executives set a goal of doubling the company's global sales within the next five to seven years: $12 billion by 2012. It was ambitious but, they felt, doable. In 2007, they held a Global

Growth Conference to map out a new strategy. The markets Amway/ Quixtar targeted were China and India, two successful markets where they hoped to rev growth; Russia, which had proved to be a strong revenue contributor; Japan and Korea, which needed a booster shot; and North America and Latin America, which needed a rebuilding effort. The new strategy was to adopt the push-pull system—consumers would pull the merchandise in demand through the delivery chain, and the distributors would push them to consumers and bring in new recruits.

Foray into State Politics

As Doug and Steve plotted Amway's global strategy, Dick DeVos jumped into the thick of Michigan politics. Republicans were determined to take back the Michigan governorship from Democrat Jennifer Granholm, a former prosecutor and attorney general who had been battling Michigan's huge unemployment in the wake of auto industry cutbacks. Republicans saw her as vulnerable and Dick as the guy to beat her in 2006. As the heir to the Amway fortune and the former head of one of Michigan's most high-profile companies, Dick had political clout, business experience—in addition to the 25 years he had spent at Amway, he had run the business side of his dad's Orlando Magic basketball franchise—and money to finance his campaign. He ran on a platform of creating new jobs, cutting business taxes, and revising regulations that he believed hurt free enterprise. On the campaign trail, he told voters, "I speak business. I'm a job maker."[13] Dick poured an estimated $35 million into the campaign. Former First Lady Laura Bush campaigned for him, and former New York Mayor Rudy Guiliani also hit the campaign trail on his behalf.

For Democrats, Dick's business background offered an open field for attacks. They seized on Dick's track record and ran TV commercials blasting Amway for investing more than $200 million in China while laying off 1,400 workers in Michigan. One ad showed Amway's factory in Guangdong, China. "Good for Dick DeVos. But how's it working for you?" the voiceover asked. Former presidential candidate John Kerry campaigned for Granholm and sent a letter to voters portraying DeVos as a right-wing extremist who donated to causes such as opponents of women's rights and the school voucher movement that supports using public money for private and parochial school tuition. (The Van Andels supported conservative causes, too: the Jay and Betty Van Andel Foundation helped fund a creationist research center, located in the Arizona desert, that bears their name; its goal is to challenge the theory of evolution at the technical level and develop a creationist model of the world's origins.) Kerry described Dick as a long-time Bush ally who put "the full weight of his personal fortune behind people and policies that have made life harder for Michigan families—from shipping jobs overseas to trade agreements that hurt Michigan's economy." He and Democrats also charged that the DeVos family was among a group of ultra-wealthy families who ran a "stealth campaign" pushing the repeal of the estate tax. The watchdog groups Public Citizen, Congress Watch, and United for a Fair Economy produced a report that included the DeVoses and Van Andels on a list of super-wealthy families who had campaigned to kill the estate tax. The study pointed out that Alticor had lobbied on the estate tax every year since 1998, as did the U.S. Chamber of Commerce, on whose board Steve represented the family business. In 2005, *Forbes* had estimated Rich DeVos's net worth at $3.4 billion, meaning family heirs would save about $1.3 billion if the estate tax were repealed, the report concluded.[14] Democrats further warned voters that Dick DeVos, with his vast wealth, wanted to use the Michigan governorship to jump into national politics and perhaps even run for president.[15]

Republicans fought back, pointing out that Amway's international business had brought billions of dollars in revenue back to Michigan and helped save jobs. But in a state reeling from job losses and pent-up anger about jobs overseas, especially to Asia, the Democrats' message resonated with voters. Despite spending a chunk of his personal fortune in the state's most expensive gubernatorial race ever, DeVos didn't even come close to beating Granholm. She won with 56 percent of the vote to DeVos's 42 percent. Some political observers said DeVos's connections to Amway ended up costing him the election.[16] Dick and Betsy DeVos remain politically active, bankrolling conservative groups and pet issues such as school vouchers. A political action committee that Dick had chaired, Restoring the American Dream, was funded by the Yagers, Britts, and other Amway Diamonds. Dick declined to run for Michigan governor in 2010.

A Second Rebranding

State politics aside, Amway had a bigger group of people to win over, those who voted with their pocketbooks—consumers. The Quixtar name change in North America proved confusing to many of them. When consumers wanted to visit the Web site, most of them typed www.amway.com. The Quixtar name had never really caught on, and even eight years after leaving it behind, the Amway brand was stronger than the company realized.

Even Steve Lieberman, now the managing director of Amway Global, had never heard of Quixtar when a recruiter told him about a job opening there. "I said, 'Quixtar? I've never heard of Quixtar,'" Lieberman recalled. "So I went on the Internet and went, 'Oh, it's the old Amway company.' I didn't know they still existed."[17] Doug DeVos said that the company's research found that Quixtar had a recognition rate of 3 percent, while Amway's recognition rate was 76 percent. "We thought, well, if we're going to build a brand, build the brand that everybody knows," he added. "It's going to be much more successful and cost a lot less and happen a lot faster."[18]

The second rebranding—or retro branding, as Steve Van Andel called it—was to take place gradually and dovetail with Amway's 50th anniversary in 2009. Building awareness of the Amway brand would take a massive advertising and public relations effort, neither of which Amway had done much of because in the past it didn't advertise. "The public audience pretty much thought we had disappeared," Steve explained. "The only way to revive ourselves was to go out and message with them. And the messaging we're doing is, to a large degree, through advertising and sponsorships."[19]

By September 2009, Amway Global returned to the Amway name in North America. To get the word out about its new identity, Amway Global launched a multiplatform, multimillion-dollar advertising campaign in 2010 entitled, "The Power of Positive." The first of three new television commercials aired in March. The message was about making life better through Amway products, its businesses, and its community efforts around the world. The commercials aired on the TV networks and cable TV, followed by spots in magazines and newspapers. Using social media and mobile technology was a natural step for a company that had depended on one-on-one communications for decades. Amway launched an application for the Apple iPhone and iPod Touch that gave distributors tools they might need. With a free download, Amway distributors could access a complete product catalog and product information, show customers videos and demonstrate how products worked, and place orders, with or without an Internet connection. The Amway app rolled out in the United States and Canada, followed by Japan and Australia and other markets in the future.

Winning the Hearts and Minds of Customers *and* IBOs

Consumers weren't the only ones Amway targeted in the rebranding effort. Amway execs realized that they needed to keep their existing IBOs happy and keep recruiting new ones. To help beginning IBOs become profitable faster, Amway began offering larger bonuses, free freight on orders of more than $75, cash incentives for meeting volume goals, and a promise to make better products. "We are going to focus on customer needs by developing products consumers want to buy and IBOs want to sell," Jim Payne, Amway's executive vice president responsible for markets in North America, Europe, Japan, Korea, Australia, New Zealand, India, and Latin America, pledged in the "Ada-tudes" e-letter to IBOs about the business transformation. "We will invest in marketing and advertising efforts to create positive awareness initially for our products and product brands and, at the end of our transformation, for our business opportunity. In total, the company will invest more than $200 million in making this business better for all IBOs."[20]

Many IBOs liked that it might be easier to bring new distributors into their downline if beginners could make money faster. But many also were unhappy to hear the business would change its name and model again. "The name Amway gets a very negative response," an IBO named Dave said in an Internet post to Payne's announcement:

> Amway is the name that comes up when used for jokes. How would you sell this? Do you try to "hide" the name as long as you can? If you come right out and tell people it's Amway, there's an immediate knee-jerk reaction. People are turned off right away. Even though they may know nothing about

Amway, they will pull away because they have heard jokes and or negative things.[21]

Another IBO, George, predicted it would be very difficult to overcome the negativity and cynicism that had grown over the last few decades over the Amway name:

> The first thought that comes to the prospect's mind with Amway is door-to-door sales and stocking a garage full of soap. Right or wrong, that is what they think and that is nothing like the online high-tech business model of Quixtar. The first thought that comes to the prospect's mind when they hear Quixtar is that they have never heard of it. I do not see the bad in being unknown as it sets up a sort of elusiveness to people that naturally draws them in. Since the IBO can't advertise and must solely rely on word of mouth to build the business, I'm not sure where being well known is a benefit to us, seems more like a hindrance. [22]

Some IBOs worried that another name change would cause their business to lose momentum and direction. "I've been through about five big changes now, and to be honest, the overall trend has been negative," an IBO named Gordon said. He continued:

> Here's the reality that no one seems to want to address: no matter how big the bonuses get, no matter how much image advertising the corporation buys, or how great my upline says the business is going to be, the business won't really grow again until the products are desired (and the distributors are welcomed) by retail consumers. [23]

Vijay Ramakrishnan had been an IBO for only six months when the change was announced. He said:

> I find it very shocking for the name to revert back to Amway. My biggest worry is just about the name. A lot of people have not heard about Quixtar, but if they do a Google search, they will see that it is associated with Amway. Amway has a lot of negative association with the past, and that will make recruiting new IBOs

much more challenging and difficult. What about the new IBOs who have entered Quixtar in the last month or so? I don't think many of them will be happy to have a sudden reorganization.[24]

IBO "Rocky" said it was "refreshing" to see a "bold move in a techno vision with Quixtar" and didn't see the point in reverting to a name from past and "all those negative issues with the 'Big A.' This is truly disappointing, regardless of what adjustments are being made and whose tools are being handled or who makes what! Will we still be part of Quixtar??? What will happen to our websites??? Why do we need to go back to Amway????? Why??????????"[25]

More Litigation

Others were asking the same question. In 2007, the company got into a dispute with a group of Quixtar distributors who had wanted to make a break and operate on their own. Ironically, the group had come together after Alticor had ditched the Amway name in North America and adopted the Quixtar online business model and brand. High-level distributors Orrin Woodward and Chris Brady, who founded the group called TEAM, filed a class-action suit that claimed Quixtar operated as a pyramid scheme that sold products at such high prices that no one would buy them except distributors. TEAM, which stands for Together Everyone Achieves More, billed itself as a training system. It was one of the lines of affiliation providing professional development programs to support IBOs—meaning it purveyed motivational tools such as tapes, seminars, and books to Amway distributors, as well as conducted training sessions. One of the TEAM members was Randy Haugen, the distributor whom Procter & Gamble had gone after in the Satan worship rumor lawsuit detailed in Chapter 9. Haugen said that negative information on the Internet about Amway was becoming a real problem and that in the mid- to late 1990s he had been privy to several conversations with the company about the need for lower-priced products and combating "the negative" on the Internet.[26] Then Quixtar was created. Haugen said:

> None of us wanted to have a company associated with Amway in any way. We were told it was a sister company and was

disconnected. They said it would be structured in a way so that we could say to people that it isn't Amway and it would be true, that this new opportunity was not Amway in any way.[27]

In 2006, Haugen and his wife had partnered with TEAM and felt that they were moving in a positive direction. Then they heard about the company's plans to change the business model and revert to the Amway plan and name. According to Haugen, who spoke at length about the subject on a Web site that posts information about Amway and Quixtar (but is not affiliated with Amway), TEAM members wanted to part ways with Quixtar before it morphed into Amway again, but they had a "no compete" clause in their original contract.[28] They said that TEAM tried but failed to negotiate with the company for an amicable separation. A day after the TEAM IBOs filed their lawsuit in a California district court, Quixtar fired 15 IBOs, including Woodward, Brady, and Haugen, for "inappropriate business-building tactics, improper positioning of the opportunity, and use of unauthorized support materials."[29]

Amway said it kicked out the distributors because they refused to agree to more stringent rules for recruiting other distributors and selling tapes, seminars, and books. TEAM tried to enjoin Quixtar from enforcing the noncompetition and nonsolicitation part of its contracts. Quixtar got a temporary restraining order and preliminary injunction to prevent Woodward, Brady, and other IBOs involved in the suit from soliciting IBOs for another business, disparaging Quixtar and damaging its reputation, and requiring them to return proprietary and confidential line of sponsorship data. After three months of legal wrangling in the case, a federal judge in Los Angeles dismissed the suit against Quixtar. "Orrin Woodward mounted a cynical and toxic attack on our business after we terminated him, and he did his best to hurt a lot of innocent people on his way out the door," Quixtar general counsel Mike Mohr said after the ruling.[30] Then, in September 2007, Quixtar filed a lawsuit against 30 anonymous bloggers who posted what it considered disparaging remarks in blogs and online forums and in YouTube videos. The suit, filed in Ottawa County Circuit Court, identified the posters only as "John Does." According to the *Grand Rapids Press*, a representative of Alticor said the action was taken to see if any of the bloggers were plaintiffs in the TEAM lawsuit who were violating the injunction rather than individuals expressing their own opinions.[31] A judge dismissed that suit.

Amway's lawyers were busy battling another class-action suit that also began in 2007 and alleged the company and some of its top-level distributors operated an illegal pyramid scheme. Filed in California by former Quixtar distributors, the case marked the first major legal battle that Amway agreed to settle. In November 2010, the company announced that it would pay $34 million in cash and $22 million worth of products. Specifically, the proposed settlement (which was not finalized as of this writing but was expected in 2011) would cover former Amway/Quixtar IBOs between 2003 and the day the settlement is approved. Each distributor who applied for the cash and products could receive up to $20 million to pay attorney's fees, up to $5 million to refund registration fees paid by IBOs who did not continue with Quixtar/Amway after their first year, up to $15,000 in payments to those IBOs who lost more than $2,500 with Quixtar/Amway, and up to $100 worth of Amway products. The settlement's total value was placed at $100 million and included a provision that neither side disparage the other.[32]

In a letter to employees announcing the settlement, Doug DeVos and Steve Van Andel again took issue with the pyramid scheme allegations, which they called "sensationalist claims that remain unproven." But they also promised the company would take responsibility for fixing "past issues" perpetrated by its IBOs. "We regret that the experiences of some IBOs fell short of the high standards that have allowed us to help many people, from all walks of life, start successful businesses for more than 50 years," Doug and Steve said in the letter.[33] They reiterated that the company had tripled its investment in programs to educate new IBOs, more than doubled the number of professional trainers to teach "best business practices," launched a consumer advertising campaign, and improved Web sites to help IBOs and protect consumers from misrepresentation and lowered prices. The final settlement included an amended complaint that eliminated the term *pyramid scheme*.

Chapter 15

The Way Ahead

As the first decade of the twenty-first century closed and Amway celebrated its 50th anniversary, Steve Van Andel and Doug DeVos pledged to continue the entrepreneurial legacy their founding fathers began. Of course, they lead a vastly different company into the future. The second-generation CEOs launched the online venture, developed the overseas empire that now dwarfs Amway's domestic business, and have vowed to make the enterprise more about selling products and less about recruitment. Amway has said that about products and recruitment time and time again, but appealing more to consumers and broadening its customer base beyond its own distributors may be the best way to keep growing as its markets mature and the number of countries where it can spread its "business opportunity" start to diminish. Comedian Jay Leno's late-night jokes about Amway distributors rushing into former Eastern Bloc countries after the Berlin Wall fell got laughs because it spoke to a truth—much of the world is already covered with Amway distributors, with the exception of Africa and the Middle East. Those areas pose their own unique set of challenges, from political instability to periodic or sustained violence, and economic problems. But in countries with more stable governments and developing consumer markets, dreams of owning one's own business and making a better living continue to sprout. As Jay Van Andel once said, "Being rewarded in proportion to how much you do is a universal language for people around the world."[1]

Building into the Future

In that long-term vision, Amway's success depends not only on continuing to woo more people to become IBOs and appealing more directly to consumers, but also on its reputation. Its multimillion-dollar mainstream media advertising campaign is designed more to project a positive image than push a particular product line. The negative that continues to haunt the company, despite the landmark 1979 Federal Trade Commission (FTC) ruling, is whether Amway really is more about making money through recruitment and tools. By its own admission, Amway is structured like a pyramid—so are most corporations and governments. The word *scheme* means "a plan or program of action," but Merriam-Webster's definition adds, "especially a crafty or secret one."[2] The FTC has decided Amway is not an illegal pyramid scheme, but is it an ethical pyramid-shaped selling configuration?

In a June 2009 report and memorandum to President Barack Obama and members of Congress who oversee the FTC, Robert L. FitzPatrick, longtime Amway critic and president of Pyramid Scheme Alert, called the multilevel marketing (MLM) business the "Main Street Bubble."[3] Ponzi schemes such as Bernard Madoff's hedge fund collapse completely and all at once, but the Main Street Bubble collapses continuously, FitzPatrick asserts, because of the "failures"—participants who quit the MLM and stop buying the products. In a study of 10 major MLMs, including Amway, Pyramid Scheme Alert found that about 60 to 90 percent of all participants eventually quit.[4] The financial loss rate for participants in MLMs that use Amway-type pay plans is 99 percent, Pyramid Scheme Alert concluded in a report that examined payout data on 11 MLMs.[5] "Collectively and over time, the Main Street Bubble far exceeds Bernard Madoff's Wall Street fraud in scale of financial harm," FitzPatrick told Obama and Congress members. "An estimated $10 billion per year is lost by U.S. consumers. Worldwide, the figure is far higher, with most losses inflicted by U.S.-based companies."

The courts, however, have repeatedly ruled in Amway's favor when plaintiffs have claimed that the company operates an illegal pyramid scheme. Since the FTC lost its case against Amway in 1979, it has sued some MLMs and barred them from engaging in MLM programs. Its Bureau of Consumer Protection offers consumers a list of how to evaluate an MLM plan and questions to ask to avoid being sucked into a pyramid scheme.[6] But no federal law directly pertaining to pyramid schemes exists. The FTC's Amway decision set a far-reaching precedent, effectively legalizing and legitimizing MLMs. Steven Hassan, a cult expert who has studied Amway and other MLMs, and consumer advocates contend that's because the FTC has had close ties to Amway and the MLM industry, which they said enjoys "extraordinary lobbying power" from political contributions to Republican Party candidates or "extreme conservative causes."[7]

The Beltway's infamous "revolving door" between regulators, legislators, and business also exists between the FTC and law firms that represent MLMs. Before he was appointed FTC chairman by President George W. Bush in 2001, Timothy Muris worked at a law firm representing Amway and other MLMs. Muris and the FTC's former head of consumer protection, J. Howard Beales, III, worked together at the FTC in the 1980s, then became MLM lobbyists who pressured the FTC against regulating multilevel marketing. Another former director of consumer protection, Jodie Bernstein, became an Amway lobbyist. She filed submissions with the FTC about the Business Opportunity Rule on behalf of the company, urging the FTC to exempt Amway from any new rules that would require more disclosure by companies selling "business opportunities." Consumer advocates such as Jon Taylor, president of the Consumer Awareness Institute, opposed the FTC's adoption of a Business Opportunity Rule that exempts MLMs— which he called "the most fraudulent 'business opportunities' the world has ever seen"—from having to disclose information they see as vital to consumer protection.[8] For Amway and its opponents, the big question is whether the Obama administration will push for greater government scrutiny of MLMs. Hassan wrote in *the Huffington Post* that he believes it will. "With the passage of the Dodd-Frank Wall Street Reform and Consumer Protection Act, signed into law by President Obama, consumers may see the beginnings of vastly increased federal oversight and regulation of Amway and the MLM industry," he said.[9]

Regulations on the Horizon?

No doubt MLMs have exploited the human nature of people who want to believe they can get rich without doing a lot of work. The money myth has been ingrained in the American psyche from the California Gold Rush to the Las Vegas Strip to the casinos that now dot American Indian reservations to the state lotteries and television game shows such as *Who Wants to Be a Millionaire?* The motivators and tool sellers who have sold this easy vision are the real villains in the Amway story. But as one IBO said, "Amway Corporate tolerated and condoned the activities of the tool scammers as it incidentally moved millions in IBO self-consumed products. In short, they are a willing party to the deception as it earns them billions."[10]

To be sure, some people get involved with Amway, work hard at it, and are successful. But they are the minority and there is no reliable data on exactly how many others started Amway businesses with high hopes, grew disillusioned, and eventually quit. The Diamond couples smiling from the cover of *Amagram*, the company's magazine for IBOs, are not overnight Amway successes. Many have been toiling at their businesses for years. One thing that has not changed and is not likely to soon is Amway's commitment to remaining a family business. The close-knit company still fosters family ties and nepotism. The Amway Policy Board—the leadership team that guides the company—has been comprised of Rich, Jay, and their eight children—Dick, Doug, and Dan DeVos; Cheri DeVos Vander Weide; Steve, Dave, and Nan Van Andel; and Barb Van Andel Gaby. Rich and Jay long ago decided they wanted to keep Amway closely held and private. It is not required to disclose profitability figures or file financial data with the Securities and Exchange Commission, and that suits the company just fine. "This means they can do things for what they think are 'the right reasons' rather than just shareholder value, and they can also take a longer viewpoint," as an international IBO put it."[11] Remaining private also shields the company from public scrutiny.

■ ■ ■

The way ahead is fraught with new challenges, and whether Amway survives another 50 years hinges on whether it can continue expanding its MLM model and spreading its message of hope and entrepreneurialism in the United States, North America, and around the world. But as Alexander Pope famously wrote in his *An Essay on Man*, "Hope springs eternal. . . ."[12]

Notes

Introduction

1. The Amway 50th anniversary celebration in Las Vegas was filmed by Alticor Communications Department and uploaded by Amway Global TV on YouTube.
2. Ibid.
3. Ibid.
4. See Van Andel's address at www.digitalillusionsllc.com/Amway_50th_Anniversary.php.
5. 50th anniversary video.
6. *Amway—In Their Own Words,* video produced by Alticor.

Chapter 1

1. Direct Selling Association, "DSA Releases 2009 Sales and Salesforce Figures," press release, July 22, 2010.
2. See www.trumpnetwork.com.
3. Pat Williams with Jim Denney, *How to Be Like Rich DeVos* (Deerfield Beach, FL: Health Communications, 2004), 149.

4. Stephen Butterfield, *Amway: The Cult of Free Enterprise* (Boston: South End Press, 1985), 3.

5. "Amway's Second Generation of Chief Executives—Steve Van Andel and Doug DeVos—Not Resting on Their Laurels," *Grand Rapids Press*, May 18, 2009.

6. Richard DeVos, *Compassionate Capitalism: People Helping People Help Themselves* (New York: Dutton, 1993), 4.

7. Ibid.

8. Steve Van Andel gave the breakdown of Amway's U.S. and international business in an interview with Emily Fredrix, Associated Press retail writer. The Q-and-A format article, "Amway CEOs Talk Global Growth, Fathers' Lessons," was published May 27, 2010, in *USA Today*.

9. David L. Kuhn, *A World of Opportunity* (Ada, MI: Amway, 2009), 166.

10. Chris Knape, "Amway Reports Record 2010 Sales of $9.2 Billion," *Grand Rapids Press*, February 17, 2011.

11. Chris Knape, "Amway Executive Finds 'Tremendous Potential' in China," *Grand Rapids Press*, April 21, 2010. Cheng made the comments in a speech to the World Affairs Councils of Western Michigan in Cascade Township, Michigan.

12. Ibid.

13. Ibid.

14. Alticor Inc. news release, "Amway Parent Grows to $9.2 Billion in 2010," PR Newswire, February 17, 2011.

15. Ranked by Euromonitor International, a global market research company, in its report "The World Market for OTC Healthcare," January 2008.

16. Brian Budzynski and Jeff Falk, "20 to Know," *Global Cosmetic Industry*, January 5, 2010.

17. *Fortune* magazine's 2010 ranking of the Fortune 500, May 3, 2010.

18. Scott DeCarlo, Andrea D. Murphy, and John J. Ray, "America's Largest Private Companies," *Forbes,* November 3, 2010.

19. "The World's Billionaires," *Forbes*, March 10, 2010.

20. Richard L. Lesher wrote the foreword to James W. Robinson's *Empire of Freedom: The Amway Story and What It Means to You* (Rocklin, CA: Prima Publishing, 1997), vii.

21. Rich DeVos with Charles Paul Conn, *Believe!* (New York: Berkley, 1985).

22. See the article and discussion thread at http://moneywatch.bnet.com/career-advice/blog/other-8-hours/why-you-should-join-amway/919/.

23. Amway's 16-page brochure, "A Business Opportunity for Entrepreneurs," makes the disclosure on page 11 in the footnotes. See a copy at www.amway.com/

en/ResourceCenterDocuments/Visitor/opp-amw-cat-v-en--AmwayGlobal BusinessOpportunityBrochure.pdf.

24. Jay Van Andel, *An Enterprising Life* (New York: HarperCollins, 1998), xviii.

25. Rich DeVos, *Hope from My Heart: Ten Lessons for Life* (Nashville, TN: J. Countryman, 2000), 31.

26. Butterfield, *Amway: The Cult of Free Enterprise*, 20.

27. Robinson, *Empire of Freedom*.

28. Rich DeVos, *Compassionate Capitalism*, 90.

29. Ibid., 96.

30. Kuhn, *A World of Opportunity*, 91.

31. Nicole Woolsey Biggart, *Charismatic Capitalism: Direct Selling Organizations in America* (Chicago: University of Chicago Press, 1989; reprint, 1990), 2.

32. Avon Products Inc. 2009 Form 10-K filed with the U.S. Securities and Exchange Commission.

33. Ibid.

34. The "$100 Million Club" listing of direct-selling companies with global corporate wholesale revenue of $100 million or more is at DirectSelling News.com.

35. Ibid.

36. Kuhn, *A World of Opportunity*, 172.

37. Federal Trade Commission, "Final Order, Opinion, Etc., in Regard to Alleged Violation of the Federal Trade Commission Act," May 8, 1979, p. 618.

38. Chris Knape, "Amway Agrees to Pay $56 Million, Settle Case Alleging It Operates a 'Pyramid Scheme," *Grand Rapids Press*, November 3, 2010.

39. Van Andel, *An Enterprising Life,* 97.

40. Amway's rebranding process is described in Chapter 8, "A New Platform for Growth," in Kuhn, *A World of Opportunity,* 171.

41. Kuhn, *A World of Opportunity*, 172.

42. "Premier Wen Declares Shanghai World Expo Closed," Expo web site news story, October 31, 2010.

43. Ibid.

Chapter 2

1. Van Andel, *An Enterprising Life*, 1. The story of his Dutch heritage, his early years, and beyond are detailed in his memoir.

2. Carl Smith, "The Plan of Chicago," in James R. Grossman, Ann Durkin Keating, and Janice L. Reiff (Eds.), *Encyclopedia of Chicago* (Chicago: University of Chicago Press, 2004).

3. Upton Sinclair, *The Jungle: The Uncensored Version* (Tucson, AZ: See Sharp Press, 2003*)*, 20.

4. 1923 and 1924 Gray Motor Corporation advertisements.

5. Van Andel, *An Enterprising Life*, 2–3.

6. Ibid., 3.

7. Ibid.

8. Ibid., 7.

9. Kuhn, *A World of Opportunity*, 106.

10. Van Andel, *An Enterprising Life*, 8.

11. DeVos, *Compassionate Capitalism*, 141.

12. Williams with Denney, *How to Be Like Rich DeVos*, 182.

13. Ibid.

14. Ibid.

15. DeVos, *Compassionate Capitalism*, 72.

16. Williams with Denney, *How to Be Like Rich DeVos*, 50.

17. Williams with Denney, *How to Be Like Rich DeVos*, 10.

18. DeVos, *Hope from My Heart*, 29.

19. Ibid.

20. Rich DeVos, *Ten Powerful Phrases for Positive People* (New York: Center Street, 2008), 35.

21. DeVos with Conn, *Believe!*, 20.

22. Van Andel, *An Enterprising Life*, 8.

23. DeVos, *Hope from My Heart*, 28.

24. Ibid.

25. Williams with Denney, *How to Be Like Rich DeVos*, 140.

26. DeVos, *Hope from My Heart*, 28.

27. DeVos, *Compassionate Capitalism*, 142.

28. DeVos, *Ten Powerful Phrases for Positive People*, 33.

29. Van Andel, *An Enterprising Life*, 9.

30. Kuhn, *A World of Opportunity*, 108.

31. Van Andel, *An Enterprising Life*, 10.

32. Williams with Denney, *How to Be Like Rich DeVos*, 29.

33. Van Andel, *An Enterprising Life*, 10–12.

34. Van Andel, *An Enterprising Life*, 13.

35. Kuhn, *A World of Opportunity*, 108.

36. Ibid.

37. Van Andel, *An Enterprising Life*, 38.

38. DeVos, *Hope from My Heart*, 38.

39. Kuhn, *A World of Opportunity*, 109.

Chapter 3

1. Van Andel, *An Enterprising Life*, 16.

2. DeVos, *Hope from My Heart*, 42.

3. Van Andel, *An Enterprising Life*, 17.

4. Ibid.

5. Van Andel, *An Enterprising Life*, 15.

6. DeVos, *Hope from My Heart*, 39.

7. Ibid.

8. Van Andel, *An Enterprising Life*, 24.

9. DeVos, *Hope from My Heart*, 39.

10. Ibid., 40.

11. Ibid.

12. Williams with Denney, *How to Be Like Rich DeVos*, 43.

13. Van Andel, *An Enterprising Life*, 32.

14. Williams with Denney, *How to Be Like Rich DeVos*, 43.

15. Van Andel, *An Enterprising Life*, 36.

16. Ibid., 38.

17. Williams with Denney, *How to Be Like Rich DeVos*, 51.

18. The early history of Nutrilite was covered in Kuhn, *A World of Opportunity*, the book Amway self-published in 2009 to commemorate Amway's 50th anniversary; 188.

19. Van Andel, *An Enterprising Life*, 39.

20. Ibid., 45.

21. Ibid., 46.

22. Ibid.

23. Ibid.

24. Ibid.

25. Rich DeVos in the foreword to Van Andel, *An Enterprising Life*, xi.

26. Van Andel, *An Enterprising Life*, xviii.

Chapter 4

1. Rima Dombrow Apple, *Vitamania: Vitamins in American Culture* (Piscataway, NJ: Rutgers University Press, 1996), 87. Bayer purchased Miles Laboratories in 1978.

2. Oral history transcript of interview with William W. Goodrich, former U.S. Food and Drug Administration general counsel, as part of series of oral history interviews on the FDA's history. Interviewed by Ronald T. Ottes and Fred L. Lofsvold on October 15, 1986.

3. Van Andel, *An Enterprising Life*, 40.

4. Ibid.

5. Van Andel, *An Enterprising Life*, 40–41.

6. Ibid., 41.

7. Ibid., 201.

8. DeVos, *Hope from My Heart*, 32.

9. Van Andel, *An Enterprising Life*, 44.

10. Goodrich oral history, FDA archives, 71.

11. Ibid.

12. Direct Selling Association consumer information.

13. National Consumers League brochure, "Pyramid Schemes: Don't Let One Collapse on You."

14. Ibid.

15. Goodrich oral history, 71.

16. Ibid., 72.

17. Kuhn, *A World of Opportunity,* 120.

18. Goodrich oral history, 72.

19. Van Andel, *An Enterprising Life*, 50.

20. Ibid.

21. Ibid., 51.

22. Ibid., 53.

23. Ibid., 57.

Chapter 5

1. DeVos, *Hope from My Heart,* 91.

2. DeVos, *Compassionate Capitalism,* 2.

3. DeVos, *Ten Powerful Phrases for Positive People,* 123–124.

4. See the Federal Trade Commission's "Guides for the Use of Environmental Marketing Claims," Section 5 of the Federal Trade Commission Act to Environmental Advertising and Marketing Practices, July 1992.

5. Van Andel, *An Enterprising Life,* 177.

6. Kuhn, *A World of Opportunity,* 124.

7. Ibid.

8. "Amway's Second Generation of Chief Executives—Steve Van Andel and Doug DeVos—Not Resting on Their Laurels," *Grand Rapids Press,* May 18, 2009.

9. FTC order, 638.

10. Ibid.

11. Amway Career Manual.

12. Ibid.

13. Ibid.

14. Van Andel, *An Enterprising Life,* 60.

15. Amway's business rules of conduct and career manual were detailed in the Federal Trade Commission's 1979 final order on the Amway case. They are paraphrased here.

16. 1975 Amway Career Manual, 37.

17. Kuhn, *A World of Opportunity,* 125.

18. Ibid.

19. Van Andel, *An Enterprising Life,* 61.

20. Wilbur Cross, *The Definitive Story of Amway Corporation* (New York: Berkeley Books, 1999), 25.

21. Bill Vlasic and Mary Beth Regan, "Amway II: The Kids Take Over," *BusinessWeek,* February 16, 1996.

22. DeVos, *Ten Powerful Phrases for Positive People,* 7.

23. Van Andel, *An Enterprising Life,* 66.

24. Ibid., 67.

25. Amway Career Manual.

26. *An Enterprising Life,* p. 57.

Chapter 6

1. "Inventor of the Week: Earl Tupper," Massachusetts Institute of Technology, MIT School of Engineering online archive, January 2000.

2. Ibid.

3. An engaging history of Tupperware can be found in Laurie Kahn-Leavitt's documentary "Tupperware!" for a segment of Public Broadcasting Service's *The American Experience,* first broadcast on December 11, 2003. The transcript is available at www.pbs.org, and the documentary is available online and from Netflix.

4. "Five Decades of Change," Tupperware Web site, www.tupperware.com.

5. PBS Tupperware documentary.

6. Ibid.

7. Kuhn, *A World of Opportunity*, 130.

8. Ibid.

9. Ibid.

10. Ibid.

11. Ibid.

12. 86 F.T.C. 1106, *In the matter of Koscot Interplanetary Inc., et al.* Order, opinion etc., in regard to alleged violation of the Federal Trade Commission Act and Section 2 of the Clayton Act. Docket 888. Complaint, May 24, 1972; final order, Nov. 18, 1975.

13. Ibid.

14. Ibid.

15. Robert L. FitzPatrick and Joyce K. Reynolds, *False Profits: Seeking Financial and Spiritual Deliverance in Multi-Level Marketing and Pyramid Schemes* (Charlotte, NC: Herald Press, 1997). FitzPatrick and Reynolds discuss the Airplane Game and its ramifications in Section II, pp. 55–114.

16. Van Andel, *An Enterprising Life*, 71.

17. Prepared statement of Debra A. Valentine, general counsel for the U.S. Federal Trade Commission, presented at the International Monetary Fund's seminar on current legal issues affecting central banks, in Washington, D.C., on May 13, 1998.

18. Ibid.

19. Ibid.

20. Van Andel, *An Enterprising Life*, 73.

21. FTC final order, 631.

22. Adam Bernstein, "Amway Co-Founder Jay Van Andel Dies at 80," *Washington Post*, December 8, 2004.

23. FTC final order, 706.

24. Valentine statement.

25. Van Andel, *An Enterprising Life,* 70.

26. Patrick J. Smith, *The Dark Side of the Pyramid* (Longwood, FL: Xulon Press, 2003), 79.

27. Federal Trade Commission news release, "FTC Proposes New Business Opportunity Rule," April 5, 2006.

28. Letter from Bruce A. Craig, Esq., to David C. Vladeck, director of the Bureau of Consumer Protection, Federal Trade Commission, dated June 24, 2009.

29. Van Andel, *An Enterprising Life*, 72.

30. Ibid., 75–76.

31. Ibid., 74–75.

32. Ibid., 76.

33. Ibid., 77.

34. FitzPatrick and Reynolds, *False Profits*, 19.

35. DeVos, *Hope from My Heart*, 17.

36. Ibid., 18–19.

Chapter 7

1. Kuhn, *A World of Opportunity,* 145.

2. Van Andel, *An Enterprising Life,* 151.

3. *State of Wisconsin v. Amway Corporation, Inc., a Michigan corporation, and Wayland C. Behnke, Dean M. Fliss, Benedetto Lanza, John C. Haugner, Jr., all Amway Direct Distributors dba World Wide Diamond,* July 28, 1982, in Milwaukee County Circuit Court.

4. *State of Wisconsin v. Amway et al.,* Count II, Table I, 7.

5. Van Andel, *An Enterprising Life,* 79.

6. *State of Wisconsin v. Amway et al.,* Count IV, 9.

7. Van Andel, *An Enterprising Life,* p. 80.

8. Ibid.

9. Ibid., 83.

10. Wilbur Cross, *Amway: The True Story of the Company that Transformed the Lives of Millions* (New York: Berkley Boos, 1999), 31.

11. Van Andel, *An Enterprising Life,* 81.

12. Ibid., 95.

13. Ibid., 96.

14. Ibid., 100.

15. Rich DeVos, "Directly Speaking," January 1983, Amway Cassette Series VA-2160, side A.

16. Ibid.

17. Van Andel, *An Enterprising Life,* 102.

18. Ibid.

19. Ibid.

20. "Directly Speaking," January 1983, side B.

21. Van Andel, *An Enterprising Life,* 164.

22. DeVos, "Directly Speaking," January 1983.

23. Ibid.

24. Ibid., 146.

25. Ibid., 147.

26. Civil Action No. 86-1360 (District of Columbia), FTC Docket No. D-9023. See also U.S. Federal Trade Commission 1986 Annual Report, 60-61, and FTC news release, "Amway Corp. to Pay $100,000 Civil Penalty, Settling FTC Charges It Failed to Make Required Earnings Disclosures in Newspaper Ad," May 19, 1986.

27. Van Andel, *An Enterprising Life,* 104.

28. Ibid.

29. Paul Farhi, "In Avon and Amway, a Culture Clash," *Washington Post,* May 4, 1989.

30. Kuhn, *A World of Opportunity,* 146.

Chapter 8

1. Amway IBOs use the term *kingpin* to describe the distributors at the top of the Amway pyramid of distributors. Most of them entered the Amway business decades ago and have established rules about lines of sponsorship. Some also have side businesses that sell motivational tools and hold functions such as seminars and rallies.

2. Cynthia Stewart-Copier, "The King of Network Marketing: A Conversation with Amway's Dexter Yager," *Network Marketing Lifestyle*, January 2001. The descriptions of Yager are cover lines from the magazine cover.

3. See Dexter and Birdie Yager's Web site, www.dexandbirdieyager.com.

4. Ibid.

5. Ibid.

6. Ibid.

7. Ibid.

8. Ibid.

9. Rich DeVos, "Directly Speaking," January 1983, side A.

10. Van Andel, *An Enterprising Life,* 99.

11. Part Three of a 1982 interview between Mike Wallace and Dexter Yager. Excerpts were shown as part of the *60 Minutes* investigation of Amway.

12. Ibid.

13. "Breaking the Point Barrier," *Business Owner,* November/December 2000.

14. Dexter R.Yager, Sr., with Doyle Yager, *The Business Handbook: A Guide to Building Your Own Successful Amway Business* (Charlotte, NC: Internet Services Corp., 1985), 53.

15. Ibid., 485–501.

16. Ibid., 487.

17. Ibid., 501.

18. For a list of all the global sales leaders, see Kuhn, *A World of Opportunity,* 90–91.

19. *John and Stacy Hanrahan, Brian Bohrer, and Mark and Lori Mensack v. William Britt, individually and dba American Multimedia, Inc.; Britt Motivation, Inc.; Britt Leasing, Inc.; Britt Management, Inc.; Britt Resources, Inc.; Executives Unlimited, Inc.; Executive Planners, Inc. and Dexter Yager, individually and dba Yager Enterprises; Dexter R. Yager, Sr. & Family Enterprises, Inc.; D & B Yager Enterprises, Inc.; Dexter Yager Securities, Inc.; Dexter Yager Motivation, Inc., Internet Services Corporation; Internet Services, Inc.; International Communication Corporation of America; Yager Resort Properties, Inc.; Dreambuilders Review and Amway Corporation, Inc.,* U.S. District Court for the Eastern District of Pennsylvania, filed July 20, 1994.

20. "Amway: The Untold Story," www.cs.cmu.edu/~dst/Amway/AUS/itcbsmaa.htm.

21. Butterfield, *Amway: The Cult of Free Enterprise,* 20.

22. Ibid., 21.

23. Ibid., 20

24. Ibid., 17.

25. Ibid., 37.

26. Ibid., 103.

27. Ibid., 178.

28. Ibid., 179.

29. Ibid., 183.

30. Ruth Carter, *Amway Motivational Organizations: Behind the Smoke and Mirrors* (Winter Park, FL: Backstreet, 1999), 1.

31. Ibid., 134.

32. Ibid.

33. Ibid.

34. Ibid.

35. Eric Scheibeler, *Merchants of Deception* (self-published, 2006), 8.

36. Ibid., 13.

37. Ibid., 15.

38. Ibid.

39. Ibid., 46.

40. Ibid., 203.

41. *60 Minutes* interview with Rich DeVos, 1982.

Chapter 9

1. Historical information about the company's founders is from Procter & Gamble, "A Company History, 1837–Today." Another reliable source is *Rising Tide: Lessons from 165 Years of Brand Building at Procter & Gamble,* by Davis Dyer, Frederick Dalzell, and Rowena Olegario (Harvard Business Press, 2004), who were given access to the company's archives.

2. Psalms 45, verse 8.

3. The rumors are addressed in detail in *The Procter & Gamble Company and The Procter & Gamble Distributing Company v. Amway Corporation and The Amway Distributors Association, et al.,* filed in the U.S. District Court for the Southern District in Houston, Texas, on July 16, 1997.

4. Procter & Gamble news release, "P&G Files Suit Over False Rumors," August 28, 1995.

5. *Amway v. Procter & Gamble* civil complaint filed in the U.S. District Court, Western District of Michigan, October 13, 1998.

6. Ibid.

7. Ibid.

8. Ibid.

9. "Utah Amway Dealer Again Faces P&G Suit," *Salt Lake Tribune*, August 25, 2000.

10. Procter & Gamble corporate news release, August 28, 1995.

11. Ibid.

12. *The Procter & Gamble Company and The Procter & Gamble Distributing Company v. Amway Corporation, The Amway Distributors Association, Ja-Ri Corporation, et al.,* filed in the U.S. District Court for the Southeastern District of Texas, July 16, 1997.

13. www.amwaywiki.com.

14. *Procter & Gamble v. Amway et al.,* July 16, 1997.

15. Ibid.

16. Ibid.

17. Amway press release, "Amway Statement about Subpoenas, Sidney Schwartz and P&G," May 8, 1999.

18. Ibid.

19. Geanne Rosenberg, "P&G Suit against Amway Is Revived," *New York Times*, March 27, 2001.

20. Associated Press, "Procter & Gamble Wins $19 Million Lawsuit over Satanism Rumors," March 20, 2007.

Chapter 10

1. Van Andel, *An Enterprising Life*, 135.

2. Ibid., 136.

3. Jay Van Andel discussed meeting Reagan and Reagan's policies in *An Enterprising Life*, Chapter 16, 169–171.

4. Ibid., 171.

5. Ibid., 153.

6. "MLM Industry Icon Doug Wead Joins XanGo," www.youtube.com.

7. Van Andel, *An Enterprising Life*, xvii.

8. Richard DeVos $1,000 campaign contribution, September 18, 1992, reported to the Federal Election Commission.

9. Center for Responsive Politics, "Heavy Hitters," 2010 report available at www.opensecrets.org. Data if based on information released by the Federal Election Commission.

10. Robert Moore, "Club 100: Over 100 Americans Gave Moore Than $100,000 to State Political Parties," Center for Public Integrity, November 21, 2002; see www.publicintegrity.org/articles/entry/405/.

11. Center for Responsive Politics, "Heavy Hitters" report.

12. DeVos, *Hope from My Heart*, 20–21.

13. Ibid., 22.

14. Tony Perry, "Amway's $1.3 Million to Fund GOP Convention TV Coverage," *Los Angeles Times*, July 26, 1996.

15. Bill Vlasic with Douglas Harbrecht and Mary Beth Regan, "The GOP Way Is the Amway," *BusinessWeek*, August 12, 1996.

16. Center for Responsive Politics, "Heavy Hitters" report.

17. Josh Goldstein, "So Far '97 Is a Good Year for Republican Fundraising," *Philadelphia Inquirer*, May 23, 1997.

18. Williams with Denney, *How to Be Like Rich DeVos*, ix.

19. Van Andel, *An Enterprising Life*, 200.

20. Kuhn, *A World of Opportunity*, 154.

21. Ibid.

22. Robinson, *Empire of Freedom*, 66.

23. David D. Kirkpatrick, "Club of the Most Powerful Gathers in Strictest Privacy," *New York Times*, August 28, 2004.

24. 2002 Hudson Institute Annual Report, 6–7.

25. The Van Andels' role in the U.S. Chamber is discussed in Kuhn, *A World of Opportunity*, 166.

26. Center for Responsive Politics.

27. Rachel Burstein and Kerry Lauerman, "She Did It Amway," *Mother Jones,* September/October 1996,

28. See myrick.house.gov.

29. *Roll Call*, September 6, 1997.

30. Charles Lewis, "The Buying of the President 2000," Center for Public Integrity's quadrennial investigation of how money shapes presidential campaigns, January 1, 2000.

Chapter 11

1. DeVos, *Compassionate Capitalism,* 4.

2. "Russia Acquires Amway Distributorship," *The Onion,* June 9, 2001.

3. DeVos, *Compassionate Capitalism*, 5.

4. Ibid., 3.

5. Van Andel, *An Enterprising Life*, 105.

6. Interview with William S. Pinckney as told to Malini Goyal, "Amway Learns in India," *Forbes India*, July 16, 2010.

7. Gale Eisenstodt and Hiroko Katayama, "Soap and Hope in Tokyo," *Forbes*, September 3, 1990, 62.

8. DeVos, *Compassionate Capitalism*, 4.

9. Eisenstodt and Katayama, "Soap and Hope in Tokyo."

10. Kuhn, *A World of Opportunity*, 148.

11. Tower Records, *Pulse* magazine, April 1995.

12. Brian Salsberg, "The New Japanese Consumer," *McKinsey Quarterly*, March 2010. John Parker was one of three executives interviewed on camera for a segment called "Learning From the Japanese Consumer: Three Executives on Next-Generation Marketing." The other executives were from Disney and Domino's.

13. Kuhn, *A World of Opportunity*, 147.

14. Nicole Woolsey Biggart, *Charismatic Capitalism: Direct Selling Organizations* (Chicago: University of Chicago Press, 1989), 148–150.

15. Michael Schuman, "Amway Finds It's Washed Over in a South Korea Soap Drama," *Wall Street Journal*, October 22, 1997, A-16.

16. Ibid.

17. This scene is paraphrased from Kuhn, *A World of Opportunity*, 100–105.

18. Ibid.

19. "Amway Learns in India."

20. Ibid.

21. See the list of Amway's global sales leaders in Kuhn, *A World of Opportunity*, 90–91.

22. Jim Downing, "Amway: Selling Dreams," *Athens News*, June 30, 2003.

23. "Amway Back to Business in State," *Times of India*, September 30, 2006.

24. "Amway Learns in India."

25. "Amway India Registers 25% Annual Growth," *Business Standard*, February 4, 2010.

26. "Amway Planning Second Facility in India," *Economic Times*, September 12, 2010.

27. "Amway Learns in India."

28. Ibid.

29. Otilia Haraga, "Amway Finds Its Way on Ugly Market," *Business Review*, November 1, 2010.

30. See www.amwaywatch.com/eastern-europe.

Chapter 12

1. Kuhn, *A World of Opportunity*, 152.

2. Nancy Crawley, "Former Secretary Builds Amway Sales Empire in Asia," *Grand Rapids Press*, May 31, 2009.

3. "Eva Cheng Becomes Mainstay of Amway China," *Women of China*, September 9, 2008.

4. Kuhn, *A World of Opportunity*, 155.

5. Cheng delivered a speech, "Amway China—Growing in Cultural Cross Currents," to the Second Asian Symposium on Direct Selling in Hong Kong from November 12 to 13, 2007. The transcript is available at www.hkdsa .org.hk/symposium/2007/program/material/EvaCheng.pdf.

6. Kuhn, *A World of Opportunity*, 141.

7. David Barboza, "Direct Selling Flourishes in China," *New York Times*, December 25, 2009.

8. Cheng HKDSA speech.

9. Ibid.

10. Leslie Chang, "Once-Barred Amway Becomes Booming Business in China," *Wall Street Journal*, March 12, 2003.

11. Crawley, "Former Secretary Builds Amway Sales Empire in Asia."

12. Cheng HKDSA speech.

13. "Eva Cheng Becomes Mainstay of Amway China."

14. Ibid.

15. Rob Gifford, *China Road: A Journey into the Future of a Rising Power* (New York: Random House, 2007).

16. Cheng ranked 88th on the list, published in *Forbes* magazine on August 27, 2008, and 93rd on the 2009 list, published on August 19, 2009.

17. The video of Charlie Lee Kim Soon's and Linda Ng Kwee Choo's rise to Amway fame is posted on www.youtube.com.

18. Xinhua, "China's Largest 'Pyramid' Scheme Nets 170,000 People," *China Daily*, August 31, 2007.

19. Mark O'Neill reported on the riot for the *Asia Sentinel*, "A Chinese Pyramid Scheme Built on an Anthill," December 3, 2007.

20. See ChinaCSR.com, "China's Direct-Selling Enterprises Sign Self-Discipline Pact," April 20, 2010.

21. Ibid.

Chapter 13

1. Williams with Denney, *How to Be Like Rich DeVos*, 291.

2. Ibid., xi.

3. DeVos, *Hope from My Heart*, 17.

4. Ibid., 114.

5. Ibid., 115.

6. Williams with Denney, *How to Be Like Rich DeVos*, xi.

7. "Billionaire Thanks God for His NHS Heart," *London Daily Mail*, March 1, 1999.

8. DeVos, *Hope from My Heart,* 12.

9. Kuhn, *A World of Opportunity*, 158.

10. Ibid., 154.

11. Ibid.

12. Jenn Gidman, "Amway/Quixtar Rebranding Scheme?" BrandChannel.com, November 24, 2008.

13. "Top 100 Internet Retailers," National Retail Federation, *STORES*, September 1, 2000.

14. Bob Tedeschi, "Some Online Retail Surprises," *New York Times*, July 22, 2002.

15. Ibid.

16. "Quixtar Sets New Single-Day and Single-Month Sales Records," PR Newswire, April 5, 2004.

17. *Business 2.0* magazine, December 2001, 45.

18. Tedeschi, "Some Online Retail Surprises."

19. Ibid.

20. *Nitro Distributing Inc., West Palm Convention Services Inc., Netco Inc., Schmitz & Associates Inc., and U-Can-II Inc. v. Alticor Inc., Amway Corp., and Quixtar,* filed in U.S. District Court for the Western District of Missouri, St. Joseph (Mo.) Division.

21. Ibid.

22. Interview with former Quixtar IBO, July 2010.

23. Letter to Doug DeVos, dated June 26, 2003.

24. See a transcript at www.msnbc.msn.com/id/4375477/ns/dateline_nbc_consumer_alert.

25. Ibid.

26. Chris Hansen, "In Pursuit of the Almighty Dollar," *Dateline NBC* (NBC News), May 7, 2004.

27. Ibid.

28. Letter to *Dateline NBC* from Ken McDonald, dated July 11, 2003.

29. Letter to *Dateline NBC* from Ken McDonald, dated July 16, 2003.

30. Letter to *Dateline NBC* from Ken McDonald, dated September 16, 2003.

31. IBO comment to Ada-tudes e-letter, July 7, 2007.

32. IBO comment from "Tex" on Ada-tudes e-letter, July 17, 2007.

Chapter 14

1. Blair made the comments in a video message to members of the Direct Selling Association for the group's annual conference held May 5–6, 1999.

2. *BERR v. Amway (UK) Limited,* approved judgment, May 14, 2008.

3. *The Secretary of State for Business Enterprise and Regulatory Reform and Amway (UK) Ltd.,* Neutral Citation, Case. No. 2651, 2652, and 2653 of 2007 in the High Court of Justice, Chancery Division, Royal Courts of Justice.

4. David Brown of the *Times* covered the court proceedings. The quoted comments are taken from his report, "Marketing Group Merely 'Selling a Dream,'" published on November 27, 2007.

5. Note to global Amway directors from Steve Van Andel and Doug DeVos, dated November 9, 2007.

6. Appeal ruling.

7. Electronic message dispersed to Amway employees on May 14, 2008, at 9:15 A.M.

8. Ibid.

9. Mark Cunningham made the comments before the court on November 26, 2007, as quoted by David Brown in the *Sunday Times,* "Marketing Group Merely 'Selling a Dream,'" November 27, 2007. See also the *Secretary of State for Business, Enterprise & Regulatory Reform v. Amway,* Court of Appeal dismissal, January 29, 2009.

10. Kuhn, *A World of Opportunity,* 168.

11. "Amway's Second Generation of Chief Executives—Steve Van Andel and Doug DeVos—Not Resting on Their Laurels."

12. Emily Fredrix, Associated Press Retail Writer, "Amway CEOs Talk about Global Growth, Fathers' Lessons," *USA Today*, May 27, 2010.

13. John Gallagher, "DeVos' Run Puts Amway in Spotlight," *Detroit Free Press*, September 24, 2006.

14. "Spending Millions to Save Billions: The Campaign of the Super Wealthy to Kill the Estate Tax," report by Public Citizen, Congress Watch, and United for a Fair Economy, April 2006.

15. John Kerry, "Battleground Michigan" letter, July 2006.

16. See Margaret Cronin Fisk's report on Bloomberg.com, "DeVos May Lose Michigan Votes for Putting Amway Jobs in China," October 23, 2006.

17. Associated Press, "Amway Angling for a Comeback in U.S.," *Holland Sentinel*, December 27, 2008.

18. Ibid.

19. Kuhn, *A World of Opportunity*, 172.

20. Ada-tudes e-letter on Amway's business transformation, posted by Jim Payne, July 3, 2007.

21. Comments to Ada-tudes e-letter, July 4, 2007.

22. Comments from IBO George to Ada-tunes e-letter, July 16, 2007.

23. Comments from IBO Gordon on Ada-tudes e-letter, August 20, 2007.

24. IBO Vijay Ramakrishnan comments on Ada-tudes e-letter, August 9, 2007.

25. IBO "Rocky" comments on Ada-tudes e-letter, August 7, 2007.

26. "Resigned Double Diamond Randy Haugen Speaks," www.cs.cmu.edu, September 6, 2007.

27. Ibid.

28. "Resigned Amway Quixtar Double Diamond Randy Haugen Speaks," www.amquix.info, no date.

29. "Quixtar Takes Swift Action to Protect Its Business," Quixtar news release, dated August 10, 2007.

30. "Federal District Court in California Dismisses Class-Action Suit against Quixtar," PR Newswire release, October 5, 2007.

31. "Amway Sues to ID Source of Negative Web Content," *Grand Rapids Press*, October 12, 2007.

32. Chris Knape, "Amway Agrees to Pay $56 Million, Settle Case Alleging It Operates a 'Pyramid Scheme,'" *Grand Rapids Press*, November 3, 2010.

33. "A Letter from Amway President Doug DeVos and Chairman Steve Van Andel to Amway Employees," November 3, 2010.

Chapter 15

1. *Amway—In Their Own Words,* video produced by Alticor.

2. *Merriam-Webster Dictionary,* 2011.

3. Robert L. FitzPatrick, "The Main Street Bubble," report and memorandum to President Barack Obama and members of Congress overseeing the Federal Trade Commission, June 15, 2009.

4. "Study of Ten Major MLMs and Amway/Quixtar Show Huge Consumer Losses and Pyramid Recruitment," Pyramid Scheme Alert, June 2008.

5. "The Myth of MLM Income Opportunity," Pyramid Scheme Alert.

6. "The Bottom Line About Multi-Level Marketing Plans," Federal Trade Commission, Bureau of Consumer Protection.

7. Steven Hassan, "Beware the 'Main Street Bubble' of Multi-Level Marketing Groups Without U.S. Government Protection," *Huffington Post,* February 2, 2011.

8. Comments from Jon Taylor to the Federal Trade Commission about the Business Opportunity Rule, June 30, 2008.

9. Hassan, "Beware the 'Main Street Bubble' of Multi-Level Marketing Groups Without U.S. Government Protection."

10. Interview with Amway IBO, December 9, 2010.

11. Ibid.

12. Alexander Pope, *An Essay on Man,* Epistle I, 1733.

Selected Bibliography

Books

Andrews, John. *Ain't It Great? A Look Inside Amway*. Bloomington, IN: 1st Books Library, 2001.

Apple, Rima Dombrow. *Vitamania: Vitamins in American Culture*. Piscataway, NJ: Rutgers University Press, 1996.

Biggart, Nicole Woolsey. *Charismatic Capitalism: Direct Selling Organizations in America*. Chicago: University of Chicago Press, 1989. Reprint, 1990.

Butterfield, Stephen. *Amway: The Cult of Free Enterprise*. Boston: South End Press, 1985.

Carey, Charles W., Jr., *American Inventors, Entrepreneurs & Business Visionaries*. New York: Facts on File, 2002.

Carter, Ruth. *Amway Motivational Organizations: Behind the Smoke and Mirrors*. Winter Park, FL: Backstreet, 1999.

Cassidy, John. *Dot.con: How America Lost Its Mind and Money in the Internet Era*. New York: Harper Perennial, 2003.

Conn, Charles Paul. *The Dream that Will Not Die: The Rest of the Story Behind the Amway Phenomenon*. Boston: Commonwealth Books, 1996.

___. *The Possible Dream: A Candid Look at Amway*. New York: Berkley, 1987.

___. *Promises to Keep: The Amway Phenomenon and How It Works*. New York: G. P. Putnam's Sons, 1985.

Cross, Wilbur. *Amway: The True Story of the Company that Transformed the Lives of Millions*. New York: Berkley Books, 1999.

___, and Gordon Olson. *Commitment to Excellence: The Remarkable Amway Story*. Elmsford, NY: Benjamin Company, 1986.

DeVos, Rich, with Charles Paul Conn. *Believe!* 10th Anniversary ed. New York: Berkley, 1985.

___. *Compassionate Capitalism: People Helping People Help Themselves*. New York: Dutton, 1993.

___. *Hope from My Heart: Ten Lessons for Life*. Nashville: J. Countryman, 2000.

___. *Ten Powerful Phrases for Positive People*. New York: Center Street, 2008.

FitzPatrick, Robert L., and Joyce K. Reynolds. *False Profits: Seeking Financial and Spiritual Deliverance in Mulit-Level Marketing and Pyramid Schemes*. Charlotte, NC: Herald Press, 1997.

Gifford, Rob. *China Road: A Journey into the Future of a Rising Power*. New York: Random House, 2007.

Helmstetter, Shad. *American Victory: The Real Story of Today's Amway*. Tucson, AZ: Chapel & Croft, 1997.

Kealing, Bob. *Tupperware Unsealed: Brownie Wise, Earl Tupper, and the Home Party Pioneers*. Gainesville, FL: University Press of Florida, 2008.

Kuhn, David L. *A World of Opportunity: Amway* (50th anniversary special edition). Ada, MI: Amway Corporation, 2009.

Lewis, Charles, and The Center for Public Integrity. *The Buying of the President 2000*. New York: Harper Perennial, 2000.

Poe, Richard. *Wave 3: The New Era in Network Marketing*. Rocklin, CA: Prima, 1994. Reprint, 2001.

Robinson, James W. *Empire of Freedom: The Amway Story and What It Means to You*. Rocklin, CA: Prima, 1997.

Scheibeler, Eric. *Merchants of Deception*. Self-published, 2006.

Sinclair, Upton. *The Jungle: The Uncensored Original Edition*. Tucson, AZ: See Sharp Press, 2003.

Skubick, Tim. *See Dick and Jen Run*. Ann Arbor, MI: University of Michigan Press and Petoskey Publishing, Traverse City, 2006.

Smith, Patrick J. *The Dark Side of the Pyramid*. Longwood, FL: Xulon Press, 2003.

Smith, Rodney K. *Multilevel Marketing: A Lawyer Looks at Amway, Shaklee, and Other Direct Sales Organizations*. Grand Rapids, MI: Baker Book House, 1984.

Van Andel, Jay. *An Enterprising Life*. New York: HarperCollins, 1998.

Williams, Pat, with Jim Denney. *How to Be Like Rich DeVos*. Deerfield Beach, FL: Heath Communications, 2004.

Xardel, Dominique. *The Direct Selling Revolution: Understanding the Growth of the Amway Corporation*. Cambridge, MA: Blackwell, 1993.

Yager, Dexter. *The Business Handbook: A Guide to Building Your Own Successful Amway Business*. Internet Services Corp., 1985.

Articles

"Amway Back to Business in State." *Times of India,* September 30, 2006.

"Amway Launches iPhone Application." DirectSellingNews.com, February 2010.

"Amway Representatives Are Knocking on Doors Again." *South China Morning Post*, July 28, 1998.

"Amway Takes a Bold Step into Cyber-Selling." *Cosmetics International*, June 25, 1999.

"Amway Tries Energy." *Crain's Detroit Business*, November 16, 1998.

"Amway's Way." *Time*, May 29, 1979.

Arnold, David J., John A. Quelch, Yoshinori Fujikawa, and Patrick Reinmoller. "Case Study: Amway Japan Ltd." *Harvard Business Review*, February 23, 1998.

Associated Press. "Amway Angling for a Comeback in the U.S." *Holland Sentinel*, December 27, 2008.

___. "Another Aide Leaves Amway." *New York Times*, March 21, 1984.

___. "Chinese Officials Ban Direct Marketing," April 22, 1998.

Barboza, David. "Direct Selling Flourishes in China." *New York Times*, December 25, 2009.

Barnes, Brooks. "Amway Adds Entertainment to Product Line." *New York Times*, November 20, 2007.

Behar, Richard. "Cleaning Up." *Forbes*, March 25, 1985.

Bernstein, Adam. "Amway Co-Founder Jay Van Andel Dies at 80." *Washington Post*, December 8, 2004.

Bott, Jennifer. "Amway Changes Name, Mission." *Detroit Free Press*, October 25, 2000.

Brooks, Arthur C. "Door-to-Door Faith: The Co-founder of Amway Shares a Faith in More Than His Products." *Wall Street Journal*, April 21, 2006.

Brown, David. "Marketing Group Merely 'Selling a Dream.'" *Sunday Times*, November 27, 2007.

Burstein, Rachel, and Kerry Lauerman. "She Did It Amway." *Mother Jones*, September–October 1996.

Chang, Leslie. "Once-Barred Amway Becomes Booming Business in China." *Wall Street Journal*, March 12, 2003.

Cole, Robert J. "Avon Offer Is Official: Amway Bids $39 a Share." *New York Times*, May 11, 1989.

Crawley, Nancy. "Former Secretary Builds Amway Sales Empire in Asia." *Grand Rapids Press*, May 31, 2009.

Davey, Monica. "In the Race for Governor of Michigan, the Struggling Economy Is Topic A." *New York Times*, October 9, 2006.

Delaney, Timothy Q. "Coming Clean on E-Mail Discovery." *ABA Journal*, December 1999.

Downing, Jim. "Amway: Selling Dreams in India." *Athens News*, June 30, 2003.

DuBois, Shelley. "How Amway Weathered the Storm, One Sale at a Time." *Fortune*, July 30, 2010.

Eisenstodt, Gale, and Hiroko Katayama, "Soap and Hope in Tokyo." *Forbes*, September 3, 1990.

Farhi, Paul. "In Avon and Amway, a Culture Clash." *Washington Post*, May 4, 1989.

Fisk, Margaret Cronin. "DeVos May Lose Michigan Votes for Putting Amway Jobs in China." Bloomberg.com, October 23, 2006.

FitzPatrick, Robert L. "The Case for Reopening the Amway Pyramid Scheme Case." Self-published report, 1999.

Freitag, Michael. "Amway Withdraws Avon Offer." *New York Times*, May 18, 1989.

"FTC Fines Amway Korea, KSDIC for False Ads." *Korea Herald News*, November 5, 1997.

Gallagher, John. "DeVos' Run Puts Amway in Spotlight." *Detroit Free Press*, September 24, 2006.

Gearan, Anne. "Amway Loses U.S. Supreme Court Appeal with P&G." Associated Press, October 1, 2001.

Gellene, Denise. "Westwood, Amway Settle Suit over Mutual Network." *Los Angeles Times*, May 7, 1986.

Gidman, Jenn. "Amway/Quixtar Rebranding Scheme?" *Brand Channel*, November 24, 2008.

Goldstein, Josh. "So Far '97 Is a Good Year for Republican Fundraising." *Philadelphia Inquirer*, May 23, 1997.

Goodenow, Gary Langan, Sr. "The SEC and Multilevel Marketing." *MLM Watch*, August 16, 2004.

Gopwani, Jewel. "Ada, Mich.–Based Direct–Sales Firm Finds Fortune in Asia." *Detroit Free Press*, October 22, 2004.

Goyal, Malini. "Amway Learns in India." *Forbes India*, July 16, 2010.

Grant, Linda. "How Amway's Two Founders Cleaned Up: Strong Overseas Sales Helped Richard DeVos and Jay Van Andel Add Billions to Their Fortunes." *U.S. News & World Report*, October 31, 1994.

Holzinger, Albert G. "Selling America to the Japanese." *Nation's Business*, October 1990.

Huang, Daohen. "Who's at the Door? Direct Selling May Open Future to Rural Youth." *Beijing Today*, January 18, 2010.

Ivins, Molly. "Congress Distributes a Tax Break to Amway." *Fort Worth Star-Telegram*, August 7, 1997.

"Japan Consumer Agency Asks Amway to Reconsider Sales Methods." *Dow Jones News Service,* July 7, 1998.

Kirby, James. "Amway May Be the First to Trip in Direct Selling Merry-Go-Round." *The Age*, December 8, 2007.

Kirkbride, Rob. "Alticor Sales Soar 27 Percent." *Grand Rapids Press*, October 21, 2004.

___. "Alticor Still Value-Driven under New Leadership." *Grand Rapids Press*, October 18, 2002.

___. "The Style of Doug DeVos." *Grand Rapids Press*, January 25, 2004.

Kirkpatrick, David. "Club of the Most Powerful Gathers in Strictest Privacy." *New York Times*, August 28, 2004.

Klebnikov, Paul. "The Power of Positive Inspiration." *Forbes*, December 9, 1991.

Knape, Chris. "Amway Agrees to Pay $56 Million, Settle Case Alleging It Operates a 'Pyramid Scheme.'" *Grand Rapids Press*, November 3, 2010.

___. "Amway Celebrates Golden Anniversary with Deep Local Roots and a Global Reach." *Grand Rapids Press*, May 17, 2009.

___. "Amway Executive Finds 'Tremendous Potential' in China." *Grand Rapids Press*, April 21, 2010.

Kroll, Christina. "Latin Beat: Amway Launches Personal Care Lines for Latin American Market." *Global Cosmetics Industry*, February 27, 2009.

Lo, Elaine Y. M., and Andy K. H. Yip, "Direct Selling in China Now Formally Regulated." Mayer Brown International LLP legal update, October 31, 2005.

MacLeod, Calum. "China's New Rules Open Door to Amway, Avon, Others." *USA Today*, November 30, 2005.

Miller, Brian. "Inside the Wonder of Amway: How to Get Rich Selling Toothpaste to Yourself." *Seattle Weekly*, January 5, 2000.

Morgello, Clem, "Richard Johnson of Amway Japan: Challenging Japan's Sales Culture." *Institutional Investor*, May 1994.

Moore, Robert. "Club 100: Over 100 Americans Gave More Than $100,000 to State Political Parties." Center for Public Integrity, November 21, 2002.

Morrill, Jim, and Nancy Stancil. "Amway the Yager Way." *Charlotte Observer*, March 19, 1995.

Muller, Joann. "Amway Tailors Marketing Approach to Individual Foreign Cultures." *Journal of Commerce and Commercial*, July 8, 1991.

"N.B.A. Orlando Team Sold." *New York Times*, September 20, 1991.

Norton, Amy. "Physician Peddlers." *Physician's Weekly*, January 5, 1998.

O'Donnell, Jayne. "Some Multilevel Salespeople Ask: What Profits?" *USA Today*, February 7, 2011.

O'Neill, Marlk. "A Chinese Pyramid Scheme Built on an Anthill." *Asia Sentinel*, December 3, 2007.

___. "Amway Makes Retail Switch, Avon Wavers." *South China Morning Post*, April 29, 1998.

Ono, Yumiko. "On a Mission: Amway Grows Abroad, Sending 'Ambassadors' to Spread the Word." *Wall Street Journal*, May 14, 1997.

Perlez, Jane. "Ban on Film Has Poland Debating Censorship." *New York Times*, June 14, 1998.

Perry, Tony. "Amway's $1.3 Million to Fund GOP Convention TV Coverage." *Los Angeles Times*, July 26, 1996.

Risen, James. "Blackwater Chief at Nexus of Military and Business." *New York Times*, October 8, 2007.

Rosenberg, Geanne. "P. & G. Suit Against Amway Is Revived." *New York Times*, March 27, 2001.

"Russia Acquires Amway Distributorship." *The Onion*, June 9, 2001.

Ruzicka, Milan. "Amway Wins Converts in Former East Bloc." *Journal of Commerce and Commercial*, June 3, 1994.

Salsberg, Brian. "The New Japanese Consumer." *McKinsey Quarterly*, March 2010.

Schuman, Michael. "Amway Finds It's Washed Over in a South Korea Soap Drama." *Wall Street Journal*, October 22,1997.

Shirouzu, Norihiko. "Analysts See Bumpy Road for Shares of Amway Japan." *Wall Street Journal*, June 16, 1998.

Stoiber, Julie. "Amway Proposes Settling Lawsuit." *Philadelphia Enquirer*, August 17, 1996.

Tate, Nancy Ken. "Amway's Green Roots Go Deep." *American Demographics*, April 1991.

Tedeschi, Bob. "Some Online Retail Surprises." *New York Times*, July 22, 2002.

Thomas, Landon. "Jay Van Andel Dies at 80; A Co-Founder of Amway." *New York Times*, December 8, 2004.

Tumulty, Karen. "Politics Can Be Risky Business for a CEO." *Washington Post*, June 11, 2010.

Urguhart, John. "Amway, Canada Reach Settlement in Customs Dispute." *Wall Street Journal*, September 25, 1989.

Vlasic, Bill, and Mary Beth Regan, "Amway II: The Kids Take Over." *BusinessWeek*, February 16, 1998.

___, with Douglas Harbrecht and Mary Beth Regan, "The GOP Way Is the Amway." *BusinessWeek*, August 12, 1996.

Woutat, Donald. "Amway Distributors Clean Up on New Market in East Europe." *Los Angeles Times*, July 10, 1991.

Oral History

Goodrich, William W. Interview conducted by Ronald T. Ottes and Fred L. Lofsvold, October 15, 1986. U.S. Food & Drug Administration archives.

Selected Court Cases and Government Reports

Amway v. Procter & Gamble, Case No. 1:98-CV-726, filed in the U.S. District Court, Western District of Michigan, October 13, 1998.

Federal Trade Commission, Docket 9023, Complaint, March 25, 1975, Final Order, May 8, 1979, *In the Matter of Amway Corporation, Inc., et al.*

John and Stacy Hanrahan, Brian Bohrer, and Mark and Lori Mensack v. William Britt, individually and d.b.a. American Multimedia, Inc.; Britt Motivation, Inc.; Britt Leasing, Inc.; Britt Management, Inc.; Britt Resources, Inc.; Executives Unlimited, Inc.; Executive Planners, Inc. and Dexter Yager, individually and d.b.a. Yager Enterprises; Dexter R. Yager, Sr. & Family Enterprises, Inc.; D & B Yager Enterprises, Inc.; Dexter Yager Securities, Inc.; Dexter Yager Motivation, Inc., Internet Services Corporation; Internet Services, Inc.; International Communication Corporation of America; Yager Resort Properties, Inc.; Dreambuilders Review; and Amway Corporation, Inc. Civil Action No. 94-4615 filed in the U.S. District Court for the Eastern District of Pennsylvania, July 20, 1994.

Gerald Hayden and Edda Hayden v. Dexter Yager; Yager Enterprises; Continuing Distributor Education Network; Distribution Marketing Technologies; Downeast Networking

Services, Inc.; Network of Business Opportunity Entrepreneurs; Don Wilson; Nancy Wilson; Colombo Disalvatore; Karen Disalvatore; Disalvatore Network Marketing; Amway Corporation; Amway Distributor Association; Edward Postma; and David Kruer. Filed in the U.S. District Court, District of Connecticut, July 27, 1997.

Ministry of Commerce, the People's Republic of China. "MOFCOM: China Has Approved 19 Chinese and Foreign-Invested Enterprises to Engage in Direct Selling Business," May 8, 2007.

_____. "Regulations on Administrations of Direct Sales," November 25, 2005.

Jeff Pokorny and Larry Blenn v. Quixtar, Inc., James Ron Puryear Jr., Georgia Lee Puryear, and World Wide Group, L.L.C.; Britt Worldwide, L.L.C, American Multimedia, Inc., Britt Management, Inc., Bill Brill and Peggy Britt. Case No. C-07-0201 filed in the U.S. District District, Northern District of California, January 10, 2007.

The Procter & Gamble Company, et al, v. Amway Corporation, et al., Civil Action No. H-97-2384 filed in the U.S. District Court for the Southern District of Texas, Houston Division, July 16, 1997.

The Procter & Gamble Company, et al., v. Randy L. Haugen, et al., and Amway Corporation, Case No. 1:95 CV-0094 K filed in the U. S. District Court for the District of Utah, Central Division, August 28, 1995.

Quixtar Inc. and Amway Corporation v. Eric N. Scheibeler, Case No. CV-00374-MM filed in the U.S. District for the Middle District of Pennsylvania, February 27, 2007.

The Secretary of State for Business Enterprise and Regulatory Reform and Amway (UK) Ltd., Neutral Citation, Case. No. 2651, 2652, and 2653 of 2007 in the High Court of Justice, Chancery Division, Royal Courts of Justice, May 14, 2008.

Tim Foley, individually, Connie Foley, individually, et al., v. Mahaleel Lee Luster, individually, d.b.a. Go Diamond Productions, d.b.a. Lustervision, U.S. Court of Appeals for the Eleventh Circuit, No. 99-14123, D.C. Docket No. 96-00175-DIV-ORL-3ABF-18, May 2, 2011.

Valentine, Debra A. "Pyramid Schemes," *Current Developments in Monetary and Financial Law,* Vol. I. Washington, D.C.: International Monetary Fund, 1999.

State of Wisconsin v. Amway Corporation, Inc., et al., Case No. 589806 filed in the State of Wisconsin Circuit Court, Milwaukee County, July 28, 1992.

Orrin Woodward, Billy Florence, Don Wilson, Tim Marks, Chuck Cullent, Kirk Birtles, Randy Haugen, Chris Brady, Jim Martin, Aron Radosa, Chuck Goetschel, David Brandy, Benjamin L. Dickie, Bruce Gilbank, and Mike Martensen v. Quixtar, Inc., Case No. CV-07-05194 filed in the U.S. District Court, Central District of California, Western Division, August 9, 2007.

Selected Internet Sites

www.amway.com/EN—Amway's global corporate Web site.

www.amwaytalk—Amway discussion site.

www.amwaywatch.com—The latest Amway news from around the world, with links to corporate and independent blogs.

www.amwaywiki.com—A wiki encyclopedia of Amway facts, sales data, listings of thousands of top achievers, and other information.

www.opportunityzone—Amway corporate blog.

www.thetruthaboutamway.com—Independent blog maintained by an Amway business owner. It's a good site to visit for discussion, opinion, facts, myths, and news, positive and negative, about Amway's business around the world.

Videos and Broadcasts

Adopting Amway's American Dream—China, Journeyman Pictures, November 2, 2007.

Amway 50th Anniversary Celebration in Las Vegas, recorded by Alticor Inc., May 27, 2009.

DeVos, Rich, "Directly Speaking," Tape One, Amway Cassette Series VA-2160, January 1983.

_____. "Directly Speaking," Tape Two, Amway Cassette Series VA-2160, March 1983.

Hansen, Chris. "In Pursuit of the Almighty Dollar," *Dateline NBC* (NBC News), May 7, 2004.

Kahn-Leavitt, Laurie. *The American Experience: Tupperware!* Public Broadcasting Service, December 11, 2003.

Wallace, Mike. "Soap and Hope," *60 Minutes* (CBS News), January 1983.

About the Author

Kathryn A. Jones has written about business for more than 25 years for such publications as the *New York Times*, *Texas Monthly*, and the *Harvard Business School Bulletin*. She lives in Glen Rose, Texas, southwest of Fort Worth.

Index